Korean Genealogy Guide

*A resource to help English speakers
discover Korean ancestors…*

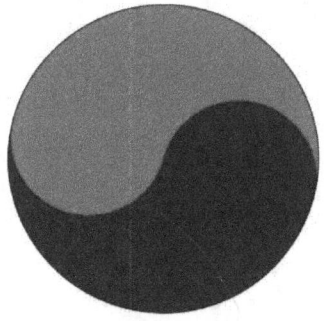

Jason Howard

DEDICATION

*This book is dedicated to my precious children.
May you and your decedents continue the journey we
started to discover and remember your ancestors...*

CONTENTS

Introduction

Korean family registries are great treasures. They contain precious genealogies that help families remember their ancestors. They also preserve the history and culture of the Korean people. They are treasured by individuals seeking to discover their own roots and historians wishing to discover the carefully preserved history of Korea.

This book is intended to help those who want to research Korean ancestry. Korean language fluency would certainly aide in a quest to discover Korean roots, but it is not a requirement. This guide provides the information necessary for an English speaker to parse and interpret basic genealogical information from Korean family registries (JokBo). The instruction, definitions, and tables that follow provide a solid foundation for Korean genealogy research. Additionally, the tools necessary to launch deeper studies into the language and family histories are introduced.

Interpretation of genealogical information in Korean family registry records is the goal of this book. This goal is realized in the last chapter. Sample records are explored to introduce common structures and patterns in Korean family registries.

There are a few concepts that must be understood to accomplish successful interpretation of family registries. For example, JokBo records are written in HanJa characters. Accordingly, this guide starts with an introduction of basic concepts about the Korean language, including HanJa and HanGul writing. Techniques for looking up definitions via the internet are introduced. Additionally, tables of the most frequently used HanJa characters are provided. The tables serve as a reference that will enable beginners to immediately begin exploring and understanding genealogical records even before mastering the language. The tables are also quite useful for fluent Korean speakers, too, as they cover concepts and HanJa characters that are not commonly used in daily life but are essential for interpreting family registries.

Korean names can be written in HanJa characters, which reveal beautiful meanings. They can also be written in HanGul characters, which reveal the Korean pronunciation. Tables of Korean family names and the HanJa characters used in Korean names are provided. Generally the genealogical records are in HanJa, and these tables can aide in discovering pronunciations and the easily typed HanGul version that can be used to search online dictionaries for meanings.

The dates and numbering systems used in family registries are not the common western systems used in daily life today. Tables enabling translation of HanJa numbers are provided. Additionally, the concepts and tables necessary to decipher lunar calendar years are provided. Even those fluent in Korean will find this reference particularly useful. The lunar year tables simplify genealogical research dramatically.

A basic knowledge of Korean history is needed both to appreciate and to understand older genealogical records. Knowing the history enriches an understanding of the lives of the ancestors recorded in family registries. In some cases just discovering the years in which the ancestors lived requires recognizing the names of monarchs and knowing the years they reigned. For example, some years are recorded in terms of a king or emperor's reign, such as "the 10th year of the reign of king SaeJong" or "the 39th year of the 60-year lunar cycle under the reign of king JongJung." A table of monarchs and their ruling years is provided to help genealogists convert these records into western solar calendar years.

The tables and information provided are a solid foundation upon which to begin interpreting genealogical records. The locations of growing online databases of Korean genealogical records are also provided as a great starting point.

Readers are encouraged to collaborate online. A growing community of Korean genealogy enthusiasts can share discoveries, share additional resources, submit and answer questions, and help each other discover Korean roots.

A good starting point is http://KoreanGenealogy.org.

1 - Korean Writing

Korea has a long and rich history. Korean language, culture, and history are inseparable. This book does not attempt to separate them. As you study the Korean language, you see the collective experience of the Korean people over thousands of years of precious culture and history.

HanJa Characters

The Korean people and their language have existed for thousands of years. Early on, they used Chinese characters to write the Korean language. The pronunciations and grammar were different than Chinese. They were using those written characters to represent their own language. When Chinese-like characters are used by Koreans in this way, they refer to the characters as "HanJa."

Today HanJa is not required when writing Korean, but it is still used in formal and traditional writing. All words can be represented by pure Korean HanGul letters, but only words with Chinese roots can be represented by HanJa characters. About 80% of Korean words can be represented by HanJa. Typically, Chinese root words are two syllables represented by two HanJa characters.

There are thousands of HanJa characters. Many share the same Korean pronunciation, but each has its own meaning. Each HanJa character represents a single syllable. However, the HanJa characters are not phonetic -- they do not contain any clues about pronunciation. They contain rich clues about meaning. In fact, a primary use of HanJa is to specify meanings, especially in cases when multiple HanJa characters share the same pronunciation.

For Korean words with HanJa roots, the HanJa representation provides the exact meaning. The HanGul version provides the exact pronunciation. The HanGul version is significantly easier to use, but both are required to fully understand the word. For example, if searching for meanings online it is much easier to search based on the phonetic HanGul version, select the correct HanJa character based on the search results, and then learn the meaning.

Korean high school students memorize thousands of HanJa characters. Truly mastering HanJa, however, requires even higher levels of study. Learning the most common HanJa root characters can enhance Korean vocabulary study significantly; this is similar to how studying Greek or Latin root words helps build English vocabulary. An excellent resource is the book "Handbook of Korean Vocabulary" (Handbook of Korean Vocabulary: A Resource for Word Recognition and Comprehension, by Miho Choo and William O'Grady, 1996, Center for Korean Studies), which has hundreds of vocabulary words organized by common root characters. It also has a useful section of Korean root words, which do not have HanJa representations. http://hanja.naver.com is a good online source for HanJa study.

A good example of a HanJa character is the root syllable "Han." The HanGul version of this syllable is 한, which specifies the pronunciation "Han" (ㅎ =h, ㅏ =a, ㄴ =n; ㅎ + ㅏ + ㄴ = 한). The HanJa version is 韓, which means Korea. You can combine the root 韓 with other syllables to create many two-syllable words, as shown in the following table:

Table 1.1: Examples of HanJa Vocabulary with Common Roots

HanJa	HanGul	Pronunciation	Definition
韓國	한국	**Han**Guk	Korean Country
韓契	한글	**Han**Gul	Korean Writing
韓食	한식	**Han**Shik	Korean Food
南韓	남한	Nam**Han**	South Korea
北韓	북한	Buk**Han**	North Korea
韓子	한자	**Han**Ja	Korean Characters

As you study HanJa you will notice that some characters are simple and some are complex. The complex HanJa are usually a combination of several simple HanJa into one character. For example, the simple HanJa for roof and tree are put together into a more complex HanJa character representing the Song family name. Understanding the characters that make up a complex HanJa symbol provides a deeper understanding of the meaning. In the following example, one interprets the imagery of a family tree under one roof, which evokes deeper insights about the meaning of the family name "Song."

Table 1.2: Examples of Simple and Compound HanJa

HanJa	HanGul	Pronunciation	Definition
宀	면	Myeon	Roof, Home
木	목	Mok	Tree
宋	송	Song	Song *(family name)*

HanGul Letters

The Korean people have a long history of valuing education. The Great King SaeJong recognized that HanJa was a barrier to literacy for many in the working class. They lacked the education, resources, and time required to memorize thousands of HanJa characters. He developed a simple form of writing called "HanGul" (Korean Writing) to solve this problem.

HanGul is simple, scientific, and phonetic. It is made up of 24 simple characters that represent sounds. They can be combined into compound letters to make up all 40 sounds used in the Korean language.

Sometimes it is useful for foreigners to attempt to write Korean words with English letters. This is called Romanization. There are several standard Romanization methods that can be used to represent Korean words in English. The standard adopted by the South Korean Ministry of Culture and Tourism in the year 2000 is the Revised Romanization method. The sounds of the Korean language are not identical to the sounds of the English language, so no Romanization method will be perfect. This book does not strictly adhere to the standard methods in an attempt to write the English form of words that is most likely to result in a non-Korean speaker pronouncing the word correctly.

A serious study of the Korean language should start with memorization of the HanGul letters in Tables 1.3 – 1.4 and their correct pronunciations. However, genealogy can be interpreted without memorization by using these tables a reference.

HanGul Syllables

HanGul letters are combined into syllables. Syllables start with a consonant, one of which can be a silent consonant placeholder if the syllable actually starts with a vowel sound. Every syllable must have a vowel, which can be simple or compound. A syllable can optionally end with one or two additional consonants.

Tables 1.5 – 1.23 show all possible combinations of HanGul letters into syllables. Note that if you memorize the HanGul letters in Tables 1.3 - 1.4 you can read syllables without using the tables of syllables. The tables can be used as a pronunciation guide. They can also be used to learn how to properly format syllables made up of multiple HanGul letters.

Table 1.3: HanGul Consonant Letters

HanGul Letter	English Transliteration	Consonant Type	Pronunciation Guide
ㄱ	g, k	Single	g, k
ㄲ	gg	Double	stronger g than ㄱ
ㄴ	n	Single	n
ㄷ	d, t	Single	d, t
ㄸ	dd	Double	stronger d than ㄷ
ㄹ	r, l	Single	r, l
ㅁ	m	Single	m
ㅂ	b, p	Single	b, p
ㅃ	bb	Double	stronger b than ㅂ
ㅅ	s, sh	Single	s, sh
ㅆ	ss	Double	stronger s than ㅅ
ㅇ	(silent), ng	Single	(silent) , 'ng'
ㅈ	j	Single	j
ㅉ	jj	Double	stronger j than ㅈ
ㅊ	ch	Single	ch
ㅋ	k	Single	stronger k than ㄱ
ㅌ	t	Single	stronger t than ㄷ
ㅍ	p	Single	stronger p than ㅂ
ㅎ	h	Single	h

Table 1.4: HanGul Vowel Letters

HanGul Letter	English Transliteration	Vowel Type	Pronunciation Guide
ㅏ	a	Simple	a in father
ㅐ	ae	Compound	e in beg
ㅑ	ya	Simple	ya in yarn
ㅒ	yae	Compound	ye in yes
ㅓ	eo	Simple	u in luck
ㅔ	ae	Compound	e in neck
ㅕ	yeo	Simple	you in young
ㅖ	yae	Compound	ye in yes
ㅗ	o	Simple	o in go
ㅘ	wa	Compound	wa in wand
ㅙ	wae	Compound	whe in when
ㅚ	oy	Compound	oy in oyster
ㅛ	yo	Simple	yo in yo-yo
ㅜ	u	Simple	u in tune
ㅝ	weo	Compound	wha in what
ㅞ	wae	Compound	wea in weapon
ㅟ	wi	Compound	we in we
ㅠ	yu	Simple	you in you
ㅡ	eu	Simple	e in the
ㅢ	ui	Compound	eo in people
ㅣ	i	Simple	e in be

Table 1.5: HanGul Syllables Starting with ㄱ (g)

Each cell shows the HanGul syllable followed by its romanization. The leading consonant is ㄱ (g).

ㄱ g	vowel	(base)	ㄱ g	ㄲ gg	ㄳ gs	ㄴ n	ㄵ nj	ㄶ nh	ㄷ d	ㄹ l	ㄺ lg	ㄻ lm	ㄼ lb	ㄽ ls	ㄾ lt
ㄱ g	ㅏ a	가 ga	각 gag	갂 gagg	갃 gags	간 gan	갅 ganj	갆 ganh	갇 gad	갈 gal	갉 galg	갊 galm	갋 galb	갌 gals	갍 galt
ㄱ g	ㅐ ae	개 gae	객 gaeg	갞 gaegg	갟 gaegs	갠 gaen	갡 gaenj	갢 gaenh	갣 gaed	갤 gael	갥 gaelg	갦 gaelm	갧 gaelb	갨 gaels	갩 gaelt
ㄱ g	ㅑ ya	갸 gya	갹 gyag	갺 gyagg	갻 gyags	갼 gyan	갽 gyanj	갾 gyanh	갿 gyad	걀 gyal	걁 gyalg	걂 gyalm	걃 gyalb	걄 gyals	걅 gyalt
ㄱ g	ㅒ yae	걔 gyae	걕 gyaeg	걖 gyaegg	걗 gyaegs	걘 gyaen	걙 gyaenj	걚 gyaenh	걛 gyaed	걜 gyael	걝 gyaelg	걞 gyaelm	걟 gyaelb	걠 gyaels	걡 gyaelt
ㄱ g	ㅓ eo	거 geo	걱 geog	걲 geogg	걳 geogs	건 geon	걵 geonj	걶 geonh	걷 geod	걸 geol	걹 geolg	걺 geolm	걻 geolb	걼 geols	걽 geolt
ㄱ g	ㅔ e	게 ge	겍 geg	겎 gegg	겏 gegs	겐 gen	겑 genj	겒 genh	겓 ged	겔 gel	겕 gelg	겖 gelm	겗 gelb	겘 gels	겙 gelt
ㄱ g	ㅕ yeo	겨 gyeo	격 gyeog	겪 gyeogg	겫 gyeogs	견 gyeon	겭 gyeonj	겮 gyeonh	겯 gyeod	결 gyeol	겱 gyeolg	겲 gyeolm	겳 gyeolb	겴 gyeols	겵 gyeolt
ㄱ g	ㅖ ye	계 gye	곅 gyeg	곆 gyegg	곇 gyegs	곈 gyen	곉 gyenj	곊 gyenh	곋 gyed	곌 gyel	곍 gyelg	곎 gyelm	곏 gyelb	곐 gyels	곑 gyelt
ㄱ g	ㅗ o	고 go	곡 gog	곢 gogg	곣 gogs	곤 gon	곥 gonj	곦 gonh	곧 god	골 gol	곩 golg	곪 golm	곫 golb	곬 gols	곭 golt
ㄱ g	ㅘ wa	과 gwa	곽 gwag	곾 gwagg	곿 gwags	관 gwan	괁 gwanj	괂 gwanh	괃 gwad	괄 gwal	괅 gwalg	괆 gwalm	괇 gwalb	괈 gwals	괉 gwalt
ㄱ g	ㅙ wae	괘 gwae	괙 gwaeg	괚 gwaegg	괛 gwaegs	괜 gwaen	괝 gwaenj	괞 gwaenh	괟 gwaed	괠 gwael	괡 gwaelg	괢 gwaelm	괣 gwaelb	괤 gwaels	괥 gwaelt
ㄱ g	ㅚ oe	괴 goe	괵 goeg	괶 goegg	괷 goegs	괸 goen	괹 goenj	괺 goenh	괻 goed	괼 goel	괽 goelg	괾 goelm	괿 goelb	굀 goels	굁 goelt
ㄱ g	ㅛ yo	교 gyo	굑 gyog	굒 gyogg	굓 gyogs	굔 gyon	굕 gyonj	굖 gyonh	굗 gyod	굘 gyol	굙 gyolg	굚 gyolm	굛 gyolb	굜 gyols	굝 gyolt
ㄱ g	ㅜ u	구 gu	국 gug	굮 gugg	굯 gugs	군 gun	굱 gunj	굲 gunh	굳 gud	굴 gul	굵 gulg	굶 gulm	굷 gulb	굸 guls	굹 gult
ㄱ g	ㅝ weo	궈 gweo	궉 gweog	궊 gweogg	궋 gweogs	권 gweon	궍 gweonj	궎 gweonh	궏 gweod	궐 gweol	궑 gweolg	궒 gweolm	궓 gweolb	궔 gweols	궕 gweolt
ㄱ g	ㅞ we	궤 gwe	궥 gweg	궦 gwegg	궧 gwegs	궨 gwen	궩 gwenj	궪 gwenh	궫 gwed	궬 gwel	궭 gwelg	궮 gwelm	궯 gwelb	궰 gwels	궱 gwelt
ㄱ g	ㅟ wi	귀 gwi	귁 gwig	귂 gwigg	귃 gwigs	귄 gwin	귅 gwinj	귆 gwinh	귇 gwid	귈 gwil	귉 gwilg	귊 gwilm	귋 gwilb	귌 gwils	귍 gwilt
ㄱ g	ㅠ yu	규 gyu	귝 gyug	귞 gyugg	귟 gyugs	균 gyun	귡 gyunj	귢 gyunh	귣 gyud	귤 gyul	귥 gyulg	귦 gyulm	귧 gyulb	귨 gyuls	귩 gyult
ㄱ g	ㅡ eu	그 geu	극 geug	긎 geugg	긏 geugs	근 geun	긑 geunj	긒 geunh	긓 geud	글 geul	긅 geulg	긆 geulm	긇 geulb	금 geuls	급 geult
ㄱ g	ㅢ yi	긔 gyi	긕 gyig	긖 gyigg	긗 gyigs	긘 gyin	긙 gyinj	긚 gyinh	긛 gyid	긜 gyil	긝 gyilg	긞 gyilm	긟 gyilb	긠 gyils	긡 gyilt
ㄱ g	ㅣ i	기 gi	긱 gig	긲 gigg	긳 gigs	긴 gin	긵 ginj	긶 ginh	긷 gid	길 gil	긹 gilg	긺 gilm	긻 gilb	긼 gils	긽 gilt

ㄱ / g		ㄿ lp	ㅀ lh	ㅁ m	ㅂ b	ㅄ bs	ㅅ s	ㅆ ss	ㅇ ng	ㅈ j	ㅊ ch	ㅋ k	ㅌ t	ㅍ p	ㅎ h
g	ㅏ a	갎 galp	갏 galh	감 gam	갑 gab	값 gabs	갓 gas	갔 gass	강 gang	갖 gaj	갗 gach	갘 gak	같 gat	갚 gap	갛 gah
g	ㅐ ae	갪 gaelp	갫 gaelh	갬 gaem	갭 gaeb	갮 gaebs	갯 gaes	갰 gaess	갱 gaeng	갲 gaej	갳 gaech	갴 gaek	갵 gaet	갶 gaep	갷 gaeh
g	ㅑ ya	걆 gyalp	걇 gyalh	걈 gyam	걉 gyab	걊 gyabs	걋 gyas	걌 gyass	걍 gyang	걎 gyaj	걏 gyach	걐 gyak	걑 gyat	걒 gyap	걓 gyah
g	ㅒ yae	걢 gyaelp	걣 gyaelh	걤 gyaem	걥 gyaeb	걦 gyaebs	걧 gyaes	걨 gyaess	걩 gyaeng	걪 gyaej	걫 gyaech	걬 gyaek	걭 gyaet	걮 gyaep	걯 gyaeh
g	ㅓ eo	걾 geolp	걿 geolh	검 geom	겁 geob	겂 geobs	것 geos	겄 geoss	겅 geong	겆 geoj	겇 geoch	겈 geok	겉 geot	겊 geop	겋 geoh
g	ㅔ e	겚 gelp	겛 gelh	겜 gem	겝 geb	겞 gebs	겟 ges	겠 gess	겡 geng	겢 gej	겣 gech	겤 gek	겥 get	겦 gep	겧 geh
g	ㅕ yeo	겶 gyeolp	겷 gyeolh	겸 gyeom	겹 gyeob	겺 gyeobs	겻 gyeos	겼 gyeoss	경 gyeong	겾 gyeoj	겿 gyeoch	곀 gyeok	곁 gyeot	곂 gyeop	곃 gyeoh
g	ㅖ ye	곒 gyelp	곓 gyelh	곔 gyem	곕 gyeb	곖 gyebs	곗 gyes	곘 gyess	곙 gyeng	곚 gyej	곛 gyech	곜 gyek	곝 gyet	곞 gyep	곟 gyeh
g	ㅗ o	곮 golp	곯 golh	곰 gom	곱 gob	곲 gobs	곳 gos	곴 goss	공 gong	곶 goj	곷 goch	곸 gok	곹 got	곺 gop	곻 goh
g	ㅘ wa	괊 gwalp	괋 gwalh	괌 gwam	괍 gwab	괎 gwabs	괏 gwas	괐 gwass	광 gwang	괒 gwaj	괓 gwach	괔 gwak	괕 gwat	괖 gwap	괗 gwah
g	ㅙ wae	괦 gwaelp	괧 gwaelh	괨 gwaem	괩 gwaeb	괪 gwaebs	괫 gwaes	괬 gwaess	괭 gwaeng	괮 gwaej	괯 gwaech	괰 gwaek	괱 gwaet	괲 gwaep	괳 gwaeh
g	ㅚ oe	굂 goelp	굃 goelh	굄 goem	굅 goeb	굆 goebs	굇 goes	굈 goess	굉 goeng	굊 goej	굋 goech	굌 goek	굍 goet	굎 goep	굏 goeh
g	ㅛ yo	굞 gyolp	굟 gyolh	굠 gyom	굡 gyob	굢 gyobs	굣 gyos	굤 gyoss	굥 gyong	굦 gyoj	굧 gyoch	굨 gyok	굩 gyot	굪 gyop	굫 gyoh
g	ㅜ u	굺 gulp	굻 gulh	굼 gum	굽 gub	굾 gubs	굿 gus	궀 guss	궁 gung	궂 guj	궃 guch	궄 guk	궅 gut	궆 gup	궇 guh
g	ㅝ weo	궖 gweolp	궗 gweolh	궘 gweom	궙 gweob	궚 gweobs	궛 gweos	궜 gweoss	권 gweong	궞 gweoj	궟 gweoch	궠 gweok	궡 gweot	궢 gweop	궣 gweoh
g	ㅞ we	궲 gwelp	궳 gwelh	궴 gwem	궵 gweb	궶 gwebs	궷 gwes	궸 gwess	궹 gweng	궺 gwej	궻 gwech	궼 gwek	궽 gwet	궾 gwep	궿 gweh
g	ㅟ wi	귎 gwilp	귏 gwilh	귐 gwim	귑 gwib	귒 gwibs	귓 gwis	귔 gwiss	귕 gwing	귖 gwij	귗 gwich	귘 gwik	귙 gwit	귚 gwip	귛 gwih
g	ㅠ yu	귪 gyulp	귫 gyulh	귬 gyum	귭 gyub	귮 gyubs	귯 gyus	귰 gyuss	귱 gyung	귲 gyuj	귳 gyuch	귴 gyuk	귵 gyut	귶 gyup	귷 gyuh
g	ㅡ eu	긆 geulp	긇 geulh	금 geum	급 geub	긊 geubs	긋 geus	긌 geuss	긍 geung	긎 geuj	긏 geuch	긐 geuk	긑 geut	긒 geup	긓 geuh
g	ㅢ yi	긢 gyilp	긣 gyilh	긤 gyim	긥 gyib	긦 gyibs	긧 gyis	긨 gyiss	긩 gying	긪 gyij	긫 gyich	긬 gyik	긭 gyit	긮 gyip	긯 gyih
g	ㅣ i	긾 gilp	긿 gilh	김 gim	깁 gib	깂 gibs	깃 gis	깄 giss	깅 ging	깆 gij	깇 gich	깈 gik	깉 git	깊 gip	깋 gih

Table 1.6: HanGul Syllables Starting with ㄲ (gg)

		ㄱ g	ㄲ gg	ㄳ gs	ㄴ n	ㄵ nj	ㄶ nh	ㄷ d	ㄹ l	ㄺ lg	ㄻ lm	ㄼ lb	ㄽ ls	ㄾ lt
ㄲ gg	ㅏ a	까 gga	깍 ggag	깏 ggagg	깐 ggags	깐 ggan	깕 gganj	깗 gganh	깐 ggad	깔 ggal	깕 ggalg	깖 ggalm	깗 ggalb	깗 ggals	깚 ggalt
ㄲ gg	ㅐ ae	깨 ggae	깩 ggaeg	깪 ggaegg	깫 ggaegs	깬 ggaen	깭 ggaenj	깮 ggaenh	깯 ggaed	깰 ggael	깱 ggaelg	깲 ggaelm	깳 ggaelb	깴 ggaels	깵 ggaelt
ㄲ gg	ㅑ ya	꺄 ggya	꺅 ggyag	꺆 ggyagg	꺇 ggyags	꺈 ggyan	꺉 ggyanj	꺊 ggyanh	꺋 ggyad	꺌 ggyal	꺍 ggyalg	꺎 ggyalm	꺏 ggyalb	꺐 ggyals	꺑 ggyalt
ㄲ gg	ㅒ yae	꺠 ggyae	꺡 ggyaeg	꺢 ggyaegg	꺣 ggyaegs	꺤 ggyaen	꺥 ggyaenj	꺦 ggyaenh	꺧 ggyaed	꺨 ggyael	꺩 ggyaelg	꺪 ggyaelm	꺫 ggyaelb	꺬 ggyaels	꺭 ggyaelt
ㄲ gg	ㅓ eo	꺼 ggeo	꺽 ggeog	꺾 ggeogg	꺿 ggeogs	껀 ggeon	껁 ggeonj	껂 ggeonh	껃 ggeod	껄 ggeol	껅 ggeolg	껆 ggeolm	껇 ggeolb	껈 ggeols	껉 ggeolt
ㄲ gg	ㅔ e	께 gge	껙 ggeg	껚 ggegg	껛 ggegs	껜 ggen	껝 ggenj	껞 ggenh	껟 gged	껠 ggel	껡 ggelg	껢 ggelm	껣 ggelb	껤 ggels	껥 ggelt
ㄲ gg	ㅕ yeo	껴 ggyeo	껵 ggyeog	껶 ggyeogg	껷 ggyeogs	껸 ggyeon	껹 ggyeonj	껺 ggyeonh	껻 ggyeod	껼 ggyeol	껽 ggyeolg	껾 ggyeolm	껿 ggyeolb	꼀 ggyeols	꼁 ggyeolt
ㄲ gg	ㅖ ye	꼐 ggye	꼑 ggyeg	꼒 ggyegg	꼓 ggyegs	꼔 ggyen	꼕 ggyenj	꼖 ggyenh	꼗 ggyed	꼘 ggyel	꼙 ggyelg	꼚 ggyelm	꼛 ggyelb	꼜 ggyels	꼝 ggyelt
ㄲ gg	ㅗ o	꼬 ggo	꼭 ggog	꼮 ggogg	꼯 ggogs	꼰 ggon	꼱 ggonj	꼲 ggonh	꼳 ggod	꼴 ggol	꼵 ggolg	꼶 ggolm	꼷 ggolb	꼸 ggols	꼹 ggolt
ㄲ gg	ㅘ wa	꽈 ggwa	꽉 ggwag	꽊 ggwagg	꽋 ggwags	꽌 ggwan	꽍 ggwanj	꽎 ggwanh	꽏 ggwad	꽐 ggwal	꽑 ggwalg	꽒 ggwalm	꽓 ggwalb	꽔 ggwals	꽕 ggwalt
ㄲ gg	ㅙ wae	꽤 ggwae	꽥 ggwaeg	꽦 ggwaegg	꽧 ggwaegs	꽨 ggwaen	꽩 ggwaenj	꽪 ggwaenh	꽫 ggwaed	꽬 ggwael	꽭 ggwaelg	꽮 ggwaelm	꽯 ggwaelb	꽰 ggwaels	꽱 ggwaelt
ㄲ gg	ㅚ oe	꾀 ggoe	꾁 ggoeg	꾂 ggoegg	꾃 ggoegs	꾄 ggoen	꾅 ggoenj	꾆 ggoenh	꾇 ggoed	꾈 ggoel	꾉 ggoelg	꾊 ggoelm	꾋 ggoelb	꾌 ggoels	꾍 ggoelt
ㄲ gg	ㅛ yo	꾜 ggyo	꾝 ggyog	꾞 ggyogg	꾟 ggyogs	꾠 ggyon	꾡 ggyonj	꾢 ggyonh	꾣 ggyod	꾤 ggyol	꾥 ggyolg	꾦 ggyolm	꾧 ggyolb	꾨 ggyols	꾩 ggyolt
ㄲ gg	ㅜ u	꾸 ggu	꾹 ggug	꾺 ggugg	꾻 ggugs	꾼 ggun	꾽 ggunj	꾾 ggunh	꾿 ggud	꿀 ggul	꿁 ggulg	꿂 ggulm	꿃 ggulb	꿄 gguls	꿅 ggult
ㄲ gg	ㅝ weo	꿔 ggweo	꿕 ggweog	꿖 ggweogg	꿗 ggweogs	꿘 ggweon	꿙 ggweonj	꿚 ggweonh	꿛 ggweod	꿜 ggweol	꿝 ggweolg	꿞 ggweolm	꿟 ggweolb	꿠 ggweols	꿡 ggweolt
ㄲ gg	ㅞ we	꿰 ggwe	꿱 ggweg	꿲 ggwegg	꿳 ggwegs	꿴 ggwen	꿵 ggwenj	꿶 ggwenh	꿷 ggwed	꿸 ggwel	꿹 ggwelg	꿺 ggwelm	꿻 ggwelb	꿼 ggwels	꿽 ggwelt
ㄲ gg	ㅟ wi	뀌 ggwi	뀍 ggwig	뀎 ggwigg	뀏 ggwigs	뀐 ggwin	뀑 ggwinj	뀒 ggwinh	뀓 ggwid	뀔 ggwil	뀕 ggwilg	뀖 ggwilm	뀗 ggwilb	뀘 ggwils	뀙 ggwilt
ㄲ gg	ㅠ yu	뀨 ggyu	뀩 ggyug	뀪 ggyugg	뀫 ggyugs	뀬 ggyun	뀭 ggyunj	뀮 ggyunh	뀯 ggyud	뀰 ggyul	뀱 ggyulg	뀲 ggyulm	뀳 ggyulb	뀴 ggyuls	뀵 ggyult
ㄲ gg	ㅡ eu	끄 ggeu	끅 ggeug	끆 ggeugg	끇 ggeugs	끈 ggeun	끉 ggeunj	끊 ggeunh	끋 ggeud	끌 ggeul	끍 ggeulg	끎 ggeulm	끏 ggeulb	끐 ggeuls	끑 ggeult
ㄲ gg	ㅢ yi	끼 ggyi	끽 ggyig	끾 ggyigg	끿 ggyigs	낀 ggyin	낁 ggyinj	낂 ggyinh	낃 ggyid	낄 ggyil	낅 ggyilg	낆 ggyilm	낇 ggyilb	낈 ggyils	낉 ggyilt
ㄲ gg	ㅣ i	끼 ggi	끽 ggig	끾 ggigg	끿 ggigs	낀 ggin	낁 gginj	낂 gginh	낃 ggid	낄 ggil	낅 ggilg	낆 ggilm	낇 ggilb	낈 ggils	낉 ggilt

ㄲ gg		ㄾ lp	ㅀ lh	ㅁ m	ㅂ b	ㅄ bs	ㅅ s	ㅆ ss	ㅇ ng	ㅈ j	ㅊ ch	ㅋ k	ㅌ t	ㅍ p	ㅎ h
ㄲ gg	ㅏ a	깖 ggalp	깛 ggalh	깜 ggam	깝 ggab	깞 ggabs	깟 ggas	깠 ggass	깡 ggang	깢 ggaj	깣 ggach	깍 ggak	깥 ggat	깦 ggap	깧 ggah
ㄲ gg	ㅐ ae	깲 ggaelp	깷 ggaelh	깸 ggaem	깹 ggaeb	깺 ggaebs	깻 ggaes	깼 ggaess	깽 ggaeng	깾 ggaej	깿 ggaech	깩 ggaek	깯 ggaet	깶 ggaep	깳 ggaeh
ㄲ gg	ㅑ ya	꺎 ggyalp	꺓 ggyalh	꺔 ggyam	꺕 ggyab	꺖 ggyabs	꺗 ggyas	꺘 ggyass	꺙 ggyang	꺚 ggyaj	꺛 ggyach	꺅 ggyak	꺝 ggyat	꺞 ggyap	꺟 ggyah
ㄲ gg	ㅒ yae	꺲 ggyaelp	꺷 ggyaelh	꺸 ggyaem	꺹 ggyaeb	꺺 ggyaebs	꺻 ggyaes	꺼 ggyaess	꺽 ggyaeng	꺾 ggyaej	꺿 ggyaech	꺩 ggyaek	꺭 ggyaet	꺮 ggyaep	꺳 ggyaeh
ㄲ gg	ㅓ eo	껆 ggeolp	껋 ggeolh	껌 ggeom	껍 ggeob	껎 ggeobs	껏 ggeos	껐 ggeoss	껑 ggeong	껒 ggeoj	껓 ggeoch	꺽 ggeok	껕 ggeot	껖 ggeop	껗 ggeoh
ㄲ gg	ㅔ e	껲 ggelp	껷 ggelh	껨 ggem	껩 ggeb	껪 ggebs	껫 gges	껬 ggess	껭 ggeng	껮 ggej	껯 ggech	껙 ggek	껟 gget	껨 ggep	껳 ggeh
ㄲ gg	ㅕ yeo	꼆 ggyeolp	꼋 ggyeolh	껺 ggyeom	껻 ggyeob	껾 ggyeobs	껸 ggyeos	껹 ggyeoss	껵 ggyeong	껹 ggyeoj	꼇 ggyeoch	껵 ggyeok	껻 ggyeot	껾 ggyeop	껿 ggyeoh
ㄲ gg	ㅖ ye	꼲 ggyelp	꼷 ggyelh	꼄 ggyem	꼅 ggyeb	꼆 ggyebs	꼍 ggyes	꼍 ggyess	꼉 ggyeng	꼊 ggyej	꼋 ggyech	꼅 ggyek	꼍 ggyet	꼎 ggyep	꼏 ggyeh
ㄲ gg	ㅗ o	꼶 ggolp	꼻 ggolh	꼼 ggom	꼽 ggob	꼾 ggobs	꼿 ggos	꽀 ggoss	꽁 ggong	꽂 ggoj	꽃 ggoch	꼭 ggok	꽅 ggot	꼾 ggop	꽇 ggoh
ㄲ gg	ㅘ wa	꽒 ggwalp	꽗 ggwalh	꽘 ggwam	꽙 ggwab	꽚 ggwabs	꽛 ggwas	꽜 ggwass	꽝 ggwang	꽞 ggwaj	꽟 ggwach	꽉 ggwak	꽡 ggwat	꽢 ggwap	꽣 ggwah
ㄲ gg	ㅙ wae	꽲 ggwaelp	꽷 ggwaelh	꽸 ggwaem	꽹 ggwaeb	꽺 ggwaebs	꽻 ggwaes	꽼 ggwaess	꽽 ggwaeng	꽾 ggwaej	꽿 ggwaech	꽥 ggwaek	꽩 ggwaet	꽪 ggwaep	꽮 ggwaeh
ㄲ gg	ㅚ oe	꾆 ggoelp	꾋 ggoelh	꾀 ggoem	꾁 ggoeb	꾂 ggoebs	꾃 ggoes	꾄 ggoess	꾅 ggoeng	꾆 ggoej	꾇 ggoech	꾁 ggoek	꾈 ggoet	꾉 ggoep	꾋 ggoeh
ㄲ gg	ㅛ yo	꾶 ggyolp	꾻 ggyolh	꾬 ggyom	꾭 ggyob	꾮 ggyobs	꾯 ggyos	꾰 ggyoss	꾱 ggyong	꾲 ggyoj	꾳 ggyoch	꾝 ggyok	꾵 ggyot	꾶 ggyop	꾷 ggyoh
ㄲ gg	ㅜ u	꿇 ggulp	꿇 ggulh	꿈 ggum	꿉 ggub	꿊 ggubs	꿋 ggus	꿌 gguss	꿍 ggung	꿎 gguj	꿏 gguch	꾹 gguk	꿑 ggut	꿈 ggup	꿓 gguh
ㄲ gg	ㅝ weo	꿞 ggweolp	꿣 ggweolh	꿤 ggweom	꿥 ggweob	꿦 ggweobs	꿧 ggweos	꿨 ggweoss	꿩 ggweong	꿪 ggweoj	꿫 ggweoch	꿕 ggweok	꿝 ggweot	꿞 ggweop	꿟 ggweoh
ㄲ gg	ㅞ we	꿲 ggwelp	꿷 ggwelh	꿸 ggwem	꿹 ggweb	꿺 ggwebs	꿻 ggwes	꿼 ggwess	꿽 ggweng	꿾 ggwej	꿿 ggwech	꿱 ggwek	꿵 ggwet	꿶 ggwep	꿿 ggweh
ㄲ gg	ㅟ wi	뀂 ggwilp	뀇 ggwilh	뀀 ggwim	뀁 ggwib	뀂 ggwibs	뀃 ggwis	뀄 ggwiss	뀅 ggwing	뀆 ggwij	뀇 ggwich	뀁 ggwik	뀈 ggwit	뀉 ggwip	뀋 ggwih
ㄲ gg	ㅠ yu	뀶 ggyulp	뀻 ggyulh	뀸 ggyum	뀹 ggyub	뀺 ggyubs	뀻 ggyus	뀼 ggyuss	뀽 ggyung	뀾 ggyuj	뀿 ggyuch	뀩 ggyuk	뀵 ggyut	뀶 ggyup	뀷 ggyuh
ㄲ gg	ㅡ eu	끎 ggeulp	끓 ggeulh	끔 ggeum	끕 ggeub	끖 ggeubs	끗 ggeus	끘 ggeuss	끙 ggeung	끚 ggeuj	끛 ggeuch	끅 ggeuk	끝 ggeut	끞 ggeup	끟 ggeuh
ㄲ gg	ㅢ yi	끫 ggyilp	끫 ggyilh	끰 ggyim	끱 ggyib	끲 ggyibs	끳 ggyis	끴 ggyiss	끵 ggying	끶 ggyij	끷 ggyich	끡 ggyik	끝 ggyit	끞 ggyip	끻 ggyih
ㄲ gg	ㅣ i	낆 ggilp	낋 ggilh	낌 ggim	낍 ggib	낎 ggibs	낏 ggis	꼈 ggiss	낑 gging	낒 ggij	낓 ggich	끽 ggik	낕 ggit	낍 ggip	낗 ggih

Table 1.7: HanGul Syllables Starting with ㄴ (n)

		ㄱ	ㄲ	ㄳ	ㄴ	ㄵ	ㄶ	ㄷ	ㄹ	ㄺ	ㄻ	ㄼ	ㄽ	ㄾ
		g	gg	gs	n	nj	nh	d	l	lg	lm	lb	ls	lt
ㄴ n	ㅏ a	나 na	낙 nag	낚 nagg	낛 nags	난 nan	낝 nanj	낞 nanh	낟 nad	날 nal	낡 nalg	낢 nalm	낣 nalb	낤 nals	낥 nalt
ㄴ n	ㅐ ae	내 nae	낵 naeg	낶 naegg	낷 naegs	낸 naen	낹 naenj	낺 naenh	낻 naed	낼 nael	낽 naelg	낾 naelm	낿 naelb	냀 naels	냁 naelt
ㄴ n	ㅑ ya	냐 nya	냑 nyag	냒 nyagg	냓 nyags	냔 nyan	냕 nyanj	냖 nyanh	냗 nyad	냘 nyal	냙 nyalg	냚 nyalm	냛 nyalb	냜 nyals	냝 nyalt
ㄴ n	ㅒ yae	냬 nyae	냭 nyaeg	냮 nyaegg	냯 nyaegs	냰 nyaen	냱 nyaenj	냲 nyaenh	냳 nyaed	냴 nyael	냵 nyaelg	냶 nyaelm	냷 nyaelb	냸 nyaels	냹 nyaelt
ㄴ n	ㅓ eo	너 neo	넉 neog	넊 neogg	넋 neogs	넌 neon	넍 neonj	넎 neonh	넏 neod	널 neol	넑 neolg	넒 neolm	넓 neolb	넔 neols	넕 neolt
ㄴ n	ㅔ e	네 ne	넥 neg	넦 negg	넧 negs	넨 nen	넩 nenj	넪 nenh	넫 ned	넬 nel	넭 nelg	넮 nelm	넯 nelb	넰 nels	넱 nelt
ㄴ n	ㅕ yeo	녀 nyeo	녁 nyeog	녂 nyeogg	녃 nyeogs	년 nyeon	녅 nyeonj	녆 nyeonh	녇 nyeod	녈 nyeol	녉 nyeolg	녊 nyeolm	녋 nyeolb	녌 nyeols	녍 nyeolt
ㄴ n	ㅖ ye	녜 nye	녝 nyeg	녞 nyegg	녟 nyegs	녠 nyen	녡 nyenj	녢 nyenh	녣 nyed	녤 nyel	녥 nyelg	녦 nyelm	녧 nyelb	녨 nyels	녩 nyelt
ㄴ n	ㅗ o	노 no	녹 nog	녺 nogg	녻 nogs	논 non	녽 nonj	녾 nonh	녿 nod	놀 nol	놁 nolg	놂 nolm	놃 nolb	놄 nols	놅 nolt
ㄴ n	ㅘ wa	놔 nwa	놕 nwag	놖 nwagg	놗 nwags	놘 nwan	놙 nwanj	놚 nwanh	놛 nwad	놜 nwal	놝 nwalg	놞 nwalm	놟 nwalb	놠 nwals	놡 nwalt
ㄴ n	ㅙ wae	놰 nwae	놱 nwaeg	놲 nwaegg	놳 nwaegs	놴 nwaen	놵 nwaenj	놶 nwaenh	놷 nwaed	놸 nwael	놹 nwaelg	놺 nwaelm	놻 nwaelb	놼 nwaels	놽 nwaelt
ㄴ n	ㅚ oe	뇌 noe	뇍 noeg	뇎 noegg	뇏 noegs	뇐 noen	뇑 noenj	뇒 noenh	뇓 noed	뇔 noel	뇕 noelg	뇖 noelm	뇗 noelb	뇘 noels	뇙 noelt
ㄴ n	ㅛ yo	뇨 nyo	뇩 nyog	뇪 nyogg	뇫 nyogs	뇬 nyon	뇭 nyonj	뇮 nyonh	뇯 nyod	뇰 nyol	뇱 nyolg	뇲 nyolm	뇳 nyolb	뇴 nyols	뇵 nyolt
ㄴ n	ㅜ u	누 nu	눅 nug	눆 nugg	눇 nugs	눈 nun	눉 nunj	눊 nunh	눋 nud	눌 nul	눍 nulg	눎 nulm	눏 nulb	눐 nuls	눑 nult
ㄴ n	ㅝ weo	눠 nweo	눡 nweog	눢 nweogg	눣 nweogs	눤 nweon	눥 nweonj	눦 nweonh	눧 nweod	눨 nweol	눩 nweolg	눪 nweolm	눫 nweolb	눬 nweols	눭 nweolt
ㄴ n	ㅞ we	눼 nwe	눽 nweg	눾 nwegg	눿 nwegs	뉀 nwen	뉁 nwenj	뉂 nwenh	뉃 nwed	뉄 nwel	뉅 nwelg	뉆 nwelm	뉇 nwelb	뉈 nwels	뉉 nwelt
ㄴ n	ㅟ wi	뉘 nwi	뉙 nwig	뉚 nwigg	뉛 nwigs	뉜 nwin	뉝 nwinj	뉞 nwinh	뉟 nwid	뉠 nwil	뉡 nwilg	뉢 nwilm	뉣 nwilb	뉤 nwils	뉥 nwilt
ㄴ n	ㅠ yu	뉴 nyu	뉵 nyug	뉶 nyugg	뉷 nyugs	뉸 nyun	뉹 nyunj	뉺 nyunh	뉻 nyud	뉼 nyul	뉽 nyulg	뉾 nyulm	뉿 nyulb	늀 nyuls	늁 nyult
ㄴ n	ㅡ eu	느 neu	늑 neug	늒 neugg	늓 neugs	는 neun	늕 neunj	늖 neunh	늗 neud	늘 neul	늙 neulg	늚 neulm	늛 neulb	늜 neuls	늝 neult
ㄴ n	ㅢ yi	늬 nyi	늭 nyig	늮 nyigg	늯 nyigs	늰 nyin	늱 nyinj	늲 nyinh	늳 nyid	늴 nyil	늵 nyilg	늶 nyilm	늷 nyilb	늸 nyils	늹 nyilt
ㄴ n	ㅣ i	니 ni	닉 nig	닊 nigg	닋 nigs	닌 nin	닍 ninj	닎 ninh	닏 nid	닐 nil	닑 nilg	닒 nilm	닓 nilb	닔 nils	닕 nilt

ㄴ n		ㄿ lp	ㅀ lh	ㅁ m	ㅂ b	ㅄ bs	ㅅ s	ㅆ ss	ㅇ ng	ㅈ j	ㅊ ch	ㅋ k	ㅌ t	ㅍ p	ㅎ h
ㄴ n	ㅏ a	nalp	nalh	nam	nab	nabs	nas	nass	nang	naj	nach	nak	nat	nap	nah
ㄴ n	ㅐ ae	naelp	naelh	naem	naeb	naebs	naes	naess	naeng	naej	naech	naek	naet	naep	naeh
ㄴ n	ㅑ ya	nyalp	nyalh	nyam	nyab	nyabs	nyas	nyass	nyang	nyaj	nyach	nyak	nyat	nyap	nyah
ㄴ n	ㅒ yae	nyaelp	nyaelh	nyaem	nyaeb	nyaebs	nyaes	nyaess	nyaeng	nyaej	nyaech	nyaek	nyaet	nyaep	nyaeh
ㄴ n	ㅓ eo	neolp	neolh	neom	neob	neobs	neos	neoss	neong	neoj	neoch	neok	neot	neop	neoh
ㄴ n	ㅔ e	nelp	nelh	nem	neb	nebs	nes	ness	neng	nej	nech	nek	net	nep	neh
ㄴ n	ㅕ yeo	nyeolp	nyeolh	nyeom	nyeob	nyeobs	nyeos	nyeoss	nyeong	nyeoj	nyeoch	nyeok	nyeot	nyeop	nyeoh
ㄴ n	ㅖ ye	nyelp	nyelh	nyem	nyeb	nyebs	nyes	nyess	nyeng	nyej	nyech	nyek	nyet	nyep	nyeh
ㄴ n	ㅗ o	nolp	nolh	nom	nob	nobs	nos	noss	nong	noj	noch	nok	not	nop	noh
ㄴ n	ㅘ wa	nwalp	nwalh	nwam	nwab	nwabs	nwas	nwass	nwang	nwaj	nwach	nwak	nwat	nwap	nwah
ㄴ n	ㅙ wae	nwaelp	nwaelh	nwaem	nwaeb	nwaebs	nwaes	nwaess	nwaeng	nwaej	nwaech	nwaek	nwaet	nwaep	nwaeh
ㄴ n	ㅚ oe	noelp	noelh	noem	noeb	noebs	noes	noess	noeng	noej	noech	noek	noet	noep	noeh
ㄴ n	ㅛ yo	nyolp	nyolh	nyom	nyob	nyobs	nyos	nyoss	nyong	nyoj	nyoch	nyok	nyot	nyop	nyoh
ㄴ n	ㅜ u	nulp	nulh	num	nub	nubs	nus	nuss	nung	nuj	nuch	nuk	nut	nup	nuh
ㄴ n	ㅝ weo	nweolp	nweolh	nweom	nweob	nweobs	nweos	nweoss	nweong	nweoj	nweoch	nweok	nweot	nweop	nweoh
ㄴ n	ㅞ we	nwelp	nwelh	nwem	nweb	nwebs	nwes	nwess	nweng	nwej	nwech	nwek	nwet	nwep	nweh
ㄴ n	ㅟ wi	nwilp	nwilh	nwim	nwib	nwibs	nwis	nwiss	nwing	nwij	nwich	nwik	nwit	nwip	nwih
ㄴ n	ㅠ yu	nyulp	nyulh	nyum	nyub	nyubs	nyus	nyuss	nyung	nyuj	nyuch	nyuk	nyut	nyup	nyuh
ㄴ n	ㅡ eu	neulp	neulh	neum	neub	neubs	neus	neuss	neung	neuj	neuch	neuk	neut	neup	neuh
ㄴ n	ㅢ yi	nyilp	nyilh	nyim	nyib	nyibs	nyis	nyiss	nying	nyij	nyich	nyik	nyit	nyip	nyih
ㄴ n	ㅣ i	nilp	nilh	nim	nib	nibs	nis	niss	ning	nij	nich	nik	nit	nip	nih

Table 1.8: HanGul Syllables Starting with ㄷ (d)

		ㄱ	ㄲ	ㄳ	ㄴ	ㄵ	ㄶ	ㄷ	ㄹ	ㄺ	ㄻ	ㄼ	ㄽ	ㄾ
		g	gg	gs	n	nj	nh	d	l	lg	lm	lb	ls	lt
ㄷ d	ㅏ a	다 da	닥 dag	닦 dagg	닧 dags	단 dan	닩 danj	닪 danh	닫 dad	달 dal	닭 dalg	닮 dalm	닯 dalb	닰 dals	닱 dalt
ㄷ d	ㅐ ae	대 dae	댁 daeg	댂 daegg	댃 daegs	댄 daen	댅 daenj	댆 daenh	댇 daed	댈 dael	댉 daelg	댊 daelm	댋 daelb	댌 daels	댍 daelt
ㄷ d	ㅑ ya	댜 dya	댝 dyag	댞 dyagg	댟 dyags	댠 dyan	댡 dyanj	댢 dyanh	댣 dyad	댤 dyal	댥 dyalg	댦 dyalm	댧 dyalb	댨 dyals	댩 dyalt
ㄷ d	ㅒ yae	댸 dyae	댹 dyaeg	댺 dyaegg	댻 dyaegs	댼 dyaen	댽 dyaenj	댾 dyaenh	댿 dyaed	뎀 dyael	뎁 dyaelg	뎂 dyaelm	뎃 dyaelb	뎄 dyaels	뎅 dyaelt
ㄷ d	ㅓ eo	더 deo	덕 deog	덖 deogg	덗 deogs	던 deon	덙 deonj	덚 deonh	덛 deod	덜 deol	덝 deolg	덞 deolm	덟 deolb	덠 deols	덡 deolt
ㄷ d	ㅔ e	데 de	덱 deg	덲 degg	덳 degs	덴 den	덵 denj	덶 denh	덷 ded	델 del	덹 delg	덺 delm	덻 delb	덼 dels	덽 delt
ㄷ d	ㅕ yeo	뎌 dyeo	뎍 dyeog	뎎 dyeogg	뎏 dyeogs	뎐 dyeon	뎑 dyeonj	뎒 dyeonh	뎓 dyeod	뎔 dyeol	뎕 dyeolg	뎖 dyeolm	뎗 dyeolb	뎘 dyeols	뎙 dyeolt
ㄷ d	ㅖ ye	뎨 dye	뎩 dyeg	뎪 dyegg	뎫 dyegs	뎬 dyen	뎭 dyenj	뎮 dyenh	뎯 dyed	뎰 dyel	뎱 dyelg	뎲 dyelm	뎳 dyelb	뎴 dyels	뎵 dyelt
ㄷ d	ㅗ o	도 do	독 dog	돆 dogg	돇 dogs	돈 don	돉 donj	돊 donh	돋 dod	돌 dol	돍 dolg	돎 dolm	돏 dolb	돐 dols	돑 dolt
ㄷ d	ㅘ wa	돠 dwa	돡 dwag	돢 dwagg	돣 dwags	돤 dwan	돥 dwanj	돦 dwanh	돧 dwad	돨 dwal	돩 dwalg	돪 dwalm	돫 dwalb	돬 dwals	돭 dwalt
ㄷ d	ㅙ wae	돼 dwae	돽 dwaeg	돾 dwaegg	돿 dwaegs	됀 dwaen	됁 dwaenj	됂 dwaenh	됃 dwaed	됄 dwael	됅 dwaelg	됆 dwaelm	됇 dwaelb	됈 dwaels	됉 dwaelt
ㄷ d	ㅚ oe	되 doe	됙 doeg	됚 doegg	됛 doegs	된 doen	됝 doenj	됞 doenh	됟 doed	될 doel	됡 doelg	됢 doelm	됣 doelb	됤 doels	됥 doelt
ㄷ d	ㅛ yo	됴 dyo	둑 dyog	둒 dyogg	둓 dyogs	둔 dyon	둕 dyonj	둖 dyonh	둗 dyod	둘 dyol	둙 dyolg	둚 dyolm	둛 dyolb	둜 dyols	둝 dyolt
ㄷ d	ㅜ u	두 du	둑 dug	둒 dugg	둓 dugs	둔 dun	둕 dunj	둖 dunh	둗 dud	둘 dul	둙 dulg	둚 dulm	둛 dulb	둜 duls	둝 dult
ㄷ d	ㅝ weo	둬 dweo	둭 dweog	둮 dweogg	둯 dweogs	둰 dweon	둱 dweonj	둲 dweonh	둳 dweod	둴 dweol	둵 dweolg	둶 dweolm	둷 dweolb	둸 dweols	둹 dweolt
ㄷ d	ㅞ we	뒈 dwe	뒉 dweg	뒊 dwegg	뒋 dwegs	뒌 dwen	뒍 dwenj	뒎 dwenh	뒏 dwed	뒐 dwel	뒑 dwelg	뒒 dwelm	뒓 dwelb	뒔 dwels	뒕 dwelt
ㄷ d	ㅟ wi	뒤 dwi	뒥 dwig	뒦 dwigg	뒧 dwigs	뒨 dwin	뒩 dwinj	뒪 dwinh	뒫 dwid	뒬 dwil	뒭 dwilg	뒮 dwilm	뒯 dwilb	뒰 dwils	뒱 dwilt
ㄷ d	ㅠ yu	듀 dyu	듁 dyug	듂 dyugg	듃 dyugs	듄 dyun	듅 dyunj	듆 dyunh	듇 dyud	듈 dyul	듉 dyulg	듊 dyulm	듋 dyulb	듌 dyuls	듍 dyult
ㄷ d	ㅡ eu	드 deu	득 deug	듞 deugg	듟 deugs	든 deun	듡 deunj	듢 deunh	듣 deud	들 deul	듥 deulg	듦 deulm	듧 deulb	듨 deuls	듩 deult
ㄷ d	ㅢ yi	듸 dyi	듹 dyig	듺 dyigg	듻 dyigs	듼 dyin	듽 dyinj	듾 dyinh	듿 dyid	딀 dyil	딁 dyilg	딂 dyilm	딃 dyilb	딄 dyils	딅 dyilt
ㄷ d	ㅣ i	디 di	딕 dig	딖 digg	딗 digs	딘 din	딙 dinj	딚 dinh	딛 did	딜 dil	딝 dilg	딞 dilm	딟 dilb	딠 dils	딡 dilt

d		ㄿ lp	ㅀ lh	ㅁ m	ㅂ b	ㅄ bs	ㅅ s	ㅆ ss	ㅇ ng	ㅈ j	ㅊ ch	ㅋ k	ㅌ t	ㅍ p	ㅎ h
ㄷ d	ㅏ a	닲 dalp	닳 dalh	담 dam	답 dab	닶 dabs	닷 das	닸 dass	당 dang	닺 daj	닻 dach	닼 dak	닽 dat	닾 dap	닿 dah
ㄷ d	ㅐ ae	댋 daelp	댏 daelh	댐 daem	댑 daeb	댋 daebs	댓 daes	댔 daess	댕 daeng	댗 daej	댗 daech	댘 daek	댙 daet	댚 daep	댛 daeh
ㄷ d	ㅑ ya	댥 dyalp	댧 dyalh	댬 dyam	댭 dyab	댮 dyabs	댯 dyas	댰 dyass	댱 dyang	댲 dyaj	댳 dyach	댴 dyak	댵 dyat	댶 dyap	댷 dyah
ㄷ d	ㅒ yae	댉 dyaelp	댎 dyaelh	댐 dyaem	댑 dyaeb	댋 dyaebs	댓 dyaes	댔 dyaess	댕 dyaeng	댗 dyaej	댗 dyaech	댘 dyaek	댙 dyaet	댚 dyaep	댛 dyaeh
ㄷ d	ㅓ eo	덻 deolp	덿 deolh	덤 deom	덥 deob	덦 deobs	덧 deos	덨 deoss	덩 deong	덪 deoj	덫 deoch	덬 deok	덭 deot	덮 deop	덯 deoh
ㄷ d	ㅔ e	뎗 delp	뎗 delh	뎀 dem	뎁 deb	뎂 debs	뎃 des	뎄 dess	뎅 deng	뎆 dej	뎇 dech	뎈 dek	뎉 det	뎊 dep	뎋 deh
ㄷ d	ㅕ yeo	뎳 dyeolp	뎷 dyeolh	뎜 dyeom	뎝 dyeob	뎞 dyeobs	뎟 dyeos	뎠 dyeoss	뎡 dyeong	뎢 dyeoj	뎣 dyeoch	뎤 dyeok	뎥 dyeot	뎦 dyeop	뎧 dyeoh
ㄷ d	ㅖ ye	뎳 dyelp	뎷 dyelh	뎸 dyem	뎹 dyeb	뎺 dyebs	뎻 dyes	뎼 dyess	뎽 dyeng	뎾 dyej	뎿 dyech	뎤 dyek	뎥 dyet	뎦 dyep	뎧 dyeh
ㄷ d	ㅗ o	돎 dolp	돐 dolh	돔 dom	돕 dob	돖 dobs	돗 dos	돘 doss	동 dong	돚 doj	돛 doch	독 dok	돝 dot	돞 dop	돟 doh
ㄷ d	ㅘ wa	돪 dwalp	돯 dwalh	돰 dwam	돱 dwab	돲 dwabs	돳 dwas	돴 dwass	돵 dwang	돶 dwaj	돷 dwach	돸 dwak	돹 dwat	돺 dwap	돻 dwah
ㄷ d	ㅙ wae	뢜 dwaelp	뢟 dwaelh	뢤 dwaem	뢥 dwaeb	뢦 dwaebs	뢧 dwaes	뢨 dwaess	뢩 dwaeng	뢪 dwaej	뢫 dwaech	뢬 dwaek	뢭 dwaet	뢮 dwaep	뢯 dwaeh
ㄷ d	ㅚ oe	됇 doelp	됇 doelh	됨 doem	됩 doeb	됪 doebs	됫 does	됬 doess	됭 doeng	됮 doej	됯 doech	됰 doek	됱 doet	됲 doep	됳 doeh
ㄷ d	ㅛ yo	둀 dyolp	둀 dyolh	둄 dyom	둅 dyob	둆 dyobs	둇 dyos	둈 dyoss	둉 dyong	둊 dyoj	둋 dyoch	둌 dyok	둍 dyot	둎 dyop	둏 dyoh
ㄷ d	ㅜ u	둚 dulp	둛 dulh	둠 dum	둡 dub	둢 dubs	둣 dus	둤 duss	둥 dung	둦 duj	둧 duch	둨 duk	둩 dut	둪 dup	둫 duh
ㄷ d	ㅝ weo	둻 dweolp	둻 dweolh	둼 dweom	둽 dweob	둾 dweobs	둿 dweos	뒀 dweoss	뒁 dweong	뒂 dweoj	뒃 dweoch	뒄 dweok	뒅 dweot	뒆 dweop	뒇 dweoh
ㄷ d	ㅞ we	뒗 dwelp	뒗 dwelh	뒘 dwem	뒙 dweb	뒚 dwebs	뒛 dwes	뒜 dwess	뒝 dweng	뒞 dwej	뒟 dwech	뒠 dwek	뒡 dwet	뒢 dwep	뒣 dweh
ㄷ d	ㅟ wi	뒳 dwilp	뒳 dwilh	뒴 dwim	뒵 dwib	뒶 dwibs	뒷 dwis	뒸 dwiss	뒹 dwing	뒺 dwij	뒻 dwich	뒼 dwik	뒽 dwit	뒾 dwip	뒿 dwih
ㄷ d	ㅠ yu	듋 dyulp	듏 dyulh	듐 dyum	듑 dyub	듒 dyubs	듓 dyus	듔 dyuss	듕 dyung	듖 dyuj	듗 dyuch	듘 dyuk	듙 dyut	듚 dyup	듛 dyuh
ㄷ d	ㅡ eu	듧 deulp	듫 deulh	듬 deum	듭 deub	듮 deubs	듯 deus	듰 deuss	등 deung	듲 deuj	듳 deuch	듴 deuk	듵 deut	듶 deup	듷 deuh
ㄷ d	ㅢ yi	딇 dyilp	딇 dyilh	딈 dyim	딉 dyib	딊 dyibs	딋 dyis	딌 dyiss	딍 dying	딎 dyij	딏 dyich	딐 dyik	딑 dyit	딒 dyip	딓 dyih
ㄷ d	ㅣ i	딟 dilp	딟 dilh	딤 dim	딥 dib	딦 dibs	딧 dis	딨 diss	딩 ding	딪 dij	딫 dich	딬 dik	딭 dit	딮 dip	딯 dih

Table 1.9: HanGul Syllables Starting with ㄸ (dd)

ㄸ dd		ㄱ g	ㄲ gg	ㄳ gs	ㄴ n	ㄵ nj	ㄶ nh	ㄷ d	ㄹ l	ㄺ lg	ㄻ lm	ㄼ lb	ㄽ ls	ㄾ lt
ㄸ dd	ㅏ a	따 dda	딱 ddag	딲 ddagg	딳 ddags	딴 ddan	딵 ddanj	딶 ddanh	딷 ddad	딸 ddal	딹 ddalg	딺 ddalm	딻 ddalb	딼 ddals	딽 ddalt
ㄸ dd	ㅐ ae	때 ddae	땍 ddaeg	땎 ddaegg	땏 ddaegs	땐 ddaen	땑 ddaenj	땒 ddaenh	땓 ddaed	땔 ddael	땕 ddaelg	땖 ddaelm	땗 ddaelb	땘 ddaels	땙 ddaelt
ㄸ dd	ㅑ ya	땨 ddya	땩 ddyag	땪 ddyagg	땫 ddyags	땬 ddyan	땭 ddyanj	땮 ddyanh	땯 ddyad	땰 ddyal	땱 ddyalg	땲 ddyalm	땳 ddyalb	땴 ddyals	땵 ddyalt
ㄸ dd	ㅒ yae	떄 ddyae	떅 ddyaeg	떆 ddyaegg	떇 ddyaegs	떈 ddyaen	떉 ddyaenj	떊 ddyaenh	떋 ddyaed	떌 ddyael	떍 ddyaelg	떎 ddyaelm	떏 ddyaelb	떐 ddyaels	떑 ddyaelt
ㄸ dd	ㅓ eo	떠 ddeo	떡 ddeog	떢 ddeogg	떣 ddeogs	떤 ddeon	떥 ddeonj	떦 ddeonh	떧 ddeod	떨 ddeol	떩 ddeolg	떪 ddeolm	떫 ddeolb	떬 ddeols	떭 ddeolt
ㄸ dd	ㅔ e	떼 dde	떽 ddeg	떾 ddegg	떿 ddegs	뗀 dden	뗁 ddenj	뗂 ddenh	뗃 dded	뗄 ddel	뗅 ddelg	뗆 ddelm	뗇 ddelb	뗈 ddels	뗉 ddelt
ㄸ dd	ㅕ yeo	뗘 ddyeo	뗙 ddyeog	뗚 ddyeogg	뗛 ddyeogs	뗜 ddyeon	뗝 ddyeonj	뗞 ddyeonh	뗟 ddyeod	뗠 ddyeol	뗡 ddyeolg	뗢 ddyeolm	뗣 ddyeolb	뗤 ddyeols	뗥 ddyeolt
ㄸ dd	ㅖ ye	뗴 ddye	뗵 ddyeg	뗶 ddyegg	뗷 ddyegs	뗸 ddyen	뗹 ddyenj	뗺 ddyenh	뗻 ddyed	뗼 ddyel	뗽 ddyelg	뗾 ddyelm	뗿 ddyelb	똀 ddyels	똁 ddyelt
ㄸ dd	ㅗ o	또 ddo	똑 ddog	똒 ddogg	똓 ddogs	똔 ddon	똕 ddonj	똖 ddonh	똗 ddod	똘 ddol	똙 ddolg	똚 ddolm	똛 ddolb	똜 ddols	똝 ddolt
ㄸ dd	ㅘ wa	똬 ddwa	똭 ddwag	똮 ddwagg	똯 ddwags	똰 ddwan	똱 ddwanj	똲 ddwanh	똳 ddwad	똴 ddwal	똵 ddwalg	똶 ddwalm	똷 ddwalb	똸 ddwals	똹 ddwalt
ㄸ dd	ㅙ wae	똬 ddwae	뙍 ddwaeg	뙎 ddwaegg	뙏 ddwaegs	뙐 ddwaen	뙑 ddwaenj	뙒 ddwaenh	뙓 ddwaed	뙔 ddwael	뙕 ddwaelg	뙖 ddwaelm	뙗 ddwaelb	뙘 ddwaels	뙙 ddwaelt
ㄸ dd	ㅚ oe	뙤 ddoe	뙥 ddoeg	뙦 ddoegg	뙧 ddoegs	뙨 ddoen	뙩 ddoenj	뙪 ddoenh	뙫 ddoed	뙬 ddoel	뙭 ddoelg	뙮 ddoelm	뙯 ddoelb	뙰 ddoels	뙱 ddoelt
ㄸ dd	ㅛ yo	뚀 ddyo	뚁 ddyog	뚂 ddyogg	뚃 ddyogs	뚄 ddyon	뚅 ddyonj	뚆 ddyonh	뚇 ddyod	뚈 ddyol	뚉 ddyolg	뚊 ddyolm	뚋 ddyolb	뚌 ddyols	뚍 ddyolt
ㄸ dd	ㅜ u	뚜 ddu	뚝 ddug	뚞 ddugg	뚟 ddugs	뚠 ddun	뚡 ddunj	뚢 ddunh	뚣 ddud	뚤 ddul	뚥 ddulg	뚦 ddulm	뚧 ddulb	뚨 dduls	뚩 ddult
ㄸ dd	ㅝ weo	뚸 ddweo	뚹 ddweog	뚺 ddweogg	뚻 ddweogs	뚼 ddweon	뚽 ddweonj	뚾 ddweonh	뚿 ddweod	뛀 ddweol	뛁 ddweolg	뛂 ddweolm	뛃 ddweolb	뛄 ddweols	뛅 ddweolt
ㄸ dd	ㅞ we	뛔 ddwe	뛕 ddweg	뛖 ddwegg	뛗 ddwegs	뛘 ddwen	뛙 ddwenj	뛚 ddwenh	뛛 ddwed	뛜 ddwel	뛝 ddwelg	뛞 ddwelm	뛟 ddwelb	뛠 ddwels	뛡 ddwelt
ㄸ dd	ㅟ wi	뛰 ddwi	뛱 ddwig	뛲 ddwigg	뛳 ddwigs	뛴 ddwin	뛵 ddwinj	뛶 ddwinh	뛷 ddwid	뛸 ddwil	뛹 ddwilg	뛺 ddwilm	뛻 ddwilb	뛼 ddwils	뛽 ddwilt
ㄸ dd	ㅠ yu	뜌 ddyu	뜍 ddyug	뜎 ddyugg	뜏 ddyugs	뜐 ddyun	뜑 ddyunj	뜒 ddyunh	뜓 ddyud	뜔 ddyul	뜕 ddyulg	뜖 ddyulm	뜗 ddyulb	뜘 ddyuls	뜙 ddyult
ㄸ dd	ㅡ eu	뜨 ddeu	뜩 ddeug	뜪 ddeugg	뜫 ddeugs	뜬 ddeun	뜭 ddeunj	뜮 ddeunh	뜯 ddeud	뜰 ddeul	뜱 ddeulg	뜲 ddeulm	뜳 ddeulb	뜴 ddeuls	뜵 ddeult
ㄸ dd	ㅢ yi	띄 ddyi	띅 ddyig	띆 ddyigg	띇 ddyigs	띈 ddyin	띉 ddyinj	띊 ddyinh	띋 ddyid	띌 ddyil	띍 ddyilg	띎 ddyilm	띏 ddyilb	띐 ddyils	띑 ddyilt
ㄸ dd	ㅣ i	띠 ddi	띡 ddig	띢 ddigg	띣 ddigs	띤 ddin	띥 ddinj	띦 ddinh	띧 ddid	띨 ddil	띩 ddilg	띪 ddilm	띫 ddilb	띬 ddils	띭 ddilt

ㄸ dd		ᆵ lp	ᇙ lh	ㅁ m	ㅂ b	ㅄ bs	ㅅ s	ㅆ ss	ㅇ ng	ㅈ j	ㅊ ch	ㅋ k	ㅌ t	ㅍ p	ㅎ h
ㄸ dd	ㅏ a	ddalp	ddalh	ddam	ddab	ddabs	ddas	ddass	ddang	ddaj	ddach	ddak	ddat	ddap	ddah
ㄸ dd	ㅐ ae	ddaelp	ddaelh	ddaem	ddaeb	ddaebs	ddaes	ddaess	ddaeng	ddaej	ddaech	ddaek	ddaet	ddaep	ddaeh
ㄸ dd	ㅑ ya	ddyalp	ddyalh	ddyam	ddyab	ddyabs	ddyas	ddyass	ddyang	ddyaj	ddyach	ddyak	ddyat	ddyap	ddyah
ㄸ dd	ㅒ yae	ddyaelp	ddyaelh	ddyaem	ddyaeb	ddyaebs	ddyaes	ddyaess	ddyaeng	ddyaej	ddyaech	ddyaek	ddyaet	ddyaep	ddyaeh
ㄸ dd	ㅓ eo	ddeolp	ddeolh	ddeom	ddeob	ddeobs	ddeos	ddeoss	ddeong	ddeoj	ddeoch	ddeok	ddeot	ddeop	ddeoh
ㄸ dd	ㅔ e	ddelp	ddelh	ddem	ddeb	ddebs	ddes	ddess	ddeng	ddej	ddech	ddek	ddet	ddep	ddeh
ㄸ dd	ㅕ yeo	ddyeolp	ddyeolh	ddyeom	ddyeob	ddyeobs	ddyeos	ddyeoss	ddyeong	ddyeoj	ddyeoch	ddyeok	ddyeot	ddyeop	ddyeoh
ㄸ dd	ㅖ ye	ddyelp	ddyelh	ddyem	ddyeb	ddyebs	ddyes	ddyess	ddyeng	ddyej	ddyech	ddyek	ddyet	ddyep	ddyeh
ㄸ dd	ㅗ o	ddolp	ddolh	ddom	ddob	ddobs	ddos	ddoss	ddong	ddoj	ddoch	ddok	ddot	ddop	ddoh
ㄸ dd	ㅘ wa	ddwalp	ddwalh	ddwam	ddwab	ddwabs	ddwas	ddwass	ddwang	ddwaj	ddwach	ddwak	ddwat	ddwap	ddwah
ㄸ dd	ㅙ wae	ddwaelp	ddwaelh	ddwaem	ddwaeb	ddwaebs	ddwaes	ddwaess	ddwaeng	ddwaej	ddwaech	ddwaek	ddwaet	ddwaep	ddwaeh
ㄸ dd	ㅚ oe	ddoelp	ddoelh	ddoem	ddoeb	ddoebs	ddoes	ddoess	ddoeng	ddoej	ddoech	ddoek	ddoet	ddoep	ddoeh
ㄸ dd	ㅛ yo	ddyolp	ddyolh	ddyom	ddyob	ddyobs	ddyos	ddyoss	ddyong	ddyoj	ddyoch	ddyok	ddyot	ddyop	ddyoh
ㄸ dd	ㅜ u	ddulp	ddulh	ddum	ddub	ddubs	ddus	dduss	ddung	dduj	dduch	dduk	ddut	ddup	dduh
ㄸ dd	ㅝ weo	ddweolp	ddweolh	ddweom	ddweob	ddweobs	ddweos	ddweoss	ddweong	ddweoj	ddweoch	ddweok	ddweot	ddweop	ddweoh
ㄸ dd	ㅞ we	ddwelp	ddwelh	ddwem	ddweb	ddwebs	ddwes	ddwess	ddweng	ddwej	ddwech	ddwek	ddwet	ddwep	ddweh
ㄸ dd	ㅟ wi	ddwilp	ddwilh	ddwim	ddwib	ddwibs	ddwis	ddwiss	ddwing	ddwij	ddwich	ddwik	ddwit	ddwip	ddwih
ㄸ dd	ㅠ yu	ddyulp	ddyulh	ddyum	ddyub	ddyubs	ddyus	ddyuss	ddyung	ddyuj	ddyuch	ddyuk	ddyut	ddyup	ddyuh
ㄸ dd	ㅡ eu	ddeulp	ddeulh	ddeum	ddeub	ddeubs	ddeus	ddeuss	ddeung	ddeuj	ddeuch	ddeuk	ddeut	ddeup	ddeuh
ㄸ dd	ㅢ yi	ddyilp	ddyilh	ddyim	ddyib	ddyibs	ddyis	ddyiss	ddying	ddyij	ddyich	ddyik	ddyit	ddyip	ddyih
ㄸ dd	ㅣ i	ddilp	ddilh	ddim	ddib	ddibs	ddis	ddiss	dding	ddij	ddich	ddik	ddit	ddip	ddih

Table 1.10: HanGul Syllables Starting with ㄹ (r)

ㄹ / vowel	(plain)	ㄱ g	ㄲ gg	ㄳ gs	ㄴ n	ㄵ nj	ㄶ nh	ㄷ d	ㄹ l	ㄺ lg	ㄻ lm	ㄼ lb	ㄽ ls	ㄾ lt
ㄹ ㅏ (a)	라 ra	rag	ragg	rags	ran	ranj	ranh	rad	ral	ralg	ralm	ralb	rals	ralt
ㄹ ㅐ (ae)	래 rae	raeg	raegg	raegs	raen	raenj	raenh	raed	rael	raelg	raelm	raelb	raels	raelt
ㄹ ㅑ (ya)	랴 rya	ryag	ryagg	ryags	ryan	ryanj	ryanh	ryad	ryal	ryalg	ryalm	ryalb	ryals	ryalt
ㄹ ㅒ (yae)	럐 ryae	ryaeg	ryaegg	ryaegs	ryaen	ryaenj	ryaenh	ryaed	ryael	ryaelg	ryaelm	ryaelb	ryaels	ryaelt
ㄹ ㅓ (eo)	러 reo	reog	reogg	reogs	reon	reonj	reonh	reod	reol	reolg	reolm	reolb	reols	reolt
ㄹ ㅔ (e)	레 re	reg	regg	regs	ren	renj	renh	red	rel	relg	relm	relb	rels	relt
ㄹ ㅕ (yeo)	려 ryeo	ryeog	ryeogg	ryeogs	ryeon	ryeonj	ryeonh	ryeod	ryeol	ryeolg	ryeolm	ryeolb	ryeols	ryeolt
ㄹ ㅖ (ye)	례 rye	ryeg	ryegg	ryegs	ryen	ryenj	ryenh	ryed	ryel	ryelg	ryelm	ryelb	ryels	ryelt
ㄹ ㅗ (o)	로 ro	rog	rogg	rogs	ron	ronj	ronh	rod	rol	rolg	rolm	rolb	rols	rolt
ㄹ ㅘ (wa)	롸 rwa	rwag	rwagg	rwags	rwan	rwanj	rwanh	rwad	rwal	rwalg	rwalm	rwalb	rwals	rwalt
ㄹ ㅙ (wae)	뢔 rwae	rwaeg	rwaegg	rwaegs	rwaen	rwaenj	rwaenh	rwaed	rwael	rwaelg	rwaelm	rwaelb	rwaels	rwaelt
ㄹ ㅚ (oe)	뢰 roe	roeg	roegg	roegs	roen	roenj	roenh	roed	roel	roelg	roelm	roelb	roels	roelt
ㄹ ㅛ (yo)	료 ryo	ryog	ryogg	ryogs	ryon	ryonj	ryonh	ryod	ryol	ryolg	ryolm	ryolb	ryols	ryolt
ㄹ ㅜ (u)	루 ru	rug	rugg	rugs	run	runj	runh	rud	rul	rulg	rulm	rulb	ruls	rult
ㄹ ㅝ (weo)	뤄 rweo	rweog	rweogg	rweogs	rweon	rweonj	rweonh	rweod	rweol	rweolg	rweolm	rweolb	rweols	rweolt
ㄹ ㅞ (we)	뤠 rwe	rweg	rwegg	rwegs	rwen	rwenj	rwenh	rwed	rwel	rwelg	rwelm	rwelb	rwels	rwelt
ㄹ ㅟ (wi)	뤼 rwi	rwig	rwigg	rwigs	rwin	rwinj	rwinh	rwid	rwil	rwilg	rwilm	rwilb	rwils	rwilt
ㄹ ㅠ (yu)	류 ryu	ryug	ryugg	ryugs	ryun	ryunj	ryunh	ryud	ryul	ryulg	ryulm	ryulb	ryuls	ryult
ㄹ ㅡ (eu)	르 reu	reug	reugg	reugs	reun	reunj	reunh	reud	reul	reulg	reulm	reulb	reuls	reult
ㄹ ㅢ (yi)	릐 ryi	ryig	ryigg	ryigs	ryin	ryinj	ryinh	ryid	ryil	ryilg	ryilm	ryilb	ryils	ryilt
ㄹ ㅣ (i)	리 ri	rig	rigg	rigs	rin	rinj	rinh	rid	ril	rilg	rilm	rilb	rils	rilt

	ㄿ lp	ㅀ lh	ㅁ m	ㅂ b	ㅄ bs	ㅅ s	ㅆ ss	ㅇ ng	ㅈ j	ㅊ ch	ㅋ k	ㅌ t	ㅍ p	ㅎ h
ㄹ a	ralp	ralh	ram	rab	rabs	ras	rass	rang	raj	rach	rak	rat	rap	rah
ㄹ ae	raelp	raelh	raem	raeb	raebs	raes	raess	raeng	raej	raech	raek	raet	raep	raeh
ㄹ ya	ryalp	ryalh	ryam	ryab	ryabs	ryas	ryass	ryang	ryaj	ryach	ryak	ryat	ryap	ryah
ㄹ yae	ryaelp	ryaelh	ryaem	ryaeb	ryaebs	ryaes	ryaess	ryaeng	ryaej	ryaech	ryaek	ryaet	ryaep	ryaeh
ㄹ eo	reolp	reolh	reom	reob	reobs	reos	reoss	reong	reoj	reoch	reok	reot	reop	reoh
ㄹ e	relp	relh	rem	reb	rebs	res	ress	reng	rej	rech	rek	ret	rep	reh
ㄹ yeo	ryeolp	ryeolh	ryeom	ryeob	ryeobs	ryeos	ryeoss	ryeong	ryeoj	ryeoch	ryeok	ryeot	ryeop	ryeoh
ㄹ ye	ryelp	ryelh	ryem	ryeb	ryebs	ryes	ryess	ryeng	ryej	ryech	ryek	ryet	ryep	ryeh
ㄹ o	rolp	rolh	rom	rob	robs	ros	ross	rong	roj	roch	rok	rot	rop	roh
ㄹ wa	rwalp	rwalh	rwam	rwab	rwabs	rwas	rwass	rwang	rwaj	rwach	rwak	rwat	rwap	rwah
ㄹ wae	rwaelp	rwaelh	rwaem	rwaeb	rwaebs	rwaes	rwaess	rwaeng	rwaej	rwaech	rwaek	rwaet	rwaep	rwaeh
ㄹ oe	roelp	roelh	roem	roeb	roebs	roes	roess	roeng	roej	roech	roek	roet	roep	roeh
ㄹ yo	ryolp	ryolh	ryom	ryob	ryobs	ryos	ryoss	ryong	ryoj	ryoch	ryok	ryot	ryop	ryoh
ㄹ u	rulp	rulh	rum	rub	rubs	rus	russ	rung	ruj	ruch	ruk	rut	rup	ruh
ㄹ weo	rweolp	rweolh	rweom	rweob	rweobs	rweos	rweoss	rweong	rweoj	rweoch	rweok	rweot	rweop	rweoh
ㄹ we	rwelp	rwelh	rwem	rweb	rwebs	rwes	rwess	rweng	rwej	rwech	rwek	rwet	rwep	rweh
ㄹ wi	rwilp	rwilh	rwim	rwib	rwibs	rwis	rwiss	rwing	rwij	rwich	rwik	rwit	rwip	rwih
ㄹ yu	ryulp	ryulh	ryum	ryub	ryubs	ryus	ryuss	ryung	ryuj	ryuch	ryuk	ryut	ryup	ryuh
ㄹ eu	reulp	reulh	reum	reub	reubs	reus	reuss	reung	reuj	reuch	reuk	reut	reup	reuh
ㄹ yi	ryilp	ryilh	ryim	ryib	ryibs	ryis	ryiss	rying	ryij	ryich	ryik	ryit	ryip	ryih
ㄹ i	rilp	rilh	rim	rib	ribs	ris	riss	ring	rij	rich	rik	rit	rip	rih

Table 1.11: HanGul Syllables Starting with ㅁ (m)

ㅁ (m)	ㄱ g	ㄲ gg	ㄳ gs	ㄴ n	ㄵ nj	ㄶ nh	ㄷ d	ㄹ l	ㄺ lg	ㄻ lm	ㄼ lb	ㄽ ls	ㄾ lt
ㅏ a — 마 ma	막 mag	맦 magg	맧 mags	만 man	많 manj	많 manh	맏 mad	말 mal	맑 malg	맒 malm	맓 malb	맔 mals	맕 malt
ㅐ ae — 매 mae	맥 maeg	맦 maegg	맧 maegs	맨 maen	맪 maenj	맪 maenh	맫 maed	맬 mael	맭 maelg	맮 maelm	맯 maelb	맰 maels	맱 maelt
ㅑ ya — 먀 mya	먁 myag	먂 myagg	먃 myags	먄 myan	먅 myanj	먅 myanh	먇 myad	먈 myal	먉 myalg	먊 myalm	먋 myalb	먌 myals	먍 myalt
ㅒ yae — 먜 myae	먝 myaeg	먞 myaegg	먟 myaegs	먠 myaen	먡 myaenj	먡 myaenh	먣 myaed	먤 myael	먥 myaelg	먦 myaelm	먧 myaelb	먨 myaels	먩 myaelt
ㅓ eo — 머 meo	먹 meog	먺 meogg	먻 meogs	먼 meon	먾 meonj	먾 meonh	멀 meod	멀 meol	멁 meolg	멂 meolm	멃 meolb	멄 meols	멅 meolt
ㅔ e — 메 me	멕 meg	멖 megg	멗 megs	멘 men	멙 menj	멙 menh	멛 med	멜 mel	멝 melg	멞 melm	멟 melb	멠 mels	멡 melt
ㅕ yeo — 며 myeo	멱 myeog	멲 myeogg	멳 myeogs	면 myeon	멶 myeonj	멶 myeonh	멷 myeod	멸 myeol	멹 myeolg	멺 myeolm	멻 myeolb	멼 myeols	멽 myeolt
ㅖ ye — 몌 mye	몍 myeg	몎 myegg	몏 myegs	몐 myen	몑 myenj	몑 myenh	몓 myed	몔 myel	몕 myelg	몖 myelm	몗 myelb	몘 myels	몙 myelt
ㅗ o — 모 mo	목 mog	몪 mogg	몫 mogs	몬 mon	몮 monj	몮 monh	몯 mod	몰 mol	몱 molg	몲 molm	몳 molb	몴 mols	몵 molt
ㅘ wa — 와 mwa	뫅 mwag	뫆 mwagg	뫇 mwags	뫈 mwan	뫉 mwanj	뫉 mwanh	뫋 mwad	뫌 mwal	뫍 mwalg	뫎 mwalm	뫏 mwalb	뫐 mwals	뫑 mwalt
ㅙ wae — 뫠 mwae	뫡 mwaeg	뫢 mwaegg	뫣 mwaegs	뫤 mwaen	뫥 mwaenj	뫥 mwaenh	뫧 mwaed	뫨 mwael	뫩 mwaelg	뫪 mwaelm	뫫 mwaelb	뫬 mwaels	뫭 mwaelt
ㅚ oe — 뫼 moe	뫽 moeg	뫾 moegg	뫿 moegs	묀 moen	묁 moenj	묁 moenh	묃 moed	묄 moel	묅 moelg	묆 moelm	묇 moelb	묈 moels	묉 moelt
ㅛ yo — 묘 myo	묙 myog	묚 myogg	묛 myogs	묜 myon	묝 myonj	묝 myonh	묟 myod	묠 myol	묡 myolg	묢 myolm	묣 myolb	묤 myols	묥 myolt
ㅜ u — 무 mu	묵 mug	묶 mugg	뭀 mugs	문 mun	뭂 munj	뭂 munh	묻 mud	물 mul	묽 mulg	묾 mulm	뭃 mulb	뭀 muls	뭁 mult
ㅝ weo — 뭐 mweo	뭑 mweog	뭒 mweogg	뭓 mweogs	뭔 mweon	뭕 mweonj	뭕 mweonh	뭗 mweod	뭘 mweol	뭙 mweolg	뭚 mweolm	뭛 mweolb	뭜 mweols	뭝 mweolt
ㅞ we — 뭬 mwe	뭭 mweg	뭮 mwegg	뭯 mwegs	뭰 mwen	뭱 mwenj	뭱 mwenh	뭳 mwed	뭴 mwel	뭵 mwelg	뭶 mwelm	뭷 mwelb	뭸 mwels	뭹 mwelt
ㅟ wi — 뮈 mwi	뮉 mwig	뮊 mwigg	뮋 mwigs	뮌 mwin	뮍 mwinj	뮍 mwinh	뮏 mwid	뮐 mwil	뮑 mwilg	뮒 mwilm	뮓 mwilb	뮔 mwils	뮕 mwilt
ㅠ yu — 뮤 myu	뮦 myug	뮦 myugg	뮧 myugs	뮨 myun	뮩 myunj	뮩 myunh	뮫 myud	뮬 myul	뮭 myulg	뮮 myulm	뮯 myulb	뮰 myuls	뮱 myult
ㅡ eu — 므 meu	믁 meug	믂 meugg	믃 meugs	믄 meun	믅 meunj	믅 meunh	믇 meud	믈 meul	믉 meulg	믊 meulm	믋 meulb	믌 meuls	믍 meult
ㅢ yi — 믜 myi	믝 myig	믞 myigg	믟 myigs	민 myin	믡 myinj	믡 myinh	믣 myid	믤 myil	믥 myilg	믦 myilm	믧 myilb	믨 myils	믩 myilt
ㅣ i — 미 mi	믹 mig	믺 migg	믻 migs	민 min	믾 minj	믾 minh	믿 mid	밀 mil	밁 milg	밂 milm	밃 milb	밄 mils	밅 milt

		ㄿ lp	ㅀ lh	ㅁ m	ㅂ b	ㅄ bs	ㅅ s	ㅆ ss	ㅇ ng	ㅈ j	ㅊ ch	ㅋ k	ㅌ t	ㅍ p	ㅎ h
ㅁ m	ㅏ a	malp	malh	mam	mab	mabs	mas	mass	mang	maj	mach	mak	mat	map	mah
ㅁ m	ㅐ ae	maelp	maelh	maem	maeb	maebs	maes	maess	maeng	maej	maech	maek	maet	maep	maeh
ㅁ m	ㅑ ya	myalp	myalh	myam	myab	myabs	myas	myass	myang	myaj	myach	myak	myat	myap	myah
ㅁ m	ㅒ yae	myaelp	myaelh	myaem	myaeb	myaebs	myaes	myaess	myaeng	myaej	myaech	myaek	myaet	myaep	myaeh
ㅁ m	ㅓ eo	meolp	meolh	meom	meob	meobs	meos	meoss	meong	meoj	meoch	meok	meot	meop	meoh
ㅁ m	ㅔ e	melp	melh	mem	meb	mebs	mes	mess	meng	mej	mech	mek	met	mep	meh
ㅁ m	ㅕ yeo	myeolp	myeolh	myeom	myeob	myeobs	myeos	myeoss	myeong	myeoj	myeoch	myeok	myeot	myeop	myeoh
ㅁ m	ㅖ ye	myelp	myelh	myem	myeb	myebs	myes	myess	myeng	myej	myech	myek	myet	myep	myeh
ㅁ m	ㅗ o	molp	molh	mom	mob	mobs	mos	moss	mong	moj	moch	mok	mot	mop	moh
ㅁ m	ㅘ wa	mwalp	mwalh	mwam	mwab	mwabs	mwas	mwass	mwang	mwaj	mwach	mwak	mwat	mwap	mwah
ㅁ m	ㅙ wae	mwaelp	mwaelh	mwaem	mwaeb	mwaebs	mwaes	mwaess	mwaeng	mwaej	mwaech	mwaek	mwaet	mwaep	mwaeh
ㅁ m	ㅚ oe	moelp	moelh	moem	moeb	moebs	moes	moess	moeng	moej	moech	moek	moet	moep	moeh
ㅁ m	ㅛ yo	myolp	myolh	myom	myob	myobs	myos	myoss	myong	myoj	myoch	myok	myot	myop	myoh
ㅁ m	ㅜ u	mulp	mulh	mum	mub	mubs	mus	muss	mung	muj	much	muk	mut	mup	muh
ㅁ m	ㅝ weo	mweolp	mweolh	mweom	mweob	mweobs	mweos	mweoss	mweong	mweoj	mweoch	mweok	mweot	mweop	mweoh
ㅁ m	ㅞ we	mwelp	mwelh	mwem	mweb	mwebs	mwes	mwess	mweng	mwej	mwech	mwek	mwet	mwep	mweh
ㅁ m	ㅟ wi	mwilp	mwilh	mwim	mwib	mwibs	mwis	mwiss	mwing	mwij	mwich	mwik	mwit	mwip	mwih
ㅁ m	ㅠ yu	myulp	myulh	myum	myub	myubs	myus	myuss	myung	myuj	myuch	myuk	myut	myup	myuh
ㅁ m	ㅡ eu	meulp	meulh	meum	meub	meubs	meus	meuss	meung	meuj	meuch	meuk	meut	meup	meuh
ㅁ m	ㅢ yi	myilp	myilh	myim	myib	myibs	myis	myiss	mying	myij	myich	myik	myit	myip	myih
ㅁ m	ㅣ i	milp	milh	mim	mib	mibs	mis	miss	ming	mij	mich	mik	mit	mip	mih

Table 1.12: HanGul Syllables Starting with ㅂ (b)

		ㄱ g	ㄲ gg	ㄳ gs	ㄴ n	ㄵ nj	ㄶ nh	ㄷ d	ㄹ l	ㄺ lg	ㄻ lm	ㄼ lb	ㄽ ls	ㄾ lt
ㅂ b	ㅏ a	바 ba	박 bag	밖 bagg	밗 bags	반 ban	밗 banj	밣 banh	받 bad	발 bal	밝 balg	밞 balm	밟 balb	밠 bals	밡 balt
ㅂ b	ㅐ ae	배 bae	백 baeg	밲 baegg	밳 baegs	밴 baen	밶 baenj	밷 baenh	밷 baed	밸 bael	밹 baelg	밺 baelm	밻 baelb	밼 baels	밽 baelt
ㅂ b	ㅑ ya	뱌 bya	뱍 byag	뱎 byagg	뱏 byags	뱐 byan	뱑 byanj	뱒 byanh	뱓 byad	뱔 byal	뱕 byalg	뱖 byalm	뱗 byalb	뱘 byals	뱙 byalt
ㅂ b	ㅒ yae	뱨 byae	뱩 byaeg	뱪 byaegg	뱫 byaegs	뱬 byaen	뱭 byaenj	뱮 byaenh	뱯 byaed	뱰 byael	뱱 byaelg	뱲 byaelm	뱳 byaelb	뱴 byaels	뱵 byaelt
ㅂ b	ㅓ eo	버 beo	벅 beog	벆 beogg	벇 beogs	번 beon	벉 beonj	벊 beonh	벋 beod	벌 beol	벍 beolg	벎 beolm	벏 beolb	벐 beols	벑 beolt
ㅂ b	ㅔ e	베 be	벡 beg	벢 begg	벣 begs	벤 ben	벥 benj	벦 benh	벧 bed	벨 bel	벩 belg	벪 belm	벫 belb	벬 bels	벭 belt
ㅂ b	ㅕ yeo	벼 byeo	벽 byeog	벾 byeogg	벿 byeogs	변 byeon	볁 byeonj	볂 byeonh	볃 byeod	별 byeol	볅 byeolg	볆 byeolm	볇 byeolb	볈 byeols	볉 byeolt
ㅂ b	ㅖ ye	볘 bye	볙 byeg	볚 byegg	볛 byegs	볜 byen	볝 byenj	볞 byenh	볟 byed	볠 byel	볡 byelg	볢 byelm	볣 byelb	볤 byels	볥 byelt
ㅂ b	ㅗ o	보 bo	복 bog	볶 bogg	볷 bogs	본 bon	볹 bonj	볺 bonh	볻 bod	볼 bol	볽 bolg	볾 bolm	볿 bolb	봀 bols	봁 bolt
ㅂ b	ㅘ wa	봐 bwa	봑 bwag	봒 bwagg	봓 bwags	봔 bwan	봕 bwanj	봖 bwanh	봗 bwad	봘 bwal	봙 bwalg	봚 bwalm	봛 bwalb	봜 bwals	봝 bwalt
ㅂ b	ㅙ wae	봬 bwae	봭 bwaeg	봮 bwaegg	봯 bwaegs	봰 bwaen	봱 bwaenj	봲 bwaenh	봳 bwaed	봴 bwael	봵 bwaelg	봶 bwaelm	봷 bwaelb	봸 bwaels	봹 bwaelt
ㅂ b	ㅚ oe	뵈 boe	뵉 boeg	뵊 boegg	뵋 boegs	뵌 boen	뵍 boenj	뵎 boenh	뵏 boed	뵐 boel	뵑 boelg	뵒 boelm	뵓 boelb	뵔 boels	뵕 boelt
ㅂ b	ㅛ yo	뵤 byo	뵥 byog	뵦 byogg	뵧 byogs	뵨 byon	뵩 byonj	뵪 byonh	뵫 byod	뵬 byol	뵭 byolg	뵮 byolm	뵯 byolb	뵰 byols	뵱 byolt
ㅂ b	ㅜ u	부 bu	북 bug	붂 bugg	붃 bugs	분 bun	붅 bunj	붆 bunh	붇 bud	불 bul	붉 bulg	붊 bulm	붋 bulb	붌 buls	붍 bult
ㅂ b	ㅝ weo	붜 bweo	붝 bweog	붞 bweogg	붟 bweogs	붠 bweon	붡 bweonj	붢 bweonh	붣 bweod	붤 bweol	붥 bweolg	붦 bweolm	붧 bweolb	붨 bweols	붩 bweolt
ㅂ b	ㅞ we	붸 bwe	붹 bweg	붺 bwegg	붻 bwegs	붼 bwen	붽 bwenj	붾 bwenh	붿 bwed	뷀 bwel	뷁 bwelg	뷂 bwelm	뷃 bwelb	뷄 bwels	뷅 bwelt
ㅂ b	ㅟ wi	뷔 bwi	뷕 bwig	뷖 bwigg	뷗 bwigs	뷘 bwin	뷙 bwinj	뷚 bwinh	뷛 bwid	뷜 bwil	뷝 bwilg	뷞 bwilm	뷟 bwilb	뷠 bwils	뷡 bwilt
ㅂ b	ㅠ yu	뷰 byu	뷱 byug	뷲 byugg	뷳 byugs	뷴 byun	뷵 byunj	뷶 byunh	뷷 byud	뷸 byul	뷹 byulg	뷺 byulm	뷻 byulb	뷼 byuls	뷽 byult
ㅂ b	ㅡ eu	브 beu	븍 beug	븎 beugg	븏 beugs	븐 beun	븑 beunj	븒 beunh	븓 beud	블 beul	븕 beulg	븖 beulm	븗 beulb	븘 beuls	븙 beult
ㅂ b	ㅢ yi	븨 byi	븩 byig	븪 byigg	븫 byigs	븬 byin	븭 byinj	븮 byinh	븯 byid	븰 byil	븱 byilg	븲 byilm	븳 byilb	븴 byils	븵 byilt
ㅂ b	ㅣ i	비 bi	빅 big	빆 bigg	빇 bigs	빈 bin	빉 binj	빊 binh	빋 bid	빌 bil	빍 bilg	빎 bilm	빏 bilb	빐 bils	빑 bilt

b		ㄿ lp	ㅀ lh	ㅁ m	ㅂ b	ㅄ bs	ㅅ s	ㅆ ss	ㅇ ng	ㅈ j	ㅊ ch	ㅋ k	ㅌ t	ㅍ p	ㅎ h
ㅂ b	ㅏ a	balp	balh	bam	bab	babs	bas	bass	bang	baj	bach	bak	bat	bap	bah
ㅂ b	ㅐ ae	baelp	baelh	baem	baeb	baebs	baes	baess	baeng	baej	baech	baek	baet	baep	baeh
ㅂ b	ㅑ ya	byalp	byalh	byam	byab	byabs	byas	byass	byang	byaj	byach	byak	byat	byap	byah
ㅂ b	ㅒ yae	byaelp	byaelh	byaem	byaeb	byaebs	byaes	byaess	byaeng	byaej	byaech	byaek	byaet	byaep	byaeh
ㅂ b	ㅓ eo	beolp	beolh	beom	beob	beobs	beos	beoss	beong	beoj	beoch	beok	beot	beop	beoh
ㅂ b	ㅔ e	belp	belh	bem	beb	bebs	bes	bess	beng	bej	bech	bek	bet	bep	beh
ㅂ b	ㅕ yeo	byeolp	byeolh	byeom	byeob	byeobs	byeos	byeoss	byeong	byeoj	byeoch	byeok	byeot	byeop	byeoh
ㅂ b	ㅖ ye	byelp	byelh	byem	byeb	byebs	byes	byess	byeng	byej	byech	byek	byet	byep	byeh
ㅂ b	ㅗ o	bolp	bolh	bom	bob	bobs	bos	boss	bong	boj	boch	bok	bot	bop	boh
ㅂ b	ㅘ wa	bwalp	bwalh	bwam	bwab	bwabs	bwas	bwass	bwang	bwaj	bwach	bwak	bwat	bwap	bwah
ㅂ b	ㅙ wae	bwaelp	bwaelh	bwaem	bwaeb	bwaebs	bwaes	bwaess	bwaeng	bwaej	bwaech	bwaek	bwaet	bwaep	bwaeh
ㅂ b	ㅚ oe	boelp	boelh	boem	boeb	boebs	boes	boess	boeng	boej	boech	boek	boet	boep	boeh
ㅂ b	ㅛ yo	byolp	byolh	byom	byob	byobs	byos	byoss	byong	byoj	byoch	byok	byot	byop	byoh
ㅂ b	ㅜ u	bulp	bulh	bum	bub	bubs	bus	buss	bung	buj	buch	buk	but	bup	buh
ㅂ b	ㅝ weo	bweolp	bweolh	bweom	bweob	bweobs	bweos	bweoss	bweong	bweoj	bweoch	bweok	bweot	bweop	bweoh
ㅂ b	ㅞ we	bwelp	bwelh	bwem	bweb	bwebs	bwes	bwess	bweng	bwej	bwech	bwek	bwet	bwep	bweh
ㅂ b	ㅟ wi	bwilp	bwilh	bwim	bwib	bwibs	bwis	bwiss	bwing	bwij	bwich	bwik	bwit	bwip	bwih
ㅂ b	ㅠ yu	byulp	byulh	byum	byub	byubs	byus	byuss	byung	byuj	byuch	byuk	byut	byup	byuh
ㅂ b	ㅡ eu	beulp	beulh	beum	beub	beubs	beus	beuss	beung	beuj	beuch	beuk	beut	beup	beuh
ㅂ b	ㅢ yi	byilp	byilh	byim	byib	byibs	byis	byiss	bying	byij	byich	byik	byit	byip	byih
ㅂ b	ㅣ i	bilp	bilh	bim	bib	bibs	bis	biss	bing	bij	bich	bik	bit	bip	bih

Table 1.13: HanGul Syllables Starting with ㅃ (bb)

		ㄱ g	ㄲ gg	ㄳ gs	ㄴ n	ㄵ nj	ㄶ nh	ㄷ d	ㄹ l	ㄹㄱ lg	ㄹㅁ lm	ㄹㅂ lb	ㄹㅅ ls	ㄹㅌ lt
ㅃ bb	ㅏ a	빠 bba	빡 bbag	빿 bbagg	빴 bbags	빤 bban	빤 bbanj	빤 bbanh	빧 bbad	빨 bbal	빩 bbalg	빪 bbalm	빫 bbalb	빬 bbals	빭 bbalt
ㅃ bb	ㅐ ae	빼 bbae	빽 bbaeg	빾 bbaegg	빽 bbaegs	뺀 bbaen	뺁 bbaenj	뺂 bbaenh	뺃 bbaed	뺄 bbael	뺅 bbaelg	뺆 bbaelm	뺇 bbaelb	뺈 bbaels	뺉 bbaelt
ㅃ bb	ㅑ ya	뺘 bbya	뺙 bbyag	뺚 bbyagg	뺛 bbyags	뺜 bbyan	뺝 bbyanj	뺞 bbyanh	뺟 bbyad	뺠 bbyal	뺡 bbyalg	뺢 bbyalm	뺣 bbyalb	뺤 bbyals	뺥 bbyalt
ㅃ bb	ㅒ yae	뺴 bbyae	뺵 bbyaeg	뺶 bbyaegg	뺷 bbyaegs	뺸 bbyaen	뺹 bbyaenj	뺺 bbyaenh	뺻 bbyaed	뺼 bbyael	뺽 bbyaelg	뺾 bbyaelm	뺿 bbyaelb	뻀 bbyaels	뻁 bbyaelt
ㅃ bb	ㅓ eo	뻐 bbeo	뻑 bbeog	뻒 bbeogg	뻓 bbeogs	뻔 bbeon	뻕 bbeonj	뻖 bbeonh	뻗 bbeod	뻘 bbeol	뻙 bbeolg	뻚 bbeolm	뻛 bbeolb	뻜 bbeols	뻝 bbeolt
ㅃ bb	ㅔ e	뻬 bbe	뻭 bbeg	뻮 bbegg	뻯 bbegs	뻰 bben	뻱 bbenj	뻲 bbenh	뻳 bbed	뻴 bbel	뻵 bbelg	뻶 bbelm	뻷 bbelb	뻸 bbels	뻹 bbelt
ㅃ bb	ㅕ yeo	뼈 bbyeo	뼉 bbyeog	뼊 bbyeogg	뼋 bbyeogs	뼌 bbyeon	뼍 bbyeonj	뼎 bbyeonh	뼏 bbyeod	뼐 bbyeol	뼑 bbyeolg	뼒 bbyeolm	뼓 bbyeolb	뼔 bbyeols	뼕 bbyeolt
ㅃ bb	ㅖ ye	뼤 bbye	뼥 bbyeg	뼦 bbyegg	뼧 bbyegs	뼨 bbyen	뼩 bbyenj	뼪 bbyenh	뼫 bbyed	뼬 bbyel	뼭 bbyelg	뼮 bbyelm	뼯 bbyelb	뼰 bbyels	뼱 bbyelt
ㅃ bb	ㅗ o	뽀 bbo	뽁 bbog	뽂 bbogg	뽃 bbogs	뽄 bbon	뽅 bbonj	뽆 bbonh	뽇 bbod	뽈 bbol	뽉 bbolg	뽊 bbolm	뽋 bbolb	뽌 bbols	뽍 bbolt
ㅃ bb	ㅘ wa	뽜 bbwa	뽝 bbwag	뽞 bbwagg	뽟 bbwags	뽠 bbwan	뽡 bbwanj	뽢 bbwanh	뽣 bbwad	뽤 bbwal	뽥 bbwalg	뽦 bbwalm	뽧 bbwalb	뽨 bbwals	뽩 bbwalt
ㅃ bb	ㅙ wae	뽸 bbwae	뽹 bbwaeg	뽺 bbwaegg	뽻 bbwaegs	뽼 bbwaen	뽽 bbwaenj	뽾 bbwaenh	뽿 bbwaed	뾀 bbwael	뾁 bbwaelg	뾂 bbwaelm	뾃 bbwaelb	뾄 bbwaels	뾅 bbwaelt
ㅃ bb	ㅚ oe	뾔 bboe	뾕 bboeg	뾖 bboegg	뾗 bboegs	뾘 bboen	뾙 bboenj	뾚 bboenh	뾛 bboed	뾜 bboel	뾝 bboelg	뾞 bboelm	뾟 bboelb	뾠 bboels	뾡 bboelt
ㅃ bb	ㅛ yo	뾰 bbyo	뾱 bbyog	뾲 bbyogg	뾳 bbyogs	뾴 bbyon	뾵 bbyonj	뾶 bbyonh	뾷 bbyod	뾸 bbyol	뾹 bbyolg	뾺 bbyolm	뾻 bbyolb	뾼 bbyols	뾽 bbyolt
ㅃ bb	ㅜ u	뿌 bbu	뿍 bbug	뿎 bbugg	뿏 bbugs	뿐 bbun	뿑 bbunj	뿒 bbunh	뿓 bbud	뿔 bbul	뿕 bbulg	뿖 bbulm	뿗 bbulb	뿘 bbuls	뿙 bbult
ㅃ bb	ㅝ weo	뿨 bbweo	뿩 bbweog	뿪 bbweogg	뿫 bbweogs	뿬 bbweon	뿭 bbweonj	뿮 bbweonh	뿯 bbweod	뿰 bbweol	뿱 bbweolg	뿲 bbweolm	뿳 bbweolb	뿴 bbweols	뿵 bbweolt
ㅃ bb	ㅞ we	뿸 bbwe	뿹 bbweg	뿺 bbwegg	뿻 bbwegs	뿼 bbwen	뿽 bbwenj	뿾 bbwenh	뿿 bbwed	쀀 bbwel	쀁 bbwelg	쀂 bbwelm	쀃 bbwelb	쀄 bbwels	쀅 bbwelt
ㅃ bb	ㅟ wi	쀠 bbwi	쀡 bbwig	쀢 bbwigg	쀣 bbwigs	쀤 bbwin	쀥 bbwinj	쀦 bbwinh	쀧 bbwid	쀨 bbwil	쀩 bbwilg	쀪 bbwilm	쀫 bbwilb	쀬 bbwils	쀭 bbwilt
ㅃ bb	ㅠ yu	쀼 bbyu	쀽 bbyug	쀾 bbyugg	쀿 bbyugs	쁀 bbyun	쁁 bbyunj	쁂 bbyunh	쁃 bbyud	쁄 bbyul	쁅 bbyulg	쁆 bbyulm	쁇 bbyulb	쁈 bbyuls	쁉 bbyult
ㅃ bb	ㅡ eu	쁘 bbeu	쁙 bbeug	쁚 bbeugg	쁛 bbeugs	쁜 bbeun	쁝 bbeunj	쁞 bbeunh	쁟 bbeud	쁠 bbeul	쁡 bbeulg	쁢 bbeulm	쁣 bbeulb	쁤 bbeuls	쁥 bbeult
ㅃ bb	ㅢ yi	쁴 bbyi	쁵 bbyig	쁶 bbyigg	쁷 bbyigs	쁸 bbyin	쁹 bbyinj	쁺 bbyinh	쁻 bbyid	쁼 bbyil	쁽 bbyilg	쁾 bbyilm	쁿 bbyilb	삀 bbyils	삁 bbyilt
ㅃ bb	ㅣ i	삐 bbi	삑 bbig	삒 bbigg	삓 bbigs	삔 bbin	삕 bbinj	삖 bbinh	삗 bbid	삘 bbil	삙 bbilg	삚 bbilm	삛 bbilb	삜 bbils	삝 bbilt

ㅃ bb +	ㄿ lp	ㅀ lh	ㅁ m	ㅂ b	ㅄ bs	ㅅ s	ㅆ ss	ㅇ ng	ㅈ j	ㅊ ch	ㅋ k	ㅌ t	ㅍ p	ㅎ h
ㅏ a	bbalp	bbalh	bbam	bbab	bbabs	bbas	bbass	bbang	bbaj	bbach	bbak	bbat	bbap	bbah
ㅐ ae	bbaelp	bbaelh	bbaem	bbaeb	bbaebs	bbaes	bbaess	bbaeng	bbaej	bbaech	bbaek	bbaet	bbaep	bbaeh
ㅑ ya	bbyalp	bbyalh	bbyam	bbyab	bbyabs	bbyas	bbyass	bbyang	bbyaj	bbyach	bbyak	bbyat	bbyap	bbyah
ㅒ yae	bbyaelp	bbyaelh	bbyaem	bbyaeb	bbyaebs	bbyaes	bbyaess	bbyaeng	bbyaej	bbyaech	bbyaek	bbyaet	bbyaep	bbyaeh
ㅓ eo	bbeolp	bbeolh	bbeom	bbeob	bbeobs	bbeos	bbeoss	bbeong	bbeoj	bbeoch	bbeok	bbeot	bbeop	bbeoh
ㅔ e	bbelp	bbelh	bbem	bbeb	bbebs	bbes	bbess	bbeng	bbej	bbech	bbek	bbet	bbep	bbeh
ㅕ yeo	bbyeolp	bbyeolh	bbyeom	bbyeob	bbyeobs	bbyeos	bbyeoss	bbyeong	bbyeoj	bbyeoch	bbyeok	bbyeot	bbyeop	bbyeoh
ㅖ ye	bbyelp	bbyelh	bbyem	bbyeb	bbyebs	bbyes	bbyess	bbyeng	bbyej	bbyech	bbyek	bbyet	bbyep	bbyeh
ㅗ o	bbolp	bbolh	bbom	bbob	bbobs	bbos	bboss	bbong	bboj	bboch	bbok	bbot	bbop	bboh
ㅘ wa	bbwalp	bbwalh	bbwam	bbwab	bbwabs	bbwas	bbwass	bbwang	bbwaj	bbwach	bbwak	bbwat	bbwap	bbwah
ㅙ wae	bbwaelp	bbwaelh	bbwaem	bbwaeb	bbwaebs	bbwaes	bbwaess	bbwaeng	bbwaej	bbwaech	bbwaek	bbwaet	bbwaep	bbwaeh
ㅚ oe	bboelp	bboelh	bboem	bboeb	bboebs	bboes	bboess	bboeng	bboej	bboech	bboek	bboet	bboep	bboeh
ㅛ yo	bbyolp	bbyolh	bbyom	bbyob	bbyobs	bbyos	bbyoss	bbyong	bbyoj	bbyoch	bbyok	bbyot	bbyop	bbyoh
ㅜ u	bbulp	bbulh	bbum	bbub	bbubs	bbus	bbuss	bbung	bbuj	bbuch	bbuk	bbut	bbup	bbuh
ㅝ weo	bbweolp	bbweolh	bbweom	bbweob	bbweobs	bbweos	bbweoss	bbweong	bbweoj	bbweoch	bbweok	bbweot	bbweop	bbweoh
ㅞ we	bbwelp	bbwelh	bbwem	bbweb	bbwebs	bbwes	bbwess	bbweng	bbwej	bbwech	bbwek	bbwet	bbwep	bbweh
ㅟ wi	bbwilp	bbwilh	bbwim	bbwib	bbwibs	bbwis	bbwiss	bbwing	bbwij	bbwich	bbwik	bbwit	bbwip	bbwih
ㅠ yu	bbyulp	bbyulh	bbyum	bbyub	bbyubs	bbyus	bbyuss	bbyung	bbyuj	bbyuch	bbyuk	bbyut	bbyup	bbyuh
ㅡ eu	bbeulp	bbeulh	bbeum	bbeub	bbeubs	bbeus	bbeuss	bbeung	bbeuj	bbeuch	bbeuk	bbeut	bbeup	bbeuh
ㅢ yi	bbyilp	bbyilh	bbyim	bbyib	bbyibs	bbyis	bbyiss	bbying	bbyij	bbyich	bbyik	bbyit	bbyip	bbyih
ㅣ i	bbilp	bbilh	bbim	bbib	bbibs	bbis	bbiss	bbing	bbij	bbich	bbik	bbit	bbip	bbih

Table 1.14: HanGul Syllables Starting with ㅅ (s)

		ㄱ g	ㄲ gg	ㄳ gs	ㄴ n	ㄵ nj	ㄶ nh	ㄷ d	ㄹ l	ㄺ lg	ㄻ lm	ㄼ lb	ㄽ ls	ㄾ lt
ㅅ s	ㅏ a	사 sa	삭 sag	샀 sagg	삯 sags	산 san	샀 sanj	삻 sanh	삳 sad	살 sal	삵 salg	삶 salm	삻 salb	삯 sals	삻 salt
ㅅ s	ㅐ ae	새 sae	색 saeg	섁 saegg	샜 saegs	샌 saen	샞 saenj	샢 saenh	샏 saed	샐 sael	섥 saelg	섧 saelm	섧 saelb	섨 saels	섩 saelt
ㅅ s	ㅑ ya	샤 sya	샥 syag	샦 syagg	샧 syags	샨 syan	샩 syanj	샪 syanh	샫 syad	샬 syal	샭 syalg	샮 syalm	샯 syalb	샰 syals	샱 syalt
ㅅ s	ㅒ yae	섀 syae	섁 syaeg	섂 syaegg	섃 syaegs	섄 syaen	섅 syaenj	섆 syaenh	섇 syaed	섈 syael	섉 syaelg	섊 syaelm	섋 syaelb	섌 syaels	섍 syaelt
ㅅ s	ㅓ eo	서 seo	석 seog	섞 seogg	섟 seogs	선 seon	섢 seonj	섭 seonh	섣 seod	설 seol	섥 seolg	섦 seolm	섧 seolb	섨 seols	섩 seolt
ㅅ s	ㅔ e	세 se	섹 seg	섺 segg	섻 segs	센 sen	섽 senj	섾 senh	섿 sed	셀 sel	셁 selg	셂 selm	셃 selb	셄 sels	셅 selt
ㅅ s	ㅕ yeo	셔 syeo	셕 syeog	셖 syeogg	셗 syeogs	션 syeon	셙 syeonj	셚 syeonh	셛 syeod	셜 syeol	셝 syeolg	셞 syeolm	셟 syeolb	셠 syeols	셡 syeolt
ㅅ s	ㅖ ye	셰 sye	셱 syeg	셲 syegg	셳 syegs	셴 syen	셵 syenj	셶 syenh	셷 syed	셸 syel	셹 syelg	셺 syelm	셻 syelb	셼 syels	셽 syelt
ㅅ s	ㅗ o	소 so	속 sog	솎 sogg	솏 sogs	손 son	솑 sonj	솒 sonh	솓 sod	솔 sol	솕 solg	솖 solm	솗 solb	솘 sols	솕 solt
ㅅ s	ㅘ wa	솨 swa	솩 swag	솪 swagg	솫 swags	솬 swan	솭 swanj	솮 swanh	솯 swad	솰 swal	솱 swalg	솲 swalm	솳 swalb	솴 swals	솵 swalt
ㅅ s	ㅙ wae	쇄 swae	쇅 swaeg	쇆 swaegg	쇇 swaegs	쇈 swaen	쇉 swaenj	쇊 swaenh	쇋 swaed	쇌 swael	쇍 swaelg	쇎 swaelm	쇏 swaelb	쇐 swaels	쇑 swaelt
ㅅ s	ㅚ oe	쇠 soe	쇡 soeg	쇢 soegg	쇣 soegs	쇤 soen	쇥 soenj	쇦 soenh	쇧 soed	쇨 soel	쇩 soelg	쇪 soelm	쇫 soelb	쇬 soels	쇭 soelt
ㅅ s	ㅛ yo	쇼 syo	쇽 syog	쇾 syogg	쇿 syogs	숀 syon	숁 syonj	숂 syonh	숃 syod	숄 syol	숅 syolg	숆 syolm	숇 syolb	숈 syols	숉 syolt
ㅅ s	ㅜ u	수 su	숙 sug	숚 sugg	숛 sugs	순 sun	숝 sunj	숞 sunh	숟 sud	술 sul	숡 sulg	숢 sulm	숣 sulb	숤 suls	숥 sult
ㅅ s	ㅝ weo	쉬 sweo	쉭 sweog	쉮 sweogg	쉯 sweogs	쉰 sweon	쉱 sweonj	쉲 sweonh	쉳 sweod	쉴 sweol	쉵 sweolg	쉶 sweolm	쉷 sweolb	쉸 sweols	쉹 sweolt
ㅅ s	ㅞ we	쉐 swe	쉑 sweg	쉒 swegg	쉓 swegs	쉔 swen	쉕 swenj	쉖 swenh	쉗 swed	쉘 swel	쉙 swelg	쉚 swelm	쉛 swelb	쉜 swels	쉝 swelt
ㅅ s	ㅟ wi	쉬 swi	쉭 swig	쉮 swigg	쉯 swigs	쉰 swin	쉱 swinj	쉲 swinh	쉳 swid	쉴 swil	쉵 swilg	쉶 swilm	쉷 swilb	쉸 swils	쉹 swilt
ㅅ s	ㅠ yu	슈 syu	슉 syug	슊 syugg	슋 syugs	슌 syun	슍 syunj	슎 syunh	슏 syud	슐 syul	슑 syulg	슒 syulm	슓 syulb	슔 syuls	슕 syult
ㅅ s	ㅡ eu	스 seu	슥 seug	슦 seugg	슧 seugs	슨 seun	슩 seunj	슪 seunh	슫 seud	슬 seul	슭 seulg	슮 seulm	슯 seulb	슰 seuls	슱 seult
ㅅ s	ㅢ yi	싀 syi	싁 syig	싂 syigg	싃 syigs	싄 syin	싅 syinj	싆 syinh	싇 syid	싈 syil	싉 syilg	싊 syilm	싋 syilb	싌 syils	싍 syilt
ㅅ s	ㅣ i	시 si	식 sig	싞 sigg	싟 sigs	신 sin	싡 sinj	싢 sinh	싣 sid	실 sil	싥 silg	싦 silm	싧 silb	싨 sils	싩 silt

		ㄿ lp	ㅀ lh	ㅁ m	ㅂ b	ㅄ bs	ㅅ s	ㅆ ss	ㅇ ng	ㅈ j	ㅊ ch	ㅋ k	ㅌ t	ㅍ p	ㅎ h
ㅅ s	ㅏ a	salp	salh	sam	sab	sabs	sas	sass	sang	saj	sach	sak	sat	sap	sah
ㅅ s	ㅐ ae	saelp	saelh	saem	saeb	saebs	saes	saess	saeng	saej	saech	saek	saet	saep	saeh
ㅅ s	ㅑ ya	syalp	syalh	syam	syab	syabs	syas	syass	syang	syaj	syach	syak	syat	syap	syah
ㅅ s	ㅒ yae	syaelp	syaelh	syaem	syaeb	syaebs	syaes	syaess	syaeng	syaej	syaech	syaek	syaet	syaep	syaeh
ㅅ s	ㅓ eo	seolp	seolh	seom	seob	seobs	seos	seoss	seong	seoj	seoch	seok	seot	seop	seoh
ㅅ s	ㅔ e	selp	selh	sem	seb	sebs	ses	sess	seng	sej	sech	sek	set	sep	seh
ㅅ s	ㅕ yeo	syeolp	syeolh	syeom	syeob	syeobs	syeos	syeoss	syeong	syeoj	syeoch	syeok	syeot	syeop	syeoh
ㅅ s	ㅖ ye	syelp	syelh	syem	syeb	syebs	syes	syess	syeng	syej	syech	syek	syet	syep	syeh
ㅅ s	ㅗ o	solp	solh	som	sob	sobs	sos	soss	song	soj	soch	sok	sot	sop	soh
ㅅ s	ㅘ wa	swalp	swalh	swam	swab	swabs	swas	swass	swang	swaj	swach	swak	swat	swap	swah
ㅅ s	ㅙ wae	swaelp	swaelh	swaem	swaeb	swaebs	swaes	swaess	swaeng	swaej	swaech	swaek	swaet	swaep	swaeh
ㅅ s	ㅚ oe	soelp	soelh	soem	soeb	soebs	soes	soess	soeng	soej	soech	soek	soet	soep	soeh
ㅅ s	ㅛ yo	syolp	syolh	syom	syob	syobs	syos	syoss	syong	syoj	syoch	syok	syot	syop	syoh
ㅅ s	ㅜ u	sulp	sulh	sum	sub	subs	sus	suss	sung	suj	such	suk	sut	sup	suh
ㅅ s	ㅝ weo	sweolp	sweolh	sweom	sweob	sweobs	sweos	sweoss	sweong	sweoj	sweoch	sweok	sweot	sweop	sweoh
ㅅ s	ㅞ we	swelp	swelh	swem	sweb	swebs	swes	swess	sweng	swej	swech	swek	swet	swep	sweh
ㅅ s	ㅟ wi	swilp	swilh	swim	swib	swibs	swis	swiss	swing	swij	swich	swik	swit	swip	swih
ㅅ s	ㅠ yu	syulp	syulh	syum	syub	syubs	syus	syuss	syung	syuj	syuch	syuk	syut	syup	syuh
ㅅ s	ㅡ eu	seulp	seulh	seum	seub	seubs	seus	seuss	seung	seuj	seuch	seuk	seut	seup	seuh
ㅅ s	ㅢ yi	syilp	syilh	syim	syib	syibs	syis	syiss	sying	syij	syich	syik	syit	syip	syih
ㅅ s	ㅣ i	silp	silh	sim	sib	sibs	sis	siss	sing	sij	sich	sik	sit	sip	sih

Table 1.15: HanGul Syllables Starting with ㅆ (ss)

		ㄱ g	ㄲ gg	ㄳ gs	ㄴ n	ㄵ nj	ㄶ nh	ㄷ d	ㄹ l	ㄺ lg	ㄻ lm	ㄼ lb	ㄽ ls	ㄾ lt
ㅆ ss	ㅏ a	싸 ssa	싹 ssag	쌎 ssagg	쌏 ssags	싼 ssan	쌊 ssanj	쌏 ssanh	싿 ssad	쌀 ssal	쌁 ssalg	쌂 ssalm	쌃 ssalb	쌄 ssals	쌅 ssalt
ㅆ ss	ㅐ ae	쌔 ssae	쌕 ssaeg	쌖 ssaegg	쌗 ssaegs	쌘 ssaen	쌙 ssaenj	쌚 ssaenh	쌛 ssaed	쌜 ssael	쌝 ssaelg	쌞 ssaelm	쌟 ssaelb	쌠 ssaels	쌡 ssaelt
ㅆ ss	ㅑ ya	쌰 ssya	쌱 ssyag	쌲 ssyagg	쌳 ssyags	쌴 ssyan	쌵 ssyanj	쌶 ssyanh	쌷 ssyad	쌸 ssyal	쌹 ssyalg	쌺 ssyalm	쌻 ssyalb	쌼 ssyals	쌽 ssyalt
ㅆ ss	ㅒ yae	쌔 ssyae	쌕 ssyaeg	쌖 ssyaegg	쌗 ssyaegs	쌘 ssyaen	쌙 ssyaenj	쌚 ssyaenh	쌛 ssyaed	쌜 ssyael	쌝 ssyaelg	쌞 ssyaelm	쌟 ssyaelb	쌠 ssyaels	쌡 ssyaelt
ㅆ ss	ㅓ eo	써 sseo	썩 sseog	썪 sseogg	썫 sseogs	썬 sseon	썭 sseonj	썮 sseonh	썯 sseod	썰 sseol	썱 sseolg	썲 sseolm	썳 sseolb	썴 sseols	썵 sseolt
ㅆ ss	ㅔ e	쎄 sse	쎅 sseg	쎆 ssegg	쎇 ssegs	쎈 ssen	쎉 ssenj	쎊 ssenh	쎋 ssed	쎌 ssel	쎍 sselg	쎎 sselm	쎏 sselb	쎐 ssels	쎑 sselt
ㅆ ss	ㅕ yeo	쎠 ssyeo	쎡 ssyeog	쎢 ssyeogg	쎣 ssyeogs	쎤 ssyeon	쎥 ssyeonj	쎦 ssyeonh	쎧 ssyeod	쎨 ssyeol	쎩 ssyeolg	쎪 ssyeolm	쎫 ssyeolb	쎬 ssyeols	쎭 ssyeolt
ㅆ ss	ㅖ ye	쎼 ssye	쎽 ssyeg	쎾 ssyegg	쎿 ssyegs	쏀 ssyen	쏁 ssyenj	쏂 ssyenh	쏃 ssyed	쏄 ssyel	쏅 ssyelg	쏆 ssyelm	쏇 ssyelb	쏈 ssyels	쏉 ssyelt
ㅆ ss	ㅗ o	쏘 sso	쏙 ssog	쏚 ssogg	쏛 ssogs	쏜 sson	쏝 ssonj	쏞 ssonh	쏟 ssod	쏠 ssol	쏡 ssolg	쏢 ssolm	쏣 ssolb	쏤 ssols	쏥 ssolt
ㅆ ss	ㅘ wa	쏴 sswa	쏵 sswag	쏶 sswagg	쏷 sswags	쏸 sswan	쏹 sswanj	쏺 sswanh	쏻 sswad	쏼 sswal	쏽 sswalg	쏾 sswalm	쏿 sswalb	쐀 sswals	쐁 sswalt
ㅆ ss	ㅙ wae	쐐 sswae	쐑 sswaeg	쐒 sswaegg	쐓 sswaegs	쐔 sswaen	쐕 sswaenj	쐖 sswaenh	쐗 sswaed	쐘 sswael	쐙 sswaelg	쐚 sswaelm	쐛 sswaelb	쐜 sswaels	쐝 sswaelt
ㅆ ss	ㅚ oe	쐬 ssoe	쐭 ssoeg	쐮 ssoegg	쐯 ssoegs	쐰 ssoen	쐱 ssoenj	쐲 ssoenh	쐳 ssoed	쐴 ssoel	쐵 ssoelg	쐶 ssoelm	쐷 ssoelb	쐸 ssoels	쐹 ssoelt
ㅆ ss	ㅛ yo	쑈 ssyo	쑉 ssyog	쑊 ssyogg	쑋 ssyogs	쑌 ssyon	쑍 ssyonj	쑎 ssyonh	쑏 ssyod	쑐 ssyol	쑑 ssyolg	쑒 ssyolm	쑓 ssyolb	쑔 ssyols	쑕 ssyolt
ㅆ ss	ㅜ u	쑤 ssu	쑥 ssug	쑦 ssugg	쑧 ssugs	쑨 ssun	쑩 ssunj	쑪 ssunh	쑫 ssud	쑬 ssul	쑭 ssulg	쑮 ssulm	쑯 ssulb	쑰 ssuls	쑱 ssult
ㅆ ss	ㅝ weo	쒀 ssweo	쒁 ssweog	쒂 ssweogg	쒃 ssweogs	쒄 ssweon	쒅 ssweonj	쒆 ssweonh	쒇 ssweod	쒈 ssweol	쒉 ssweolg	쒊 ssweolm	쒋 ssweolb	쒌 ssweols	쒍 ssweolt
ㅆ ss	ㅞ we	쒜 sswe	쒝 ssweg	쒞 sswegg	쒟 sswegs	쒠 sswen	쒡 sswenj	쒢 sswenh	쒣 sswed	쒤 sswel	쒥 sswelg	쒦 sswelm	쒧 sswelb	쒨 sswels	쒩 sswelt
ㅆ ss	ㅟ wi	쒸 sswi	쒹 sswig	쒺 sswigg	쒻 sswigs	쒼 sswin	쒽 sswinj	쒾 sswinh	쒿 sswid	쓀 sswil	쓁 sswilg	쓂 sswilm	쓃 sswilb	쓄 sswils	쓅 sswilt
ㅆ ss	ㅠ yu	쓔 ssyu	쓕 ssyug	쓖 ssyugg	쓗 ssyugs	쓘 ssyun	쓙 ssyunj	쓚 ssyunh	쓛 ssyud	쓜 ssyul	쓝 ssyulg	쓞 ssyulm	쓟 ssyulb	쓠 ssyuls	쓡 ssyult
ㅆ ss	ㅡ eu	쓰 sseu	쓱 sseug	쓲 sseugg	쓳 sseugs	쓴 sseun	쓵 sseunj	쓶 sseunh	쓷 sseud	쓸 sseul	쓹 sseulg	쓺 sseulm	쓻 sseulb	쓼 sseuls	쓽 sseult
ㅆ ss	ㅢ yi	씨 ssyi	씩 ssyig	씪 ssyigg	씫 ssyigs	씬 ssyin	씭 ssyinj	씮 ssyinh	씯 ssyid	씰 ssyil	씱 ssyilg	씲 ssyilm	씳 ssyilb	씴 ssyils	씵 ssyilt
ㅆ ss	ㅣ i	씨 ssi	씩 ssig	씪 ssigg	씫 ssigs	씬 ssin	씭 ssinj	씮 ssinh	씯 ssid	씰 ssil	씱 ssilg	씲 ssilm	씳 ssilb	씴 ssils	씵 ssilt

ss +	ᄚ lp	ᄚ lh	ㅁ m	ㅂ b	ㅄ bs	ㅅ s	ㅆ ss	ㅇ ng	ㅈ j	ㅊ ch	ㅋ k	ㅌ t	ㅍ p	ㅎ h
a	ssalp	ssalh	ssam	ssab	ssabs	ssas	ssass	ssang	ssaj	ssach	ssak	ssat	ssap	ssah
ae	ssaelp	ssaelh	ssaem	ssaeb	ssaebs	ssaes	ssaess	ssaeng	ssaej	ssaech	ssaek	ssaet	ssaep	ssaeh
ya	ssyalp	ssyalh	ssyam	ssyab	ssyabs	ssyas	ssyass	ssyang	ssyaj	ssyach	ssyak	ssyat	ssyap	ssyah
yae	ssyaelp	ssyaelh	ssyaem	ssyaeb	ssyaebs	ssyaes	ssyaess	ssyaeng	ssyaej	ssyaech	ssyaek	ssyaet	ssyaep	ssyaeh
eo	sseolp	sseolh	sseom	sseob	sseobs	sseos	sseoss	sseong	sseoj	sseoch	sseok	sseot	sseop	sseoh
e	sselp	sselh	ssem	sseb	ssebs	sses	ssess	sseng	ssej	ssech	ssek	sset	ssep	sseh
yeo	ssyeolp	ssyeolh	ssyeom	ssyeob	ssyeobs	ssyeos	ssyeoss	ssyeong	ssyeoj	ssyeoch	ssyeok	ssyeot	ssyeop	ssyeoh
ye	ssyelp	ssyelh	ssyem	ssyeb	ssyebs	ssyes	ssyess	ssyeng	ssyej	ssyech	ssyek	ssyet	ssyep	ssyeh
o	ssolp	ssolh	ssom	ssob	ssobs	ssos	ssoss	ssong	ssoj	ssoch	ssok	ssot	ssop	ssoh
wa	sswalp	sswalh	sswam	sswab	sswabs	sswas	sswass	sswang	sswaj	sswach	sswak	sswat	sswap	sswah
wae	sswaelp	sswaelh	sswaem	sswaeb	sswaebs	sswaes	sswaess	sswaeng	sswaej	sswaech	sswaek	sswaet	sswaep	sswaeh
oe	ssoelp	ssoelh	ssoem	ssoeb	ssoebs	ssoes	ssoess	ssoeng	ssoej	ssoech	ssoek	ssoet	ssoep	ssoeh
yo	ssyolp	ssyolh	ssyom	ssyob	ssyobs	ssyos	ssyoss	ssyong	ssyoj	ssyoch	ssyok	ssyot	ssyop	ssyoh
u	ssulp	ssulh	ssum	ssub	ssubs	ssus	ssuss	ssung	ssuj	ssuch	ssuk	ssut	ssup	ssuh
weo	ssweolp	ssweolh	ssweom	ssweob	ssweobs	ssweos	ssweoss	ssweong	ssweoj	ssweoch	ssweok	ssweot	ssweop	ssweoh
we	sswelp	sswelh	sswem	ssweb	sswebs	sswes	sswess	ssweng	sswej	sswech	sswek	sswet	sswep	ssweh
wi	sswilp	sswilh	sswim	sswib	sswibs	sswis	sswiss	sswing	sswij	sswich	sswik	sswit	sswip	sswih
yu	ssyulp	ssyulh	ssyum	ssyub	ssyubs	ssyus	ssyuss	ssyung	ssyuj	ssyuch	ssyuk	ssyut	ssyup	ssyuh
eu	sseulp	sseulh	sseum	sseub	sseubs	sseus	sseuss	sseung	sseuj	sseuch	sseuk	sseut	sseup	sseuh
yi	ssyilp	ssyilh	ssyim	ssyib	ssyibs	ssyis	ssyiss	ssying	ssyij	ssyich	ssyik	ssyit	ssyip	ssyih
i	ssilp	ssilh	ssim	ssib	ssibs	ssis	ssiss	ssing	ssij	ssich	ssik	ssit	ssip	ssih

Table 1.16: HanGul Syllables Starting with ㅇ (vowel sounds)

		ㄱ g	ㄲ gg	ㄳ gs	ㄴ n	ㄵ nj	ㄶ nh	ㄷ d	ㄹ l	ㄺ lg	ㄻ lm	ㄼ lb	ㄽ ls	ㄾ lt
ㅇ	ㅏ a	아 a	악 ag	앆 agg	앇 ags	안 an	앉 anj	않 anh	앋 ad	알 al	앍 alg	앎 alm	앏 alb	앐 als	앑 alt
ㅇ	ㅐ ae	애 ae	액 aeg	앢 aegg	앣 aegs	앤 aen	앦 aenj	앧 aenh	앧 aed	앨 ael	앩 aelg	앫 aelm	앮 aelb	앬 aels	앭 aelt
ㅇ	ㅑ ya	야 ya	약 yag	앾 yagg	앿 yags	얀 yan	얁 yanj	얂 yanh	얃 yad	얄 yal	얅 yalg	얆 yalm	얇 yalb	얈 yals	얉 yalt
ㅇ	ㅒ yae	얘 yae	얙 yaeg	얚 yaegg	얛 yaegs	얜 yaen	얝 yaenj	얞 yaenh	얟 yaed	얠 yael	얡 yaelg	얢 yaelm	얣 yaelb	얤 yaels	얥 yaelt
ㅇ	ㅓ eo	어 eo	억 eog	엌 eogg	엋 eogs	언 eon	엊 eonj	엏 eonh	얻 eod	얼 eol	얽 eolg	얾 eolm	얿 eolb	엀 eols	엁 eolt
ㅇ	ㅔ e	에 e	엑 eg	엒 egg	엓 egs	엔 en	엕 enj	엖 enh	엗 ed	엘 el	엙 elg	엚 elm	엛 elb	엜 els	엝 elt
ㅇ	ㅕ yeo	여 yeo	역 yeog	엮 yeogg	엯 yeogs	연 yeon	엱 yeonj	엲 yeonh	연 yeod	열 yeol	엵 yeolg	엶 yeolm	엷 yeolb	엸 yeols	엹 yeolt
ㅇ	ㅖ ye	예 ye	옉 yeg	옊 yegg	옋 yegs	옌 yen	옍 yenj	옎 yenh	옏 yed	옐 yel	옑 yelg	옒 yelm	옓 yelb	옔 yels	옕 yelt
ㅇ	ㅗ o	오 o	옥 og	옦 ogg	옧 ogs	온 on	옩 onj	옪 onh	옫 od	올 ol	옭 olg	옮 olm	옯 olb	옰 ols	옱 olt
ㅇ	ㅘ wa	와 wa	왁 wag	왂 wagg	왃 wags	완 wan	왅 wanj	왆 wanh	왇 wad	왈 wal	왉 walg	왊 walm	왋 walb	왌 wals	왍 walt
ㅇ	ㅙ wae	왜 wae	왝 waeg	왞 waegg	왟 waegs	왠 waen	왡 waenj	왢 waenh	왣 waed	왤 wael	왥 waelg	왦 waelm	왧 waelb	왨 waels	왩 waelt
ㅇ	ㅚ oe	외 oe	왹 oeg	왺 oegg	왻 oegs	왼 oen	왽 oenj	왾 oenh	왿 oed	욀 oel	욁 oelg	욂 oelm	욃 oelb	욄 oels	욅 oelt
ㅇ	ㅛ yo	요 yo	욕 yog	욖 yogg	욗 yogs	욘 yon	욙 yonj	욚 yonh	욛 yod	욜 yol	욝 yolg	욞 yolm	욟 yolb	욠 yols	욡 yolt
ㅇ	ㅜ u	우 u	욱 ug	욲 ugg	욳 ugs	운 un	욵 unj	욶 unh	욷 ud	울 ul	욹 ulg	욺 ulm	욻 ulb	욼 uls	욽 ult
ㅇ	ㅝ weo	워 weo	웍 weog	웎 weogg	웏 weogs	원 weon	웑 weonj	웒 weonh	웓 weod	월 weol	웕 weolg	웖 weolm	웗 weolb	웘 weols	웙 weolt
ㅇ	ㅞ we	웨 we	웩 weg	웪 wegg	웫 wegs	웬 wen	웭 wenj	웮 wenh	웯 wed	웰 wel	웱 welg	웲 welm	웳 welb	웴 wels	웵 welt
ㅇ	ㅟ wi	위 wi	윅 wig	윆 wigg	윇 wigs	윈 win	윉 winj	윊 winh	윋 wid	윌 wil	윍 wilg	윎 wilm	윏 wilb	윐 wils	윑 wilt
ㅇ	ㅠ yu	유 yu	육 yug	윢 yugg	윣 yugs	윤 yun	윥 yunj	윦 yunh	윧 yud	율 yul	윩 yulg	윪 yulm	윫 yulb	윬 yuls	윭 yult
ㅇ	ㅡ eu	으 eu	윽 eug	윾 eugg	윿 eugs	은 eun	읁 eunj	읂 eunh	읃 eud	을 eul	읅 eulg	읆 eulm	읇 eulb	읈 euls	읉 eult
ㅇ	ㅢ yi	의 yi	읙 yig	읚 yigg	읛 yigs	읜 yin	읝 yinj	읞 yinh	읟 yid	읠 yil	읡 yilg	읢 yilm	읣 yilb	읤 yils	읥 yilt
ㅇ	ㅣ i	이 i	익 ig	읶 igg	읷 igs	인 in	읹 inj	읺 inh	읻 id	일 il	읽 ilg	읾 ilm	읿 ilb	잀 ils	잁 ilt

	ㄿ lp	ㅀ lh	ㅁ m	ㅂ b	ㅄ bs	ㅅ s	ㅆ ss	ㅇ ng	ㅈ j	ㅊ ch	ㅋ k	ㅌ t	ㅍ p	ㅎ h
ㅏ a	alp	alh	am	ab	abs	as	ass	ang	aj	ach	ak	at	ap	ah
ㅐ ae	aelp	aelh	aem	aeb	aebs	aes	aess	aeng	aej	aech	aek	aet	aep	aeh
ㅑ ya	yalp	yalh	yam	yab	yabs	yas	yass	yang	yaj	yach	yak	yat	yap	yah
ㅒ yae	yaelp	yaelh	yaem	yaeb	yaebs	yaes	yaess	yaeng	yaej	yaech	yaek	yaet	yaep	yaeh
ㅓ eo	eolp	eolh	eom	eob	eobs	eos	eoss	eong	eoj	eoch	eok	eot	eop	eoh
ㅔ e	elp	elh	em	eb	ebs	es	ess	eng	ej	ech	ek	et	ep	eh
ㅕ yeo	yeolp	yeolh	yeom	yeob	yeobs	yeos	yeoss	yeong	yeoj	yeoch	yeok	yeot	yeop	yeoh
ㅖ ye	yelp	yelh	yem	yeb	yebs	yes	yess	yeng	yej	yech	yek	yet	yep	yeh
ㅗ o	olp	olh	om	ob	obs	os	oss	ong	oj	och	ok	ot	op	oh
ㅘ wa	walp	walh	wam	wab	wabs	was	wass	wang	waj	wach	wak	wat	wap	wah
ㅙ wae	waelp	waelh	waem	waeb	waebs	waes	waess	waeng	waej	waech	waek	waet	waep	waeh
ㅚ oe	oelp	oelh	oem	oeb	oebs	oes	oess	oeng	oej	oech	oek	oet	oep	oeh
ㅛ yo	yolp	yolh	yom	yob	yobs	yos	yoss	yong	yoj	yoch	yok	yot	yop	yoh
ㅜ u	ulp	ulh	um	ub	ubs	us	uss	ung	uj	uch	uk	ut	up	uh
ㅝ weo	weolp	weolh	weom	weob	weobs	weos	weoss	weong	weoj	weoch	weok	weot	weop	weoh
ㅞ we	welp	welh	wem	web	webs	wes	wess	weng	wej	wech	wek	wet	wep	weh
ㅟ wi	wilp	wilh	wim	wib	wibs	wis	wiss	wing	wij	wich	wik	wit	wip	wih
ㅠ yu	yulp	yulh	yum	yub	yubs	yus	yuss	yung	yuj	yuch	yuk	yut	yup	yuh
ㅡ eu	eulp	eulh	eum	eub	eubs	eus	euss	eung	euj	euch	euk	eut	eup	euh
ㅢ yi	yilp	yilh	yim	yib	yibs	yis	yiss	ying	yij	yich	yik	yit	yip	yih
ㅣ i	ilp	ilh	im	ib	ibs	is	iss	ing	ij	ich	ik	it	ip	ih

Table 1.17: HanGul Syllables Starting with ㅈ (j)

		ㄱ g	ㄲ gg	ㄳ gs	ㄴ n	ㄵ nj	ㄶ nh	ㄷ d	ㄹ l	ㄺ lg	ㄻ lm	ㄼ lb	ㄽ ls	ㄾ lt
ㅈ j	ㅏ a	자 ja	작 jag	쟈 jagg	잤 jags	잔 jan	잪 janj	잫 janh	잗 jad	잘 jal	잙 jalg	잚 jalm	잛 jalb	잜 jals	잝 jalt
ㅈ j	ㅐ ae	재 jae	잭 jaeg	잳 jaegg	잱 jaegs	잰 jaen	잮 jaenj	잷 jaenh	잴 jaed	잴 jael	잶 jaelg	잷 jaelm	잷 jaelb	잷 jaels	잷 jaelt
ㅈ j	ㅑ ya	쟈 jya	쟉 jyag	쟊 jyagg	쟋 jyags	쟌 jyan	쟎 jyanj	쟏 jyanh	쟏 jyad	쟐 jyal	쟑 jyalg	쟒 jyalm	쟓 jyalb	쟔 jyals	쟕 jyalt
ㅈ j	ㅒ yae	쟤 jyae	쟥 jyaeg	쟦 jyaegg	쟧 jyaegs	쟨 jyaen	쟩 jyaenj	쟪 jyaenh	쟫 jyaed	쟬 jyael	쟭 jyaelg	쟮 jyaelm	쟯 jyaelb	쟰 jyaels	쟱 jyaelt
ㅈ j	ㅓ eo	저 jeo	적 jeog	젂 jeogg	젃 jeogs	전 jeon	젅 jeonj	젆 jeonh	젇 jeod	절 jeol	젉 jeolg	젊 jeolm	젋 jeolb	젌 jeols	젍 jeolt
ㅈ j	ㅔ e	제 je	젝 jeg	젞 jegg	젟 jegs	젠 jen	젡 jenj	젢 jenh	젣 jed	젤 jel	젥 jelg	젦 jelm	젧 jelb	젨 jels	젩 jelt
ㅈ j	ㅕ yeo	져 jyeo	젹 jyeog	젺 jyeogg	젻 jyeogs	젼 jyeon	젽 jyeonj	젾 jyeonh	젿 jyeod	졀 jyeol	졁 jyeolg	졂 jyeolm	졃 jyeolb	졄 jyeols	졅 jyeolt
ㅈ j	ㅖ ye	졔 jye	졕 jyeg	졖 jyegg	졗 jyegs	졘 jyen	졙 jyenj	졚 jyenh	졛 jyed	졜 jyel	졝 jyelg	졞 jyelm	졟 jyelb	졠 jyels	졡 jyelt
ㅈ j	ㅗ o	조 jo	족 jog	졲 jogg	졳 jogs	존 jon	졵 jonj	졶 jonh	졷 jod	졸 jol	졹 jolg	졺 jolm	졻 jolb	졼 jols	졽 jolt
ㅈ j	ㅘ wa	좌 jwa	좍 jwag	좎 jwagg	좏 jwags	좐 jwan	좑 jwanj	좒 jwanh	좓 jwad	좔 jwal	좕 jwalg	좖 jwalm	좗 jwalb	좘 jwals	좙 jwalt
ㅈ j	ㅙ wae	좨 jwae	좩 jwaeg	좪 jwaegg	좫 jwaegs	좬 jwaen	좭 jwaenj	좮 jwaenh	좯 jwaed	좰 jwael	좱 jwaelg	좲 jwaelm	좳 jwaelb	좴 jwaels	좵 jwaelt
ㅈ j	ㅚ oe	죄 joe	죅 joeg	죆 joegg	죇 joegs	죈 joen	죉 joenj	죊 joenh	죋 joed	죌 joel	죍 joelg	죎 joelm	죏 joelb	죐 joels	죑 joelt
ㅈ j	ㅛ yo	죠 jyo	죡 jyog	죢 jyogg	죣 jyogs	죤 jyon	죥 jyonj	죦 jyonh	죧 jyod	죨 jyol	죩 jyolg	죪 jyolm	죫 jyolb	죬 jyols	죭 jyolt
ㅈ j	ㅜ u	주 ju	죽 jug	죾 jugg	죿 jugs	준 jun	줁 junj	줂 junh	줃 jud	줄 jul	줅 julg	줆 julm	줇 julb	줈 juls	줉 jult
ㅈ j	ㅝ weo	줘 jweo	줙 jweog	줚 jweogg	줛 jweogs	줜 jweon	줝 jweonj	줞 jweonh	줟 jweod	줠 jweol	줡 jweolg	줢 jweolm	줣 jweolb	줤 jweols	줥 jweolt
ㅈ j	ㅞ we	줴 jwe	줵 jweg	줶 jwegg	줷 jwegs	줸 jwen	줹 jwenj	줺 jwenh	줻 jwed	줼 jwel	줽 jwelg	줾 jwelm	줿 jwelb	쥀 jwels	쥁 jwelt
ㅈ j	ㅟ wi	쥐 jwi	쥑 jwig	쥒 jwigg	쥓 jwigs	쥔 jwin	쥕 jwinj	쥖 jwinh	쥗 jwid	쥘 jwil	쥙 jwilg	쥚 jwilm	쥛 jwilb	쥜 jwils	쥝 jwilt
ㅈ j	ㅠ yu	쥬 jyu	쥭 jyug	쥮 jyugg	쥯 jyugs	쥰 jyun	쥱 jyunj	쥲 jyunh	쥳 jyud	쥴 jyul	쥵 jyulg	쥶 jyulm	쥷 jyulb	쥸 jyuls	쥹 jyult
ㅈ j	ㅡ eu	즈 jeu	즉 jeug	즊 jeugg	즋 jeugs	즌 jeun	즍 jeunj	즎 jeunh	즏 jeud	즐 jeul	즑 jeulg	즒 jeulm	즓 jeulb	즔 jeuls	즕 jeult
ㅈ j	ㅢ yi	즤 jyi	즥 jyig	즦 jyigg	즧 jyigs	즨 jyin	즩 jyinj	즪 jyinh	즫 jyid	즬 jyil	즭 jyilg	즮 jyilm	즯 jyilb	즰 jyils	즱 jyilt
ㅈ j	ㅣ i	지 ji	직 jig	짂 jigg	짃 jigs	진 jin	짅 jinj	짆 jinh	짇 jid	질 jil	짉 jilg	짊 jilm	짋 jilb	짌 jils	짍 jilt

		ㄿ lp	ㅀ lh	ㅁ m	ㅂ b	ㅄ bs	ㅅ s	ㅆ ss	ㅇ ng	ㅈ j	ㅊ ch	ㅋ k	ㅌ t	ㅍ p	ㅎ h
ㅈ j	ㅏ a	잟 jalp	잛 jalh	잠 jam	잡 jab	잢 jabs	잣 jas	잤 jass	장 jang	잦 jaj	잧 jach	작 jak	잩 jat	잪 jap	잫 jah
ㅈ j	ㅐ ae	잻 jaelp	잻 jaelh	잼 jaem	잽 jaeb	잾 jaebs	잿 jaes	쟀 jaess	쟁 jaeng	잿 jaej	잿 jaech	잭 jaek	잳 jaet	잺 jaep	쟁 jaeh
ㅈ j	ㅑ ya	쟓 jyalp	쟓 jyalh	쟘 jyam	쟙 jyab	쟚 jyabs	쟛 jyas	쟜 jyass	쟝 jyang	쟞 jyaj	쟟 jyach	쟉 jyak	쟡 jyat	쟢 jyap	쟣 jyah
ㅈ j	ㅒ yae	쟳 jyaelp	쟳 jyaelh	쟴 jyaem	쟵 jyaeb	쟶 jyaebs	쟷 jyaes	쟸 jyaess	쟹 jyaeng	쟺 jyaej	쟻 jyaech	쟥 jyaek	쟽 jyaet	쟾 jyaep	쟿 jyaeh
ㅈ j	ㅓ eo	젋 jeolp	젋 jeolh	점 jeom	접 jeob	젒 jeobs	젓 jeos	젔 jeoss	정 jeong	젖 jeoj	젗 jeoch	적 jeok	젙 jeot	젚 jeop	젛 jeoh
ㅈ j	ㅔ e	젫 jelp	젫 jelh	젬 jem	젭 jeb	젮 jebs	젯 jes	젰 jess	젱 jeng	젲 jej	젳 jech	젝 jek	젵 jet	젶 jep	젷 jeh
ㅈ j	ㅕ yeo	졇 jyeolp	졇 jyeolh	졈 jyeom	졉 jyeob	졊 jyeobs	졋 jyeos	졌 jyeoss	경 jyeong	졎 jyeoj	졏 jyeoch	젹 jyeok	졑 jyeot	졒 jyeop	졓 jyeoh
ㅈ j	ㅖ ye	졫 jyelp	졫 jyelh	졤 jyem	졥 jyeb	졦 jyebs	졧 jyes	졨 jyess	졩 jyeng	졪 jyej	졫 jyech	졕 jyek	졭 jyet	졮 jyep	졯 jyeh
ㅈ j	ㅗ o	졻 jolp	졻 jolh	좀 jom	좁 job	좂 jobs	좃 jos	좄 joss	종 jong	좆 joj	좇 joch	족 jok	졷 jot	졶 jop	좋 joh
ㅈ j	ㅘ wa	좳 jwalp	좳 jwalh	좜 jwam	좝 jwab	좞 jwabs	좟 jwas	좠 jwass	좡 jwang	좢 jwaj	좣 jwach	좍 jwak	좥 jwat	좦 jwap	좧 jwah
ㅈ j	ㅙ wae	쵏 jwaelp	쵏 jwaelh	쵐 jwaem	쵑 jwaeb	쵒 jwaebs	쵓 jwaes	쵔 jwaess	쵕 jwaeng	쵖 jwaej	쵗 jwaech	쵉 jwaek	쵙 jwaet	쵚 jwaep	쵛 jwaeh
ㅈ j	ㅚ oe	죏 joelp	죏 joelh	죔 joem	죕 joeb	죖 joebs	죗 joes	죘 joess	죙 joeng	죚 joej	죛 joech	죅 joek	죝 joet	죞 joep	죟 joeh
ㅈ j	ㅛ yo	죯 jyolp	죯 jyolh	죰 jyom	죱 jyob	죲 jyobs	죳 jyos	죴 jyoss	죵 jyong	죶 jyoj	죷 jyoch	죡 jyok	죹 jyot	죺 jyop	죻 jyoh
ㅈ j	ㅜ u	쥛 julp	쥛 julh	줌 jum	줍 jub	줎 jubs	줏 jus	줐 juss	중 jung	줒 juj	줓 juch	죽 juk	줕 jut	줖 jup	줗 juh
ㅈ j	ㅝ weo	줧 jweolp	줧 jweolh	줨 jweom	줩 jweob	줪 jweobs	줫 jweos	줬 jweoss	줭 jweong	줮 jweoj	줯 jweoch	줙 jweok	줱 jweot	줲 jweop	줳 jweoh
ㅈ j	ㅞ we	쥃 jwelp	쥃 jwelh	쥄 jwem	쥅 jweb	쥆 jwebs	쥇 jwes	쥈 jwess	쥉 jweng	쥊 jwej	쥋 jwech	쥅 jwek	쥍 jwet	쥎 jwep	쥏 jweh
ㅈ j	ㅟ wi	쥟 jwilp	쥟 jwilh	쥠 jwim	쥡 jwib	쥢 jwibs	쥣 jwis	쥤 jwiss	쥥 jwing	쥦 jwij	쥧 jwich	쥑 jwik	쥩 jwit	쥪 jwip	쥫 jwih
ㅈ j	ㅠ yu	쥳 jyulp	쥳 jyulh	쥼 jyum	쥽 jyub	쥾 jyubs	쥿 jyus	즀 jyuss	즁 jyung	즂 jyuj	즃 jyuch	쥭 jyuk	즅 jyut	즆 jyup	즇 jyuh
ㅈ j	ㅡ eu	즳 jeulp	즳 jeulh	즘 jeum	즙 jeub	즚 jeubs	즛 jeus	즜 jeuss	증 jeung	즞 jeuj	즟 jeuch	즉 jeuk	즡 jeut	즢 jeup	즣 jeuh
ㅈ j	ㅢ yi	즯 jyilp	즯 jyilh	짐 jyim	집 jyib	짒 jyibs	짓 jyis	짔 jyiss	징 jying	짖 jyij	짗 jyich	즥 jyik	짙 jyit	짚 jyip	짛 jyih
ㅈ j	ㅣ i	짋 jilp	짋 jilh	짐 jim	집 jib	짒 jibs	짓 jis	짔 jiss	징 jing	짖 jij	짗 jich	직 jik	짙 jit	짚 jip	짛 jih

Table 1.18: HanGul Syllables Starting with ㅉ (jj)

ㅉ jj		ㄱ g	ㄲ gg	ㄳ gs	ㄴ n	ㄵ nj	ㄶ nh	ㄷ d	ㄹ l	ㄺ lg	ㄻ lm	ㄼ lb	ㄽ ls	ㄾ lt
ㅉ jj	ㅏ a	짜 jja	짝 jjag	짞 jjagg	짠 jjags	짠 jjan	짢 jjanj	짷 jjanh	짣 jjad	짤 jjal	짥 jjalg	짦 jjalm	짧 jjalb	짨 jjals	짪 jjalt
ㅉ jj	ㅐ ae	째 jjae	짹 jjaeg	짺 jjaegg	짻 jjaegs	짼 jjaen	짽 jjaenj	짷 jjaenh	짿 jjaed	쨀 jjael	쨁 jjaelg	쨂 jjaelm	쨄 jjaelb	쨄 jjaels	쨆 jjaelt
ㅉ jj	ㅑ ya	쨔 jjya	쨕 jjyag	쨖 jjyagg	쨗 jjyags	쨘 jjyan	쨙 jjyanj	쨚 jjyanh	쨛 jjyad	쨜 jjyal	쨝 jjyalg	쨞 jjyalm	쨠 jjyalb	쨠 jjyals	쨢 jjyalt
ㅉ jj	ㅒ yae	쨰 jjyae	쨱 jjyaeg	쨲 jjyaegg	쨳 jjyaegs	쨴 jjyaen	쨵 jjyaenj	쨶 jjyaenh	쨷 jjyaed	쨸 jjyael	쨹 jjyaelg	쨺 jjyaelm	쨼 jjyaelb	쨼 jjyaels	쨾 jjyaelt
ㅉ jj	ㅓ eo	쩌 jjeo	쩍 jjeog	쩎 jjeogg	쩏 jjeogs	쩐 jjeon	쩑 jjeonj	쩒 jjeonh	쩓 jjeod	쩔 jjeol	쩕 jjeolg	쩖 jjeolm	쩘 jjeolb	쩘 jjeols	쩚 jjeolt
ㅉ jj	ㅔ e	쩨 jje	쩩 jjeg	쩪 jjegg	쩫 jjegs	쩬 jjen	쩭 jjenj	쩮 jjenh	쩯 jjed	쩰 jjel	쩱 jjelg	쩲 jjelm	쩴 jjelb	쩴 jjels	쩶 jjelt
ㅉ jj	ㅕ yeo	쪄 jjyeo	쪅 jjyeog	쪆 jjyeogg	쪇 jjyeogs	쪈 jjyeon	쪉 jjyeonj	쪊 jjyeonh	쪋 jjyeod	쪌 jjyeol	쪍 jjyeolg	쪎 jjyeolm	쪐 jjyeolb	쪐 jjyeols	쪒 jjyeolt
ㅉ jj	ㅖ ye	쪠 jjye	쪡 jjyeg	쪢 jjyegg	쪣 jjyegs	쪤 jjyen	쪥 jjyenj	쪦 jjyenh	쪧 jjyed	쪨 jjyel	쪩 jjyelg	쪪 jjyelm	쪬 jjyelb	쪬 jjyels	쪮 jjyelt
ㅉ jj	ㅗ o	쪼 jjo	쪽 jjog	쪾 jjogg	쪿 jjogs	쫀 jjon	쫁 jjonj	쫂 jjonh	쫃 jjod	쫄 jjol	쫅 jjolg	쫆 jjolm	쫈 jjolb	쫈 jjols	쫊 jjolt
ㅉ jj	ㅘ wa	쫘 jjwa	쫙 jjwag	쫚 jjwagg	쫛 jjwags	쫜 jjwan	쫝 jjwanj	쫞 jjwanh	쫟 jjwad	쫠 jjwal	쫡 jjwalg	쫢 jjwalm	쫤 jjwalb	쫤 jjwals	쫦 jjwalt
ㅉ jj	ㅙ wae	쫴 jjwae	쫵 jjwaeg	쫶 jjwaegg	쫷 jjwaegs	쫸 jjwaen	쫹 jjwaenj	쫺 jjwaenh	쫻 jjwaed	쫼 jjwael	쫽 jjwaelg	쫾 jjwaelm	쬀 jjwaelb	쬀 jjwaels	쬂 jjwaelt
ㅉ jj	ㅚ oe	쬐 jjoe	쬑 jjoeg	쬒 jjoegg	쬓 jjoegs	쬔 jjoen	쬕 jjoenj	쬖 jjoenh	쬗 jjoed	쬘 jjoel	쬙 jjoelg	쬚 jjoelm	쬜 jjoelb	쬜 jjoels	쬞 jjoelt
ㅉ jj	ㅛ yo	쬐 jjyo	쬭 jjyog	쬮 jjyogg	쬯 jjyogs	쬰 jjyon	쬱 jjyonj	쬲 jjyonh	쬳 jjyod	쬴 jjyol	쬵 jjyolg	쬶 jjyolm	쬸 jjyolb	쬸 jjyols	쬺 jjyolt
ㅉ jj	ㅜ u	쭈 jju	쭉 jjug	쭊 jjugg	쭋 jjugs	쭌 jjun	쭍 jjunj	쭎 jjunh	쭏 jjud	쭐 jjul	쭑 jjulg	쭒 jjulm	쭔 jjulb	쭔 jjuls	쭖 jjult
ㅉ jj	ㅝ weo	쭤 jjweo	쭥 jjweog	쭦 jjweogg	쭧 jjweogs	쭨 jjweon	쭩 jjweonj	쭪 jjweonh	쭫 jjweod	쭬 jjweol	쭭 jjweolg	쭮 jjweolm	쭰 jjweolb	쭰 jjweols	쭲 jjweolt
ㅉ jj	ㅞ we	쮀 jjwe	쮁 jjweg	쮂 jjwegg	쮃 jjwegs	쮄 jjwen	쮅 jjwenj	쮆 jjwenh	쮇 jjwed	쮈 jjwel	쮉 jjwelg	쮊 jjwelm	쮌 jjwelb	쮌 jjwels	쮎 jjwelt
ㅉ jj	ㅟ wi	쮜 jjwi	쮝 jjwig	쮞 jjwigg	쮟 jjwigs	쮠 jjwin	쮡 jjwinj	쮢 jjwinh	쮣 jjwid	쮤 jjwil	쮥 jjwilg	쮦 jjwilm	쮨 jjwilb	쮨 jjwils	쮪 jjwilt
ㅉ jj	ㅠ yu	쮸 jjyu	쮹 jjyug	쮺 jjyugg	쮻 jjyugs	쮼 jjyun	쮽 jjyunj	쮾 jjyunh	쮿 jjyud	쯀 jjyul	쯁 jjyulg	쯂 jjyulm	쯄 jjyulb	쯄 jjyuls	쯆 jjyult
ㅉ jj	ㅡ eu	쯔 jjeu	쯕 jjeug	쯖 jjeugg	쯗 jjeugs	쯘 jjeun	쯙 jjeunj	쯚 jjeunh	쯛 jjeud	쯜 jjeul	쯝 jjeulg	쯞 jjeulm	쯠 jjeulb	쯠 jjeuls	쯢 jjeult
ㅉ jj	ㅢ yi	쯰 jjyi	쯱 jjyig	쯲 jjyigg	쯳 jjyigs	쯴 jjyin	쯵 jjyinj	쯶 jjyinh	쯷 jjyid	쯸 jjyil	쯹 jjyilg	쯺 jjyilm	쯼 jjyilb	쯼 jjyils	쯾 jjyilt
ㅉ jj	ㅣ i	찌 jji	찍 jjig	찎 jjigg	찏 jjigs	찐 jjin	찑 jjinj	찒 jjinh	찓 jjid	찔 jjil	찕 jjilg	찖 jjilm	찘 jjilb	찘 jjils	찚 jjilt

	ㄿ lp	ㅀ lh	ㅁ m	ㅂ b	ㅄ bs	ㅅ s	ㅆ ss	ㅇ ng	ㅈ j	ㅊ ch	ㅋ k	ㅌ t	ㅍ p	ㅎ h
ㅉ jj ㅏ a	짪 jjalp	짫 jjalh	짬 jjam	짭 jjab	짮 jjabs	짯 jjas	짰 jjass	짱 jjang	짲 jjaj	짳 jjach	짴 jjak	짵 jjat	짶 jjap	짷 jjah
ㅉ jj ㅐ ae	쨆 jjaelp	쨇 jjaelh	쨈 jjaem	쨉 jjaeb	쨊 jjaebs	쨋 jjaes	쨌 jjaess	쨍 jjaeng	쨎 jjaej	쨏 jjaech	쨐 jjaek	쨑 jjaet	쨒 jjaep	쨓 jjaeh
ㅉ jj ㅑ ya	쨢 jjyalp	쨣 jjyalh	쨤 jjyam	쨥 jjyab	쨦 jjyabs	쨧 jjyas	쨨 jjyass	쨩 jjyang	쨪 jjyaj	쨫 jjyach	쨬 jjyak	쨭 jjyat	쨮 jjyap	쨯 jjyah
ㅉ jj ㅒ yae	쨾 jjyaelp	쨿 jjyaelh	쩀 jjyaem	쩁 jjyaeb	쩂 jjyaebs	쩃 jjyaes	쩄 jjyaess	쩅 jjyaeng	쩆 jjyaej	쩇 jjyaech	쩈 jjyaek	쩉 jjyaet	쩊 jjyaep	쩋 jjyaeh
ㅉ jj ㅓ eo	쩚 jjeolp	쩛 jjeolh	쩜 jjeom	쩝 jjeob	쩞 jjeobs	쩟 jjeos	쩠 jjeoss	쩡 jjeong	쩢 jjeoj	쩣 jjeoch	쩤 jjeok	쩥 jjeot	쩦 jjeop	쩧 jjeoh
ㅉ jj ㅔ e	쩶 jjelp	쩷 jjelh	쩸 jjem	쩹 jjeb	쩺 jjebs	쩻 jjes	쩼 jjess	쩽 jjeng	쩾 jjej	쩿 jjech	쪀 jjek	쪁 jjet	쪂 jjep	쪃 jjeh
ㅉ jj ㅕ yeo	쪒 jjyeolp	쪓 jjyeolh	쪔 jjyeom	쪕 jjyeob	쪖 jjyeobs	쪗 jjyeos	쪘 jjyeoss	쪙 jjyeong	쪚 jjyeoj	쪛 jjyeoch	쪜 jjyeok	쪝 jjyeot	쪞 jjyeop	쪟 jjyeoh
ㅉ jj ㅖ ye	쪮 jjyelp	쪯 jjyelh	쪰 jjyem	쪱 jjyeb	쪲 jjyebs	쪳 jjyes	쪴 jjyess	쪵 jjyeng	쪶 jjyej	쪷 jjyech	쪸 jjyek	쪹 jjyet	쪺 jjyep	쪻 jjyeh
ㅉ jj ㅗ o	쫊 jjolp	쫋 jjolh	쫌 jjom	쫍 jjob	쫎 jjobs	쫏 jjos	쫐 jjoss	쫑 jjong	쫒 jjoj	쫓 jjoch	쫔 jjok	쫕 jjot	쫖 jjop	쫗 jjoh
ㅉ jj ㅘ wa	쫦 jjwalp	쫧 jjwalh	쫨 jjwam	쫩 jjwab	쫪 jjwabs	쫫 jjwas	쫬 jjwass	쫭 jjwang	쫮 jjwaj	쫯 jjwach	쫰 jjwak	쫱 jjwat	쫲 jjwap	쫳 jjwah
ㅉ jj ㅙ wae	쬂 jjwaelp	쬃 jjwaelh	쬄 jjwaem	쬅 jjwaeb	쬆 jjwaebs	쬇 jjwaes	쬈 jjwaess	쬉 jjwaeng	쬊 jjwaej	쬋 jjwaech	쬌 jjwaek	쬍 jjwaet	쬎 jjwaep	쬏 jjwaeh
ㅉ jj ㅚ oe	쬞 jjoelp	쬟 jjoelh	쬠 jjoem	쬡 jjoeb	쬢 jjoebs	쬣 jjoes	쬤 jjoess	쬥 jjoeng	쬦 jjoej	쬧 jjoech	쬨 jjoek	쬩 jjoet	쬪 jjoep	쬫 jjoeh
ㅉ jj ㅛ yo	쬺 jjyolp	쬻 jjyolh	쬼 jjyom	쬽 jjyob	쬾 jjyobs	쬿 jjyos	쭀 jjyoss	쭁 jjyong	쭂 jjyoj	쭃 jjyoch	쭄 jjyok	쭅 jjyot	쭆 jjyop	쭇 jjyoh
ㅉ jj ㅜ u	쭖 jjulp	쭗 jjulh	쭘 jjum	쭙 jjub	쭚 jjubs	쭛 jjus	쭜 jjuss	쭝 jjung	쭞 jjuj	쭟 jjuch	쭠 jjuk	쭡 jjut	쭢 jjup	쭣 jjuh
ㅉ jj ㅝ weo	쭲 jjweolp	쭳 jjweolh	쭴 jjweom	쭵 jjweob	쭶 jjweobs	쭷 jjweos	쭸 jjweoss	쭹 jjweong	쭺 jjweoj	쭻 jjweoch	쭼 jjweok	쭽 jjweot	쭾 jjweop	쭿 jjweoh
ㅉ jj ㅞ we	쮎 jjwelp	쮏 jjwelh	쮐 jjwem	쮑 jjweb	쮒 jjwebs	쮓 jjwes	쮔 jjwess	쮕 jjweng	쮖 jjwej	쮗 jjwech	쮘 jjwek	쮙 jjwet	쮚 jjwep	쮛 jjweh
ㅉ jj ㅟ wi	쮪 jjwilp	쮫 jjwilh	쮬 jjwim	쮭 jjwib	쮮 jjwibs	쮯 jjwis	쮰 jjwiss	쮱 jjwing	쮲 jjwij	쮳 jjwich	쮴 jjwik	쮵 jjwit	쮶 jjwip	쮷 jjwih
ㅉ jj ㅠ yu	쯆 jjyulp	쯇 jjyulh	쯈 jjyum	쯉 jjyub	쯊 jjyubs	쯋 jjyus	쯌 jjyuss	쯍 jjyung	쯎 jjyuj	쯏 jjyuch	쯐 jjyuk	쯑 jjyut	쯒 jjyup	쯓 jjyuh
ㅉ jj ㅡ eu	쯢 jjeulp	쯣 jjeulh	쯤 jjeum	쯥 jjeub	쯦 jjeubs	쯧 jjeus	쯨 jjeuss	쯩 jjeung	쯪 jjeuj	쯫 jjeuch	쯬 jjeuk	쯭 jjeut	쯮 jjeup	쯯 jjeuh
ㅉ jj ㅢ yi	쯾 jjyilp	쯿 jjyilh	찀 jjyim	찁 jjyib	찂 jjyibs	찃 jjyis	찄 jjyiss	찅 jjying	찆 jjyij	찇 jjyich	찈 jjyik	찉 jjyit	찊 jjyip	찋 jjyih
ㅉ jj ㅣ i	찚 jjilp	찛 jjilh	찜 jjim	찝 jjib	찞 jjibs	찟 jjis	찠 jjiss	찡 jjing	찢 jjij	찣 jjich	찤 jjik	찥 jjit	찦 jjip	찧 jjih

Table 1.19: HanGul Syllables Starting with ㅊ (ch)

			ㄱ g	ㄲ gg	ㄳ gs	ㄴ n	ㄵ nj	ㄶ nh	ㄷ d	ㄹ l	ㄺ lg	ㄻ lm	ㄼ lb	ㄽ ls	ㄾ lt
ㅊ	ㅏ	차	착	찪	찫	찬	찭	찮	찯	찰	찱	찲	찳	찴	찵
c	a	ca	cag	cagg	cags	can	canj	canh	cad	cal	calg	calm	calb	cals	calt
ㅊ	ㅐ	채	책	챆	챇	챈	챉	챊	챋	챌	챍	챎	챏	챐	챑
c	ae	cae	caeg	caegg	caegs	caen	caenj	caenh	caed	cael	caelg	caelm	caelb	caels	caelt
ㅊ	ㅑ	챠	챡	챢	챣	챤	챥	챦	챧	챨	챩	챪	챫	챬	챭
c	ya	cya	cyag	cyagg	cyags	cyan	cyanj	cyanh	cyad	cyal	cyalg	cyalm	cyalb	cyals	cyalt
ㅊ	ㅒ	챼	챽	챾	챿	첀	첁	첂	첃	첄	첅	첆	첇	첈	첉
c	yae	cyae	cyaeg	cyaegg	cyaegs	cyaen	cyaenj	cyaenh	cyaed	cyael	cyaelg	cyaelm	cyaelb	cyaels	cyaelt
ㅊ	ㅓ	처	척	첚	첛	천	첝	첞	첟	철	첡	첢	첣	첤	첥
c	eo	ceo	ceog	ceogg	ceogs	ceon	ceonj	ceonh	ceod	ceol	ceolg	ceolm	ceolb	ceols	ceolt
ㅊ	ㅔ	체	첵	첶	첷	첸	첹	첺	첻	첼	첽	첾	첿	쳀	쳁
c	e	ce	ceg	cegg	cegs	cen	cenj	cenh	ced	cel	celg	celm	celb	cels	celt
ㅊ	ㅕ	쳐	쳑	쳒	쳓	쳔	쳕	쳖	쳗	쳘	쳙	쳚	쳛	쳜	쳝
c	yeo	cyeo	cyeog	cyeogg	cyeogs	cyeon	cyeonj	cyeonh	cyeod	cyeol	cyeolg	cyeolm	cyeolb	cyeols	cyeolt
ㅊ	ㅖ	쳬	쳭	쳮	쳯	쳰	쳱	쳲	쳳	쳴	쳵	쳶	쳷	쳸	쳹
c	ye	cye	cyeg	cyegg	cyegs	cyen	cyenj	cyenh	cyed	cyel	cyelg	cyelm	cyelb	cyels	cyelt
ㅊ	ㅗ	초	촉	촊	촋	촌	촍	촎	촏	촐	촑	촒	촓	촔	촕
c	o	co	cog	cogg	cogs	con	conj	conh	cod	col	colg	colm	colb	cols	colt
ㅊ	ㅘ	촤	촥	촦	촧	촨	촩	촪	촫	촬	촭	촮	촯	촰	촱
c	wa	cwa	cwag	cwagg	cwags	cwan	cwanj	cwanh	cwad	cwal	cwalg	cwalm	cwalb	cwals	cwalt
ㅊ	ㅙ	쵀	쵁	쵂	쵃	쵄	쵅	쵆	쵇	쵈	쵉	쵊	쵋	쵌	쵍
c	wae	cwae	cwaeg	cwaegg	cwaegs	cwaen	cwaenj	cwaenh	cwaed	cwael	cwaelg	cwaelm	cwaelb	cwaels	cwaelt
ㅊ	ㅚ	최	쵝	쵞	쵟	쵠	쵡	쵢	쵣	쵤	쵥	쵦	쵧	쵨	쵩
c	oe	coe	coeg	coegg	coegs	coen	coenj	coenh	coed	coel	coelg	coelm	coelb	coels	coelt
ㅊ	ㅛ	쵸	쵹	쵺	쵻	쵼	쵽	쵾	쵿	춀	춁	춂	춃	춄	춅
c	yo	cyo	cyog	cyogg	cyogs	cyon	cyonj	cyonh	cyod	cyol	cyolg	cyolm	cyolb	cyols	cyolt
ㅊ	ㅜ	추	축	춖	춗	춘	춙	춚	춛	출	춝	춞	춟	춠	춡
c	u	cu	cug	cugg	cugs	cun	cunj	cunh	cud	cul	culg	culm	culb	culs	cult
ㅊ	ㅝ	춰	춱	춲	춳	춴	춵	춶	춷	춸	춹	춺	춻	춼	춽
c	weo	cweo	cweog	cweogg	cweogs	cweon	cweonj	cweonh	cweod	cweol	cweolg	cweolm	cweolb	cweols	cweolt
ㅊ	ㅞ	췌	췍	췎	췏	췐	췑	췒	췓	췔	췕	췖	췗	췘	췙
c	we	cwe	cweg	cwegg	cwegs	cwen	cwenj	cwenh	cwed	cwel	cwelg	cwelm	cwelb	cwels	cwelt
ㅊ	ㅟ	취	췩	췪	췫	췬	췭	췮	췯	췰	췱	췲	췳	췴	췵
c	wi	cwi	cwig	cwigg	cwigs	cwin	cwinj	cwinh	cwid	cwil	cwilg	cwilm	cwilb	cwils	cwilt
ㅊ	ㅠ	츄	츅	츆	츇	츈	츉	츊	츋	츌	츍	츎	츏	츐	츑
c	yu	cyu	cyug	cyugg	cyugs	cyun	cyunj	cyunh	cyud	cyul	cyulg	cyulm	cyulb	cyuls	cyult
ㅊ	ㅡ	츠	측	츢	츣	츤	츥	츦	츧	츨	츩	츪	츫	츬	츭
c	eu	ceu	ceug	ceugg	ceugs	ceun	ceunj	ceunh	ceud	ceul	ceulg	ceulm	ceulb	ceuls	ceult
ㅊ	ㅢ	츼	츽	츾	츿	칀	칁	칂	칃	칄	칅	칆	칇	칈	칉
c	yi	cyi	cyig	cyigg	cyigs	cyin	cyinj	cyinh	cyid	cyil	cyilg	cyilm	cyilb	cyils	cyilt
ㅊ	ㅣ	치	칙	칚	칛	친	칝	칞	칟	칠	칡	칢	칣	칤	칥
c	i	ci	cig	cigg	cigs	cin	cinj	cinh	cid	cil	cilg	cilm	cilb	cils	cilt

ㅊ c +	ㄼ lp	ㅀ lh	ㅁ m	ㅂ b	ㅄ bs	ㅅ s	ㅆ ss	ㅇ ng	ㅈ j	ㅊ ch	ㅋ k	ㅌ t	ㅍ p	ㅎ h
ㅏ a	찳 calp	찷 calh	참 cam	찹 cab	찺 cabs	찻 cas	찼 cass	창 cang	찾 caj	찿 cach	챀 cak	챁 cat	챂 cap	챃 cah
ㅐ ae	챏 caelp	챓 caelh	챔 caem	챕 caeb	챖 caebs	챗 caes	챘 caess	챙 caeng	챚 caej	챛 caech	챜 caek	챝 caet	챞 caep	챟 caeh
ㅑ ya	챫 cyalp	챯 cyalh	챰 cyam	챱 cyab	챲 cyabs	챳 cyas	챴 cyass	챵 cyang	챶 cyaj	챷 cyach	챸 cyak	챹 cyat	챺 cyap	챻 cyah
ㅒ yae	첇 cyaelp	첋 cyaelh	첌 cyaem	첍 cyaeb	첎 cyaebs	첏 cyaes	첐 cyaess	첑 cyaeng	첒 cyaej	첓 cyaech	첔 cyaek	첕 cyaet	첖 cyaep	첗 cyaeh
ㅓ eo	첣 ceolp	첧 ceolh	첨 ceom	첩 ceob	첪 ceobs	첫 ceos	첬 ceoss	청 ceong	첮 ceoj	첯 ceoch	첰 ceok	첱 ceot	첲 ceop	첳 ceoh
ㅔ e	첿 celp	쳃 celh	쳄 cem	쳅 ceb	쳆 cebs	쳇 ces	쳈 cess	쳉 ceng	쳊 cej	쳋 cech	쳌 cek	쳍 cet	쳎 cep	쳏 ceh
ㅕ yeo	쳛 cyeolp	쳟 cyeolh	쳠 cyeom	쳡 cyeob	쳢 cyeobs	쳣 cyeos	쳤 cyeoss	쳥 cyeong	쳦 cyeoj	쳧 cyeoch	쳨 cyeok	쳩 cyeot	쳪 cyeop	쳫 cyeoh
ㅖ ye	쳷 cyelp	쳻 cyelh	쳼 cyem	쳽 cyeb	쳾 cyebs	쳿 cyes	촀 cyess	촁 cyeng	촂 cyej	촃 cyech	촄 cyek	촅 cyet	촆 cyep	촇 cyeh
ㅗ o	촓 colp	촗 colh	촘 com	촙 cob	촚 cobs	촛 cos	촜 coss	총 cong	촞 coj	촟 coch	촠 cok	촡 cot	촢 cop	촣 coh
ㅘ wa	촯 cwalp	촳 cwalh	촴 cwam	촵 cwab	촶 cwabs	촷 cwas	촸 cwass	촹 cwang	촺 cwaj	촻 cwach	촼 cwak	촽 cwat	촾 cwap	촿 cwah
ㅙ wae	쵋 cwaelp	쵏 cwaelh	쵐 cwaem	쵑 cwaeb	쵒 cwaebs	쵓 cwaes	쵔 cwaess	쵕 cwaeng	쵖 cwaej	쵗 cwaech	쵘 cwaek	쵙 cwaet	쵚 cwaep	쵛 cwaeh
ㅚ oe	쵧 coelp	쵫 coelh	쵬 coem	쵭 coeb	쵮 coebs	쵯 coes	쵰 coess	쵱 coeng	쵲 coej	쵳 coech	쵴 coek	쵵 coet	쵶 coep	쵷 coeh
ㅛ yo	춃 cyolp	춇 cyolh	춈 cyom	춉 cyob	춊 cyobs	춋 cyos	춌 cyoss	춍 cyong	춎 cyoj	춏 cyoch	춐 cyok	춑 cyot	춒 cyop	춓 cyoh
ㅜ u	춟 culp	춣 culh	춤 cum	춥 cub	춦 cubs	춧 cus	춨 cuss	충 cung	춪 cuj	춫 cuch	춬 cuk	춭 cut	춮 cup	춯 cuh
ㅝ weo	춻 cweolp	춿 cweolh	췀 cweom	췁 cweob	췂 cweobs	췃 cweos	췄 cweoss	췅 cweong	췆 cweoj	췇 cweoch	췈 cweok	췉 cweot	췊 cweop	췋 cweoh
ㅞ we	췗 cwelp	췛 cwelh	췜 cwem	췝 cweb	췞 cwebs	췟 cwes	췠 cwess	췡 cweng	췢 cwej	췣 cwech	췤 cwek	췥 cwet	췦 cwep	췧 cweh
ㅟ wi	췳 cwilp	췷 cwilh	췸 cwim	췹 cwib	췺 cwibs	췻 cwis	췼 cwiss	췽 cwing	췾 cwij	췿 cwich	츀 cwik	츁 cwit	츂 cwip	츃 cwih
ㅠ yu	츏 cyulp	츓 cyulh	츔 cyum	츕 cyub	츖 cyubs	츗 cyus	츘 cyuss	츙 cyung	츚 cyuj	츛 cyuch	츜 cyuk	츝 cyut	츞 cyup	츟 cyuh
ㅡ eu	츫 ceulp	츯 ceulh	츰 ceum	츱 ceub	츲 ceubs	츳 ceus	츴 ceuss	층 ceung	츶 ceuj	츷 ceuch	츸 ceuk	츹 ceut	츺 ceup	츻 ceuh
ㅢ yi	칇 cyilp	칋 cyilh	칌 cyim	칍 cyib	칎 cyibs	칏 cyis	칐 cyiss	칑 cying	칒 cyij	칓 cyich	칔 cyik	칕 cyit	칖 cyip	칗 cyih
ㅣ i	칣 cilp	칧 cilh	침 cim	칩 cib	칪 cibs	칫 cis	칬 ciss	칭 cing	칮 cij	칯 cich	칰 cik	칱 cit	칲 cip	칳 cih

Table 1.20: HanGul Syllables Starting with ㅋ (k)

		ㄱ g	ㄲ gg	ㄳ gs	ㄴ n	ㄵ nj	ㄶ nh	ㄷ d	ㄹ l	ㄺ lg	ㄻ lm	ㄼ lb	ㄽ ls	ㄾ lt
ㅋ k	ㅏ a	카 ka	칵 kag	칶 kagg	칷 kags	칸 kan	칹 kanj	칺 kanh	칻 kad	칼 kal	칽 kalg	칾 kalm	칿 kalb	캀 kals	캁 kalt
ㅋ k	ㅐ ae	캐 kae	캑 kaeg	캒 kaegg	캓 kaegs	캔 kaen	캕 kaenj	캖 kaenh	캗 kaed	캘 kael	캙 kaelg	캚 kaelm	캛 kaelb	캜 kaels	캝 kaelt
ㅋ k	ㅑ ya	캬 kya	캭 kyag	캮 kyagg	캯 kyags	캰 kyan	캱 kyanj	캲 kyanh	캳 kyad	캴 kyal	캵 kyalg	캶 kyalm	캷 kyalb	캸 kyals	캹 kyalt
ㅋ k	ㅒ yae	캐 kyae	캑 kyaeg	캒 kyaegg	캓 kyaegs	캔 kyaen	캕 kyaenj	캖 kyaenh	캗 kyaed	캘 kyael	캙 kyaelg	캚 kyaelm	캛 kyaelb	캜 kyaels	캝 kyaelt
ㅋ k	ㅓ eo	커 keo	컥 keog	컦 keogg	컧 keogs	컨 keon	컩 keonj	컪 keonh	컫 keod	컬 keol	컭 keolg	컮 keolm	컯 keolb	컰 keols	컱 keolt
ㅋ k	ㅔ e	케 ke	켁 keg	켂 kegg	켃 kegs	켄 ken	켅 kenj	켆 kenh	켇 ked	켈 kel	켉 kelg	켊 kelm	켋 kelb	켌 kels	켍 kelt
ㅋ k	ㅕ yeo	켜 kyeo	켠 kyeog	켬 kyeogg	켰 kyeogs	켠 kyeon	켥 kyeonj	켵 kyeonh	켣 kyeod	켤 kyeol	켥 kyeolg	켬 kyeolm	켧 kyeolb	켨 kyeols	켩 kyeolt
ㅋ k	ㅖ ye	켸 kye	켹 kyeg	켺 kyegg	켻 kyegs	켼 kyen	켽 kyenj	켾 kyenh	켿 kyed	콀 kyel	콁 kyelg	콂 kyelm	콃 kyelb	콄 kyels	콅 kyelt
ㅋ k	ㅗ o	코 ko	콕 kog	콖 kogg	콗 kogs	콘 kon	콙 konj	콚 konh	콛 kod	콜 kol	콝 kolg	콞 kolm	콟 kolb	콠 kols	콡 kolt
ㅋ k	ㅘ wa	콰 kwa	콱 kwag	콲 kwagg	콳 kwags	콴 kwan	콵 kwanj	콶 kwanh	콷 kwad	콸 kwal	콹 kwalg	콺 kwalm	콻 kwalb	콼 kwals	콽 kwalt
ㅋ k	ㅙ wae	쾌 kwae	쾍 kwaeg	쾎 kwaegg	쾏 kwaegs	쾐 kwaen	쾑 kwaenj	쾒 kwaenh	쾓 kwaed	쾔 kwael	쾕 kwaelg	쾖 kwaelm	쾗 kwaelb	쾘 kwaels	쾙 kwaelt
ㅋ k	ㅚ oe	쾨 koe	쾩 koeg	쾪 koegg	쾫 koegs	쾬 koen	쾭 koenj	쾮 koenh	쾯 koed	쾰 koel	쾱 koelg	쾲 koelm	쾳 koelb	쾴 koels	쾵 koelt
ㅋ k	ㅛ yo	쿄 kyo	콕 kyog	쿆 kyogg	쿇 kyogs	쿈 kyon	쿉 kyonj	쿊 kyonh	쿋 kyod	쿌 kyol	쿍 kyolg	쿎 kyolm	쿏 kyolb	쿐 kyols	쿑 kyolt
ㅋ k	ㅜ u	쿠 ku	쿡 kug	쿢 kugg	쿣 kugs	쿤 kun	쿥 kunj	쿦 kunh	쿧 kud	쿨 kul	쿩 kulg	쿪 kulm	쿫 kulb	쿬 kuls	쿭 kult
ㅋ k	ㅝ weo	쿼 kweo	쿽 kweog	쿾 kweogg	쿿 kweogs	퀀 kweon	퀁 kweonj	퀂 kweonh	퀃 kweod	퀄 kweol	퀅 kweolg	퀆 kweolm	퀇 kweolb	퀈 kweols	퀉 kweolt
ㅋ k	ㅞ we	퀘 kwe	퀙 kweg	퀚 kwegg	퀛 kwegs	퀜 kwen	퀝 kwenj	퀞 kwenh	퀟 kwed	퀠 kwel	퀡 kwelg	퀢 kwelm	퀣 kwelb	퀤 kwels	퀥 kwelt
ㅋ k	ㅟ wi	퀴 kwi	퀵 kwig	퀶 kwigg	퀷 kwigs	퀸 kwin	퀹 kwinj	퀺 kwinh	퀻 kwid	퀼 kwil	퀽 kwilg	퀾 kwilm	퀿 kwilb	큀 kwils	큁 kwilt
ㅋ k	ㅠ yu	큐 kyu	큑 kyug	큒 kyugg	큓 kyugs	큔 kyun	큕 kyunj	큖 kyunh	큗 kyud	큘 kyul	큙 kyulg	큚 kyulm	큛 kyulb	큜 kyuls	큝 kyult
ㅋ k	ㅡ eu	크 keu	큭 keug	큮 keugg	큯 keugs	큰 keun	큱 keunj	큲 keunh	큳 keud	클 keul	큵 keulg	큶 keulm	큷 keulb	큸 keuls	큹 keult
ㅋ k	ㅢ yi	킈 kyi	킉 kyig	킊 kyigg	킋 kyigs	킌 kyin	킍 kyinj	킎 kyinh	킏 kyid	킐 kyil	킑 kyilg	킒 kyilm	킓 kyilb	킔 kyils	킕 kyilt
ㅋ k	ㅣ i	키 ki	킥 kig	킦 kigg	킧 kigs	킨 kin	킩 kinj	킪 kinh	킫 kid	킬 kil	킭 kilg	킮 kilm	킯 kilb	킰 kils	킱 kilt

		ㄿ lp	ㅀ lh	ㅁ m	ㅂ b	ㅄ bs	ㅅ s	ㅆ ss	ㅇ ng	ㅈ j	ㅊ ch	ㅋ k	ㅌ t	ㅍ p	ㅎ h
ㅋ k	ㅏ a	칼 kalp	캃 kalh	캄 kam	캅 kab	캆 kabs	캇 kas	캈 kass	캉 kang	캊 kaj	캋 kach	칵 kak	캍 kat	캎 kap	캏 kah
ㅋ k	ㅐ ae	캟 kaelp	캟 kaelh	캠 kaem	캡 kaeb	캢 kaebs	캣 kaes	캤 kaess	캥 kaeng	캦 kaej	캧 kaech	캑 kaek	캩 kaet	캪 kaep	캫 kaeh
ㅋ k	ㅑ ya	퍍 kyalp	퍓 kyalh	캄 kyam	캽 kyab	캾 kyabs	캿 kyas	컀 kyass	컁 kyang	컂 kyaj	컃 kyach	컄 kyak	컅 kyat	컆 kyap	컇 kyah
ㅋ k	ㅒ yae	컖 kyaelp	컗 kyaelh	컒 kyaem	컓 kyaeb	컔 kyaebs	컕 kyaes	컖 kyaess	컞 kyaeng	컞 kyaej	컟 kyaech	컔 kyaek	컡 kyaet	컢 kyaep	컣 kyaeh
ㅋ k	ㅓ eo	컲 keolp	컳 keolh	컴 keom	컵 keob	컶 keobs	컷 keos	컸 keoss	컹 keong	컺 keoj	컻 keoch	컥 keok	컽 keot	컾 keop	컿 keoh
ㅋ k	ㅔ e	켎 kelp	켏 kelh	켐 kem	켑 keb	켒 kebs	켓 kes	켔 kess	켕 keng	켖 kej	켗 kech	켁 kek	켙 ket	켚 kep	켛 keh
ㅋ k	ㅕ yeo	켪 kyeolp	켫 kyeolh	켬 kyeom	켭 kyeob	켮 kyeobs	켯 kyeos	켰 kyeoss	켱 kyeong	켲 kyeoj	켳 kyeoch	켝 kyeok	켵 kyeot	켶 kyeop	켷 kyeoh
ㅋ k	ㅖ ye	켦 kyelp	켧 kyelh	켬 kyem	켭 kyeb	켮 kyebs	켯 kyes	켰 kyess	켱 kyeng	켲 kyej	켳 kyech	켝 kyek	켵 kyet	켶 kyep	켷 kyeh
ㅋ k	ㅗ o	콟 kolp	콠 kolh	콤 kom	콥 kob	콦 kobs	콧 kos	콨 koss	콩 kong	콪 koj	콫 koch	콕 kok	콭 kot	콮 kop	콯 koh
ㅋ k	ㅘ wa	퐓 kwalp	퐓 kwalh	쾀 kwam	쾁 kwab	쾂 kwabs	쾃 kwas	쾄 kwass	쾅 kwang	쾆 kwaj	쾇 kwach	쾈 kwak	쾉 kwat	쾊 kwap	쾋 kwah
ㅋ k	ㅙ wae	쾖 kwaelp	쾗 kwaelh	쾜 kwaem	쾝 kwaeb	쾞 kwaebs	쾟 kwaes	쾠 kwaess	쾡 kwaeng	쾢 kwaej	쾣 kwaech	쾤 kwaek	쾥 kwaet	쾦 kwaep	쾧 kwaeh
ㅋ k	ㅚ oe	쾲 koelp	쾳 koelh	쾸 koem	쾹 koeb	쾺 koebs	쾻 koes	쾼 koess	쾽 koeng	쾾 koej	쾿 koech	쿀 koek	쿁 koet	쿂 koep	쿃 koeh
ㅋ k	ㅛ yo	쿎 kyolp	쿏 kyolh	쿐 kyom	쿑 kyob	쿒 kyobs	쿓 kyos	쿔 kyoss	쿕 kyong	쿖 kyoj	쿗 kyoch	쿀 kyok	쿙 kyot	쿚 kyop	쿛 kyoh
ㅋ k	ㅜ u	쿪 kulp	쿫 kulh	쿰 kum	쿱 kub	쿲 kubs	쿳 kus	쿴 kuss	쿵 kung	쿶 kuj	쿷 kuch	쿡 kuk	쿹 kut	쿺 kup	쿻 kuh
ㅋ k	ㅝ weo	퀆 kweolp	퀇 kweolh	퀌 kweom	퀍 kweob	퀎 kweobs	퀏 kweos	퀐 kweoss	퀑 kweong	퀒 kweoj	퀓 kweoch	퀔 kweok	퀕 kweot	퀖 kweop	퀗 kweoh
ㅋ k	ㅞ we	퀞 kwelp	퀟 kwelh	퀘 kwem	퀙 kweb	퀚 kwebs	퀛 kwes	퀜 kwess	퀝 kweng	퀞 kwej	퀟 kwech	퀔 kwek	퀡 kwet	퀢 kwep	퀣 kweh
ㅋ k	ㅟ wi	퀲 kwilp	퀳 kwilh	퀸 kwim	퀹 kwib	퀺 kwibs	퀻 kwis	퀼 kwiss	퀽 kwing	퀾 kwij	퀿 kwich	퀵 kwik	큁 kwit	큂 kwip	큃 kwih
ㅋ k	ㅠ yu	큎 kyulp	큏 kyulh	큠 kyum	큡 kyub	큢 kyubs	큣 kyus	큤 kyuss	큥 kyung	큦 kyuj	큧 kyuch	큑 kyuk	큩 kyut	큪 kyup	큫 kyuh
ㅋ k	ㅡ eu	큲 keulp	큳 keulh	큼 keum	큽 keub	큾 keubs	큿 keus	킀 keuss	킁 keung	킂 keuj	킃 keuch	큭 keuk	킅 keut	킆 keup	킇 keuh
ㅋ k	ㅢ yi	킒 kyilp	킓 kyilh	킘 kyim	킙 kyib	킚 kyibs	킛 kyis	킜 kyiss	킝 kying	킞 kyij	킟 kyich	킙 kyik	킡 kyit	킢 kyip	킣 kyih
ㅋ k	ㅣ i	킲 kilp	킳 kilh	킴 kim	킵 kib	킶 kibs	킷 kis	킸 kiss	킹 king	킺 kij	킻 kich	킥 kik	킽 kit	킾 kip	킿 kih

Table 1.21: HanGul Syllables Starting with ㅌ (t)

ㅌ t		ㄱ g	ㄲ gg	ㄳ gs	ㄴ n	ㄵ nj	ㄶ nh	ㄷ d	ㄹ l	ㄺ lg	ㄻ lm	ㄼ lb	ㄽ ls	ㄾ lt
ㅌ t	ㅏ a	타 ta	탁 tag	탂 tagg	탃 tags	탄 tan	탅 tanj	탆 tanh	탇 tad	탈 tal	탉 talg	탊 talm	탋 talb	탌 tals	탍 talt
ㅌ t	ㅐ ae	태 tae	택 taeg	탞 taegg	탯 taegs	탠 taen	탡 taenj	탢 taenh	탣 taed	탤 tael	탥 taelg	탦 taelm	탧 taelb	탨 taels	탩 taelt
ㅌ t	ㅑ ya	탸 tya	탹 tyag	탺 tyagg	탻 tyags	탼 tyan	탽 tyanj	탾 tyanh	탿 tyad	턀 tyal	턁 tyalg	턂 tyalm	턃 tyalb	턄 tyals	턅 tyalt
ㅌ t	ㅒ yae	턔 tyae	턕 tyaeg	턖 tyaegg	턗 tyaegs	턘 tyaen	턙 tyaenj	턚 tyaenh	턛 tyaed	턜 tyael	턝 tyaelg	턞 tyaelm	턟 tyaelb	턠 tyaels	턡 tyaelt
ㅌ t	ㅓ eo	터 teo	턱 teog	턲 teogg	턳 teogs	턴 teon	턵 teonj	턶 teonh	턷 teod	털 teol	턹 teolg	턺 teolm	턻 teolb	턼 teols	턽 teolt
ㅌ t	ㅔ e	테 te	텍 teg	텎 tegg	텏 tegs	텐 ten	텑 tenj	텒 tenh	텓 ted	텔 tel	텕 telg	텖 telm	텗 telb	텘 tels	텙 telt
ㅌ t	ㅕ yeo	텨 tyeo	텩 tyeog	텪 tyeogg	텫 tyeogs	텬 tyeon	텭 tyeonj	텮 tyeonh	텯 tyeod	텰 tyeol	텱 tyeolg	텲 tyeolm	텳 tyeolb	텴 tyeols	텵 tyeolt
ㅌ t	ㅖ ye	톄 tye	톅 tyeg	톆 tyegg	톇 tyegs	톈 tyen	톉 tyenj	톊 tyenh	톋 tyed	톌 tyel	톍 tyelg	톎 tyelm	톏 tyelb	톐 tyels	톑 tyelt
ㅌ t	ㅗ o	토 to	톡 tog	톢 togg	톣 togs	톤 ton	톥 tonj	톦 tonh	톧 tod	톨 tol	톩 tolg	톪 tolm	톫 tolb	톬 tols	톭 tolt
ㅌ t	ㅘ wa	톼 twa	톽 twag	톾 twagg	톿 twags	퇀 twan	퇁 twanj	퇂 twanh	퇃 twad	퇄 twal	퇅 twalg	퇆 twalm	퇇 twalb	퇈 twals	퇉 twalt
ㅌ t	ㅙ wae	퇘 twae	퇙 twaeg	퇚 twaegg	퇛 twaegs	퇜 twaen	퇝 twaenj	퇞 twaenh	퇟 twaed	퇠 twael	퇡 twaelg	퇢 twaelm	퇣 twaelb	퇤 twaels	퇥 twaelt
ㅌ t	ㅚ oe	퇴 toe	퇵 toeg	퇶 toegg	퇷 toegs	퇸 toen	퇹 toenj	퇺 toenh	퇻 toed	퇼 toel	퇽 toelg	퇾 toelm	퇿 toelb	툀 toels	툁 toelt
ㅌ t	ㅛ yo	툐 tyo	툑 tyog	툒 tyogg	툓 tyogs	툔 tyon	툕 tyonj	툖 tyonh	툗 tyod	툘 tyol	툙 tyolg	툚 tyolm	툛 tyolb	툜 tyols	툝 tyolt
ㅌ t	ㅜ u	투 tu	툭 tug	툮 tugg	툯 tugs	툰 tun	툱 tunj	툲 tunh	툳 tud	툴 tul	툵 tulg	툶 tulm	툷 tulb	툸 tuls	툹 tult
ㅌ t	ㅝ weo	퉈 tweo	퉉 tweog	퉊 tweogg	퉋 tweogs	퉌 tweon	퉍 tweonj	퉎 tweonh	퉏 tweod	퉐 tweol	퉑 tweolg	퉒 tweolm	퉓 tweolb	퉔 tweols	퉕 tweolt
ㅌ t	ㅞ we	퉤 twe	퉥 tweg	퉦 twegg	퉧 twegs	퉨 twen	퉩 twenj	퉪 twenh	퉫 twed	퉬 twel	퉭 twelg	퉮 twelm	퉯 twelb	퉰 twels	퉱 twelt
ㅌ t	ㅟ wi	튀 twi	튁 twig	튂 twigg	튃 twigs	튄 twin	튅 twinj	튆 twinh	튇 twid	튈 twil	튉 twilg	튊 twilm	튋 twilb	튌 twils	튍 twilt
ㅌ t	ㅠ yu	튜 tyu	튝 tyug	튞 tyugg	튟 tyugs	튠 tyun	튡 tyunj	튢 tyunh	튣 tyud	튤 tyul	튥 tyulg	튦 tyulm	튧 tyulb	튨 tyuls	튩 tyult
ㅌ t	ㅡ eu	트 teu	특 teug	튺 teugg	튻 teugs	튼 teun	튽 teunj	튾 teunh	튿 teud	틀 teul	틁 teulg	틂 teulm	틃 teulb	틄 teuls	틅 teult
ㅌ t	ㅢ yi	틔 tyi	틕 tyig	틖 tyigg	틗 tyigs	틘 tyin	틙 tyinj	틚 tyinh	틛 tyid	틜 tyil	틝 tyilg	틞 tyilm	틟 tyilb	틠 tyils	틡 tyilt
ㅌ t	ㅣ i	티 ti	틱 tig	틲 tigg	틳 tigs	틴 tin	틵 tinj	틶 tinh	틷 tid	틸 til	틹 tilg	틺 tilm	틻 tilb	틼 tils	틽 tilt

		ㄿ lp	ㅀ lh	ㅁ m	ㅂ b	ㅄ bs	ㅅ s	ㅆ ss	ㅇ ng	ㅈ j	ㅊ ch	ㅋ k	ㅌ t	ㅍ p	ㅎ h
ㅌ t	ㅏ a	탋 talp	탏 talh	탐 tam	탑 tab	탒 tabs	탓 tas	탔 tass	탕 tang	탖 taj	탗 tach	탘 tak	탙 tat	탚 tap	탛 tah
ㅌ t	ㅐ ae	탷 taelp	탷 taelh	탬 taem	탭 taeb	탰 taebs	탯 taes	탰 taess	탱 taeng	탲 taej	탳 taech	택 taek	탵 taet	탶 taep	탷 taeh
ㅌ t	ㅑ ya	턅 tyalp	턅 tyalh	탐 tyam	탑 tyab	턊 tyabs	턋 tyas	턌 tyass	턍 tyang	턎 tyaj	턏 tyach	턐 tyak	턑 tyat	턒 tyap	턓 tyah
ㅌ t	ㅒ yae	턟 tyaelp	턟 tyaelh	턈 tyaem	턉 tyaeb	턐 tyaebs	턓 tyaes	턌 tyaess	턍 tyaeng	턎 tyaej	턏 tyaech	턐 tyaek	턑 tyaet	턒 tyaep	턓 tyaeh
ㅌ t	ㅓ eo	텳 teolp	텳 teolh	텀 teom	텁 teob	텂 teobs	텃 teos	텄 teoss	텅 teong	텆 teoj	텇 teoch	텈 teok	텉 teot	텊 teop	텋 teoh
ㅌ t	ㅔ e	텔 telp	텗 telh	템 tem	텝 teb	텞 tebs	텟 tes	텠 tess	텡 teng	텢 tej	텣 tech	텍 tek	텥 tet	텦 tep	텧 teh
ㅌ t	ㅕ yeo	텵 tyeolp	텵 tyeolh	텸 tyeom	텹 tyeob	텺 tyeobs	텻 tyeos	텼 tyeoss	텽 tyeong	텾 tyeoj	텿 tyeoch	톀 tyeok	톁 tyeot	톂 tyeop	톃 tyeoh
ㅌ t	ㅖ ye	톏 tyelp	톏 tyelh	톔 tyem	톕 tyeb	톖 tyebs	톗 tyes	톘 tyess	톙 tyeng	톚 tyej	톛 tyech	톅 tyek	톝 tyet	톞 tyep	톟 tyeh
ㅌ t	ㅗ o	톯 tolp	톯 tolh	톰 tom	톱 tob	톲 tobs	톳 tos	톴 toss	통 tong	톶 toj	톷 toch	톡 tok	톹 tot	톺 top	톻 toh
ㅌ t	ㅘ wa	퇇 twalp	퇇 twalh	퇌 twam	퇍 twab	퇎 twabs	퇏 twas	퇐 twass	퇑 twang	퇒 twaj	퇓 twach	퇔 twak	퇕 twat	퇖 twap	퇗 twah
ㅌ t	ㅙ wae	퇣 twaelp	퇣 twaelh	퇨 twaem	퇩 twaeb	퇪 twaebs	퇫 twaes	퇬 twaess	퇭 twaeng	퇮 twaej	퇯 twaech	퇔 twaek	퇱 twaet	퇲 twaep	퇳 twaeh
ㅌ t	ㅚ oe	툏 toelp	툏 toelh	툄 toem	툅 toeb	툆 toebs	툇 toes	툈 toess	툉 toeng	툊 toej	툋 toech	툌 toek	툍 toet	툎 toep	툏 toeh
ㅌ t	ㅛ yo	툫 tyolp	툫 tyolh	툠 tyom	툡 tyob	툢 tyobs	툣 tyos	툤 tyoss	툥 tyong	툦 tyoj	툧 tyoch	툭 tyok	툩 tyot	툪 tyop	툫 tyoh
ㅌ t	ㅜ u	퉇 tulp	퉇 tulh	툼 tum	툽 tub	툾 tubs	툿 tus	퉀 tuss	퉁 tung	퉂 tuj	퉃 tuch	툭 tuk	퉅 tut	퉆 tup	퉇 tuh
ㅌ t	ㅝ weo	퉣 tweolp	퉣 tweolh	퉘 tweom	퉙 tweob	퉚 tweobs	퉛 tweos	퉜 tweoss	퉝 tweong	퉞 tweoj	퉟 tweoch	퉠 tweok	퉡 tweot	퉢 tweop	퉣 tweoh
ㅌ t	ㅞ we	퉯 twelp	퉯 twelh	퉴 twem	퉵 tweb	퉶 twebs	퉷 twes	퉸 twess	퉹 tweng	퉺 twej	퉻 twech	퉼 twek	퉽 twet	퉾 twep	퉿 tweh
ㅌ t	ㅟ wi	튋 twilp	튋 twilh	튐 twim	튑 twib	튒 twibs	튓 twis	튔 twiss	튕 twing	튖 twij	튗 twich	튀 twik	튙 twit	튚 twip	튛 twih
ㅌ t	ㅠ yu	튧 tyulp	튧 tyulh	튬 tyum	튭 tyub	튮 tyubs	튯 tyus	튰 tyuss	튱 tyung	튲 tyuj	튳 tyuch	튝 tyuk	튵 tyut	튶 tyup	튷 tyuh
ㅌ t	ㅡ eu	틃 teulp	틃 teulh	틈 teum	틉 teub	틊 teubs	틋 teus	틌 teuss	틍 teung	틎 teuj	틏 teuch	특 teuk	틑 teut	틒 teup	틓 teuh
ㅌ t	ㅢ yi	틟 tyilp	틟 tyilh	틤 tyim	틥 tyib	틦 tyibs	틧 tyis	틨 tyiss	틩 tying	틪 tyij	틫 tyich	틬 tyik	틭 tyit	틮 tyip	틯 tyih
ㅌ t	ㅣ i	틻 tilp	틻 tilh	팀 tim	팁 tib	팂 tibs	팃 tis	팄 tiss	팅 ting	팆 tij	팇 tich	틱 tik	팉 tit	팊 tip	팋 tih

Table 1.22: HanGul Syllables Starting with ㅍ (p)

		ㄱ	ㄲ	ㄳ	ㄴ	ㄵ	ㄶ	ㄷ	ㄹ	ㄺ	ㄻ	ㄼ	ㄽ	ㄾ
		g	gg	gs	n	nj	nh	d	l	lg	lm	lb	ls	lt
ㅍ p	ㅏ a	파 pa	팍 pag	팎 pagg	팏 pags	판 pan	팑 panj	팒 panh	팓 pad	팔 pal	팕 palg	팖 palm	팗 palb	팘 pals	팙 palt
ㅍ p	ㅐ ae	패 pae	팩 paeg	팪 paegg	팫 paegs	팬 paen	팭 paenj	팮 paenh	팯 paed	팰 pael	팱 paelg	팲 paelm	팳 paelb	팴 paels	팵 paelt
ㅍ p	ㅑ ya	퍄 pya	퍅 pyag	퍆 pyagg	퍇 pyags	퍈 pyan	퍉 pyanj	퍊 pyanh	퍋 pyad	퍌 pyal	퍍 pyalg	퍎 pyalm	퍏 pyalb	퍐 pyals	퍑 pyalt
ㅍ p	ㅒ yae	퍠 pyae	퍡 pyaeg	퍢 pyaegg	퍣 pyaegs	퍤 pyaen	퍥 pyaenj	퍦 pyaenh	퍧 pyaed	퍨 pyael	퍩 pyaelg	퍪 pyaelm	퍫 pyaelb	퍬 pyaels	퍭 pyaelt
ㅍ p	ㅓ eo	퍼 peo	퍽 peog	퍾 peogg	퍿 peogs	펀 peon	펁 peonj	펂 peonh	펃 peod	펄 peol	펅 peolg	펆 peolm	펇 peolb	펈 peols	펉 peolt
ㅍ p	ㅔ e	페 pe	펙 peg	펚 pegg	펛 pegs	펜 pen	펝 penj	펞 penh	펟 ped	펠 pel	펡 pelg	펢 pelm	펣 pelb	펤 pels	펥 pelt
ㅍ p	ㅕ yeo	펴 pyeo	펵 pyeog	펶 pyeogg	펷 pyeogs	편 pyeon	펹 pyeonj	펺 pyeonh	펻 pyeod	펼 pyeol	펽 pyeolg	펾 pyeolm	펿 pyeolb	폀 pyeols	폁 pyeolt
ㅍ p	ㅖ ye	폐 pye	폑 pyeg	폒 pyegg	폓 pyegs	폔 pyen	폕 pyenj	폖 pyenh	폗 pyed	폘 pyel	폙 pyelg	폚 pyelm	폛 pyelb	폜 pyels	폝 pyelt
ㅍ p	ㅗ o	포 po	폭 pog	폮 pogg	폯 pogs	폰 pon	폱 ponj	폲 ponh	폳 pod	폴 pol	폵 polg	폶 polm	폷 polb	폸 pols	폹 polt
ㅍ p	ㅘ wa	퐈 pwa	퐉 pwag	퐊 pwagg	퐋 pwags	퐌 pwan	퐍 pwanj	퐎 pwanh	퐏 pwad	퐐 pwal	퐑 pwalg	퐒 pwalm	퐓 pwalb	퐔 pwals	퐕 pwalt
ㅍ p	ㅙ wae	퐤 pwae	퐥 pwaeg	퐦 pwaegg	퐧 pwaegs	퐨 pwaen	퐩 pwaenj	퐪 pwaenh	퐫 pwaed	퐬 pwael	퐭 pwaelg	퐮 pwaelm	퐯 pwaelb	퐰 pwaels	퐱 pwaelt
ㅍ p	ㅚ oe	푀 poe	푁 poeg	푂 poegg	푃 poegs	푄 poen	푅 poenj	푆 poenh	푇 poed	푈 poel	푉 poelg	푊 poelm	푋 poelb	푌 poels	푍 poelt
ㅍ p	ㅛ yo	표 pyo	푝 pyog	푞 pyogg	푟 pyogs	푠 pyon	푡 pyonj	푢 pyonh	푣 pyod	푤 pyol	푥 pyolg	푦 pyolm	푧 pyolb	푨 pyols	푩 pyolt
ㅍ p	ㅜ u	푸 pu	푹 pug	푺 pugg	푻 pugs	푼 pun	푽 punj	푾 punh	푿 pud	풀 pul	풁 pulg	풂 pulm	풃 pulb	풄 puls	풅 pult
ㅍ p	ㅝ weo	풔 pweo	풕 pweog	풖 pweogg	풗 pweogs	풘 pweon	풙 pweonj	풚 pweonh	풛 pweod	풜 pweol	풝 pweolg	풞 pweolm	풟 pweolb	풠 pweols	풡 pweolt
ㅍ p	ㅞ we	풰 pwe	풱 pweg	풲 pwegg	풳 pwegs	풴 pwen	풵 pwenj	풶 pwenh	풷 pwed	풸 pwel	풹 pwelg	풺 pwelm	풻 pwelb	풼 pwels	풽 pwelt
ㅍ p	ㅟ wi	퓌 pwi	퓍 pwig	퓎 pwigg	퓏 pwigs	퓐 pwin	퓑 pwinj	퓒 pwinh	퓓 pwid	퓔 pwil	퓕 pwilg	퓖 pwilm	퓗 pwilb	퓘 pwils	퓙 pwilt
ㅍ p	ㅠ yu	퓨 pyu	퓩 pyug	퓪 pyugg	퓫 pyugs	퓬 pyun	퓭 pyunj	퓮 pyunh	퓯 pyud	퓰 pyul	퓱 pyulg	퓲 pyulm	퓳 pyulb	퓴 pyuls	퓵 pyult
ㅍ p	ㅡ eu	프 peu	픅 peug	픆 peugg	픇 peugs	픈 peun	픉 peunj	픊 peunh	픋 peud	플 peul	픍 peulg	픎 peulm	픏 peulb	픐 peuls	픑 peult
ㅍ p	ㅢ yi	픠 pyi	픡 pyig	픢 pyigg	픣 pyigs	픤 pyin	픥 pyinj	픦 pyinh	픧 pyid	픨 pyil	픩 pyilg	픪 pyilm	픫 pyilb	픬 pyils	픭 pyilt
ㅍ p	ㅣ i	피 pi	픽 pig	픾 pigg	픿 pigs	핀 pin	핁 pinj	핂 pinh	핃 pid	필 pil	핅 pilg	핆 pilm	핇 pilb	핈 pils	핉 pilt

		ㄿ lp	ㅀ lh	ㅁ m	ㅂ b	ㅄ bs	ㅅ s	ㅆ ss	ㅇ ng	ㅈ j	ㅊ ch	ㅋ k	ㅌ t	ㅍ p	ㅎ h
ㅍ p	ㅏ a	퐓 palp	퐗 palh	팜 pam	팝 pab	퐶 pabs	팟 pas	팠 pass	팡 pang	팢 paj	팣 pach	팤 pak	팥 pat	팦 pap	팡 pah
ㅍ p	ㅐ ae	퟊ paelp	ퟋ ퟃ ퟇ paelh	팸 paem	팹 paeb	ퟃ paebs	팻 paes	팼 paess	팽 paeng	팾 paej	팿 paech	팩 paek	퍁 paet	퍂 paep	팽 paeh
ㅍ p	ㅑ ya	퍏 pyalp	퍓 pyalh	퍔 pyam	퍕 pyab	퍖 pyabs	퍗 pyas	퍘 pyass	퍙 pyang	퍚 pyaj	퍛 pyach	퍜 pyak	퍝 pyat	퍞 pyap	퍙 pyah
ㅍ p	ㅒ yae	퍫 pyaelp	퍯 pyaelh	퍰 pyaem	퍱 pyaeb	퍲 pyaebs	퍳 pyaes	퍴 pyaess	퍵 pyaeng	퍶 pyaej	퍷 pyaech	퍸 pyaek	퍹 pyaet	퍺 pyaep	퍵 pyaeh
ㅍ p	ㅓ eo	펇 peolp	펋 peolh	펌 peom	펍 peob	펎 peobs	펏 peos	펐 peoss	펑 peong	펒 peoj	펓 peoch	펔 peok	펕 peot	펖 peop	펑 peoh
ㅍ p	ㅔ e	펣 pelp	펧 pelh	펨 pem	펩 peb	펪 pebs	펫 pes	펫 pess	펭 peng	펮 pej	펯 pech	펰 pek	펱 pet	펲 pep	펭 peh
ㅍ p	ㅕ yeo	폏 pyeolp	폓 pyeolh	폄 pyeom	폅 pyeob	폆 pyeobs	폇 pyeos	폈 pyeoss	평 pyeong	폊 pyeoj	폋 pyeoch	폌 pyeok	폍 pyeot	폎 pyeop	평 pyeoh
ㅍ p	ㅖ ye	폫 pyelp	폯 pyelh	폠 pyem	폡 pyeb	폢 pyebs	폣 pyes	폤 pyess	폥 pyeng	폦 pyej	폧 pyech	폨 pyek	폩 pyet	폪 pyep	폥 pyeh
ㅍ p	ㅗ o	퐓 polp	퐗 polh	폼 pom	폽 pob	폾 pobs	폿 pos	퐀 poss	퐁 pong	퐂 poj	퐃 poch	퐄 pok	퐅 pot	퐆 pop	퐁 poh
ㅍ p	ㅘ wa	퐯 pwalp	퐳 pwalh	퐴 pwam	퐵 pwab	퐶 pwabs	퐷 pwas	퐸 pwass	퐹 pwang	퐺 pwaj	퐻 pwach	퐼 pwak	퐽 pwat	퐾 pwap	퐹 pwah
ㅍ p	ㅙ wae	푋 pwaelp	푏 pwaelh	푐 pwaem	푑 pwaeb	푒 pwaebs	푓 pwaes	푔 pwaess	푕 pwaeng	푖 pwaej	푗 pwaech	푘 pwaek	푙 pwaet	푚 pwaep	푕 pwaeh
ㅍ p	ㅚ oe	푧 poelp	푫 poelh	푬 poem	푭 poeb	푮 poebs	푯 poes	푰 poess	푱 poeng	푲 poej	푳 poech	푴 poek	푵 poet	푶 poep	푱 poeh
ㅍ p	ㅛ yo	푯 pyolp	푯 pyolh	푬 pyom	푭 pyob	푮 pyobs	푯 pyos	푰 pyoss	푱 pyong	푲 pyoj	푳 pyoch	푴 pyok	푵 pyot	푶 pyop	푱 pyoh
ㅍ p	ㅜ u	풻 pulp	풿 pulh	품 pum	풉 pub	풊 pubs	풋 pus	풌 puss	풍 pung	풎 puj	풏 puch	풐 puk	풑 put	풒 pup	풍 puh
ㅍ p	ㅝ weo	풟 pweolp	풣 pweolh	풤 pweom	풥 pweob	풦 pweobs	풧 pweos	풨 pweoss	풩 pweong	풪 pweoj	풫 pweoch	풬 pweok	풭 pweot	풮 pweop	풩 pweoh
ㅍ p	ㅞ we	풻 pwelp	풿 pwelh	풻 pwem	풽 pweb	풾 pwebs	풿 pwes	퓀 pwess	퓁 pweng	퓂 pwej	퓃 pwech	퓄 pwek	퓅 pwet	퓆 pwep	퓁 pweh
ㅍ p	ㅟ wi	퓇 pwilp	퓋 pwilh	퓌 pwim	퓍 pwib	퓎 pwibs	퓏 pwis	퓐 pwiss	퓑 pwing	퓒 pwij	퓓 pwich	퓔 pwik	퓕 pwit	퓖 pwip	퓑 pwih
ㅍ p	ㅠ yu	퓣 pyulp	퓧 pyulh	퓸 pyum	퓹 pyub	퓺 pyubs	퓻 pyus	퓼 pyuss	퓽 pyung	퓾 pyuj	퓿 pyuch	픀 pyuk	픁 pyut	픂 pyup	퓽 pyuh
ㅍ p	ㅡ eu	픏 peulp	픓 peulh	픔 peum	픕 peub	픖 peubs	픗 peus	픘 peuss	픙 peung	픚 peuj	픛 peuch	픜 peuk	픝 peut	픞 peup	픙 peuh
ㅍ p	ㅢ yi	픫 pyilp	픯 pyilh	픰 pyim	픱 pyib	픲 pyibs	픳 pyis	픴 pyiss	픵 pying	픶 pyij	픷 pyich	픸 pyik	픹 pyit	픺 pyip	픵 pyih
ㅍ p	ㅣ i	핇 pilp	핋 pilh	핌 pim	핍 pib	핎 pibs	핏 pis	핐 piss	핑 ping	핒 pij	핓 pich	핔 pik	핕 pit	핖 pip	핑 pih

Table 1.23: HanGul Syllables Starting with ㅎ (h)

ㅎ h		ㄱ g	ㄲ gg	ㄳ gs	ㄴ n	ㄵ nj	ㄶ nh	ㄷ d	ㄹ l	ㄺ lg	ㄻ lm	ㄼ lb	ㄽ ls	ㄾ lt
ㅎ h	ㅏ a	하 ha	학 hag	핫 hagg	핫 hags	한 han	핝 hanj	핞 hanh	핟 had	할 hal	핡 halg	핢 halm	핣 halb	핤 hals	핥 halt
ㅎ h	ㅐ ae	해 hae	핵 haeg	핶 haegg	핷 haegs	핸 haen	핹 haenj	핺 haenh	핻 haed	핼 hael	핽 haelg	핾 haelm	핿 haelb	햀 haels	햁 haelt
ㅎ h	ㅑ ya	햐 hya	햑 hyag	햒 hyagg	햓 hyags	햔 hyan	햕 hyanj	햖 hyanh	햗 hyad	햘 hyal	햙 hyalg	햚 hyalm	햛 hyalb	햜 hyals	햝 hyalt
ㅎ h	ㅒ yae	해 hyae	핵 hyaeg	햞 hyaegg	햟 hyaegs	햠 hyaen	햡 hyaenj	햢 hyaenh	햣 hyaed	햤 hyael	향 hyaelg	햦 hyaelm	햧 hyaelb	햨 hyaels	햩 hyaelt
ㅎ h	ㅓ eo	허 heo	헉 heog	헊 heogg	헋 heogs	헌 heon	헍 heonj	헎 heonh	헏 heod	헐 heol	헑 heolg	헒 heolm	헓 heolb	헔 heols	헕 heolt
ㅎ h	ㅔ e	헤 he	헥 heg	헦 hegg	헧 hegs	헨 hen	헩 henj	헪 henh	헫 hed	헬 hel	헭 helg	헮 helm	헯 helb	헰 hels	헱 helt
ㅎ h	ㅕ yeo	혀 hyeo	혁 hyeog	혂 hyeogg	혃 hyeogs	현 hyeon	혅 hyeonj	혆 hyeonh	혇 hyeod	혈 hyeol	혉 hyeolg	혊 hyeolm	혋 hyeolb	혌 hyeols	혍 hyeolt
ㅎ h	ㅖ ye	혜 hye	혝 hyeg	혞 hyegg	혟 hyegs	혠 hyen	혡 hyenj	혢 hyenh	혣 hyed	혤 hyel	혥 hyelg	혦 hyelm	혧 hyelb	혨 hyels	혩 hyelt
ㅎ h	ㅗ o	호 ho	혹 hog	혺 hogg	혻 hogs	혼 hon	혽 honj	혾 honh	혿 hod	홀 hol	홁 holg	홂 holm	홃 holb	홄 hols	홅 holt
ㅎ h	ㅘ wa	화 hwa	확 hwag	홲 hwagg	홳 hwags	환 hwan	홵 hwanj	홶 hwanh	홷 hwad	활 hwal	홹 hwalg	홺 hwalm	홻 hwalb	홼 hwals	홽 hwalt
ㅎ h	ㅙ wae	홰 hwae	홱 hwaeg	홲 hwaegg	홳 hwaegs	홴 hwaen	홵 hwaenj	홶 hwaenh	홷 hwaed	홸 hwael	홹 hwaelg	홺 hwaelm	홻 hwaelb	홼 hwaels	홽 hwaelt
ㅎ h	ㅚ oe	회 hoe	획 hoeg	홲 hoegg	홳 hoegs	횐 hoen	횑 hoenj	횒 hoenh	횓 hoed	횔 hoel	횕 hoelg	횖 hoelm	횗 hoelb	횘 hoels	횙 hoelt
ㅎ h	ㅛ yo	효 hyo	횩 hyog	횪 hyogg	횫 hyogs	횬 hyon	횭 hyonj	횮 hyonh	횯 hyod	횰 hyol	횱 hyolg	횲 hyolm	횳 hyolb	횴 hyols	횵 hyolt
ㅎ h	ㅜ u	후 hu	훅 hug	훆 hugg	훇 hugs	훈 hun	훉 hunj	훊 hunh	훋 hud	훌 hul	훍 hulg	훎 hulm	훏 hulb	훐 huls	훑 hult
ㅎ h	ㅝ weo	훠 hweo	훡 hweog	훢 hweogg	훣 hweogs	훤 hweon	훥 hweonj	훦 hweonh	훧 hweod	훨 hweol	훩 hweolg	훪 hweolm	훫 hweolb	훬 hweols	훭 hweolt
ㅎ h	ㅞ we	훼 hwe	훽 hweg	훾 hwegg	훿 hwegs	휀 hwen	휁 hwenj	휂 hwenh	휃 hwed	휄 hwel	휅 hwelg	휆 hwelm	휇 hwelb	휈 hwels	휉 hwelt
ㅎ h	ㅟ wi	휘 hwi	휙 hwig	휚 hwigg	휛 hwigs	휜 hwin	휝 hwinj	휞 hwinh	휟 hwid	휠 hwil	휡 hwilg	휢 hwilm	휣 hwilb	휤 hwils	휥 hwilt
ㅎ h	ㅠ yu	휴 hyu	휵 hyug	휶 hyugg	휷 hyugs	휸 hyun	휹 hyunj	휺 hyunh	휻 hyud	휼 hyul	휽 hyulg	휾 hyulm	휿 hyulb	흀 hyuls	흁 hyult
ㅎ h	ㅡ eu	흐 heu	흑 heug	흒 heugg	흓 heugs	흔 heun	흕 heunj	흖 heunh	흗 heud	흘 heul	흙 heulg	흚 heulm	흛 heulb	흜 heuls	흝 heult
ㅎ h	ㅢ yi	희 hyi	흭 hyig	흮 hyigg	흯 hyigs	흰 hyin	흱 hyinj	흲 hyinh	흳 hyid	흴 hyil	흵 hyilg	흶 hyilm	흷 hyilb	흸 hyils	흹 hyilt
ㅎ h	ㅣ i	히 hi	힉 hig	힊 higg	힋 higs	힌 hin	힍 hinj	힎 hinh	힏 hid	힐 hil	힑 hilg	힒 hilm	힓 hilb	힔 hils	힕 hilt

		ᆵ lp	ᆶ lh	ㅁ m	ㅂ b	ㅄ bs	ㅅ s	ㅆ ss	ㅇ ng	ㅈ j	ㅊ ch	ㅋ k	ㅌ t	ㅍ p	ㅎ h
ㅎ h	ㅏ a	halp	halh	ham	hab	habs	has	hass	hang	haj	hach	hak	hat	hap	hah
ㅎ h	ㅐ ae	haelp	haelh	haem	haeb	haebs	haes	haess	haeng	haej	haech	haek	haet	haep	haeh
ㅎ h	ㅑ ya	hyalp	hyalh	hyam	hyab	hyabs	hyas	hyass	hyang	hyaj	hyach	hyak	hyat	hyap	hyah
ㅎ h	ㅒ yae	hyaelp	hyaelh	hyaem	hyaeb	hyaebs	hyaes	hyaess	hyaeng	hyaej	hyaech	hyaek	hyaet	hyaep	hyaeh
ㅎ h	ㅓ eo	heolp	heolh	heom	heob	heobs	heos	heoss	heong	heoj	heoch	heok	heot	heop	heoh
ㅎ h	ㅔ e	help	helh	hem	heb	hebs	hes	hess	heng	hej	hech	hek	het	hep	heh
ㅎ h	ㅕ yeo	hyeolp	hyeolh	hyeom	hyeob	hyeobs	hyeos	hyeoss	hyeong	hyeoj	hyeoch	hyeok	hyeot	hyeop	hyeoh
ㅎ h	ㅖ ye	hyelp	hyelh	hyem	hyeb	hyebs	hyes	hyess	hyeng	hyej	hyech	hyek	hyet	hyep	hyeh
ㅎ h	ㅗ o	holp	holh	hom	hob	hobs	hos	hoss	hong	hoj	hoch	hok	hot	hop	hoh
ㅎ h	ㅘ wa	hwalp	hwalh	hwam	hwab	hwabs	hwas	hwass	hwang	hwaj	hwach	hwak	hwat	hwap	hwah
ㅎ h	ㅙ wae	hwaelp	hwaelh	hwaem	hwaeb	hwaebs	hwaes	hwaess	hwaeng	hwaej	hwaech	hwaek	hwaet	hwaep	hwaeh
ㅎ h	ㅚ oe	hoelp	hoelh	hoem	hoeb	hoebs	hoes	hoess	hoeng	hoej	hoech	hoek	hoet	hoep	hoeh
ㅎ h	ㅛ yo	hyolp	hyolh	hyom	hyob	hyobs	hyos	hyoss	hyong	hyoj	hyoch	hyok	hyot	hyop	hyoh
ㅎ h	ㅜ u	hulp	hulh	hum	hub	hubs	hus	huss	hung	huj	huch	huk	hut	hup	huh
ㅎ h	ㅝ weo	hweolp	hweolh	hweom	hweob	hweobs	hweos	hweoss	hweong	hweoj	hweoch	hweok	hweot	hweop	hweoh
ㅎ h	ㅞ we	hwelp	hwelh	hwem	hweb	hwebs	hwes	hwess	hweng	hwej	hwech	hwek	hwet	hwep	hweh
ㅎ h	ㅟ wi	hwilp	hwilh	hwim	hwib	hwibs	hwis	hwiss	hwing	hwij	hwich	hwik	hwit	hwip	hwih
ㅎ h	ㅠ yu	hyulp	hyulh	hyum	hyub	hyubs	hyus	hyuss	hyung	hyuj	hyuch	hyuk	hyut	hyup	hyuh
ㅎ h	ㅡ eu	heulp	heulh	heum	heub	heubs	heus	heuss	heung	heuj	heuch	heuk	heut	heup	heuh
ㅎ h	ㅢ yi	hyilp	hyilh	hyim	hyib	hyibs	hyis	hyiss	hying	hyij	hyich	hyik	hyit	hyip	hyih
ㅎ h	ㅣ i	hilp	hilh	him	hib	hibs	his	hiss	hing	hij	hich	hik	hit	hip	hih

Stroke Order and Direction

The stroke order and direction are important when drawing HanGul and HanJa characters by hand. The stroke order is particularly important when sketching a HanJa character on a computer to search for its HanGul pronunciation or definition. The following guidelines generally apply to drawing both HanGul and HanJa characters:

Stroke Direction

- o Draw individual strokes from top-to-bottom or left-to-right, when possible.

- o Right–to-left diagonals are drawn top-to-bottom and right-to-left.

Stroke Order

- o Draw horizontal strokes before vertical strokes.

- o Start with the strokes on the top and work down to the ones on the bottom.

- o Draw the left-to-right diagonals before the right-to-left diagonals.

- o Strokes that pass thru many others are drawn last.

- o For symmetric characters, draw the center stroke first, strokes left of center second, and strokes right of center last.

- o Draw very small strokes last.

- o Use 3 strokes to draw a square. Draw the left side first (top-to-bottom), draw the top (left-to-right) and right (top-to-bottom) in one stroke that includes a corner, then draw the bottom stroke (left-to-right).

- o If a stroke or group of strokes is inside a square group of strokes, draw the outside square first then the contents.

To see how any HanJa are drawn, go to http://hanja.naver.com, look up a character by typing HanGul or sketching HanJa with the mouse, then look at the "획순 보기"section to see the stroke order. You can also click on the button by that section title to see an animation demonstrating the correct stroke direction and order.

Text Direction

Both HanJa and HanGul text were traditionally written top-to-bottom and right-to-left on a page or scroll. Books were written in the opposite direction from western books. The back page of a western style book is where the first page of a traditional eastern book would start. Modern Korean writing follows the same text direction as the western world, but genealogical records normally use the traditional eastern text direction.

Korean on Computers

Genealogists studying Korean records frequently need to use Korean HanGul and HanJa characters on computers. While it is possible to use printed dictionaries, there are so many online resources that the ability to use Korean on a computer is almost essential.

The ability to read Korean HanGul and HanJa characters on computers with English operating systems is generally not difficult. Both Windows and Mac computers have free options that enable viewing Korean fonts. A Korean keyboard is also not required to write Korean HanGul and HanJa characters. There are free Korean input methods available for most versions of popular operating systems that don't require a Korean keyboard.

Korean on Windows Computers

Text and video instructions for enabling Korean on Windows 7 are found at the following web address:

http://windows.microsoft.com/en-us/windows7/Add-or-change-an-input-language

Installing the Korean input method enables the following language tool bars (shown maximized and minimized below):

You can click on the "가 Han/Eng" button to switch input methods between Korean and English. You can use a Korean keyboard or buy a pack of stickers with Korean characters on them to put on your keyboard. If you prefer not to learn to type in Korean, you can also use an on-screen keyboard by clicking on the "Soft Keyboard" icon. The following keyboard images (with and without "Shift" enabled) are shown on the screen and can be clicked with a mouse to enter HanGul characters without using a physical keyboard.

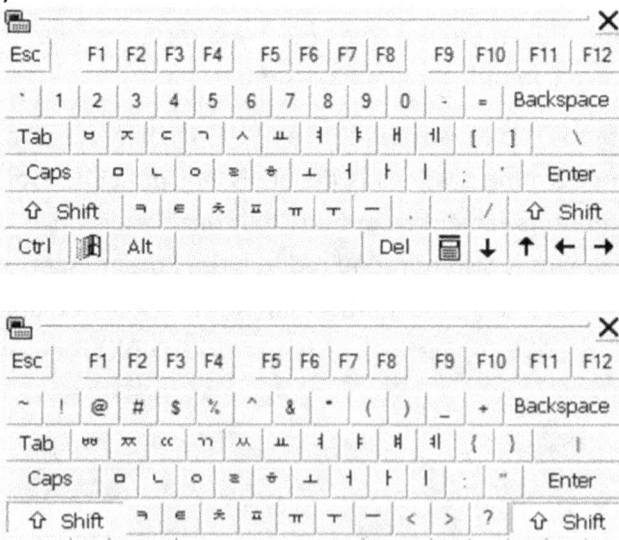

Typing (or mouse-clicking) compound vowels requires typing more than one key in cases where the compound vowel does not have its own key. The following table shows what to type to enter compound vowels that don't have their own keyboard key:

Table 1.24: How to Type Compound Vowels

Compound Vowel	Keys to Type (1st key, 2nd key)
ㅘ	ㅗ ㅏ
ㅙ	ㅗ ㅒ
ㅚ	ㅗ ㅣ
ㅝ	ㅜ ㅓ
ㅞ	ㅜ ㅖ
ㅟ	ㅜ ㅣ
ㅢ	ㅡ ㅣ

A third option for typing HanGul characters also works for HanJa characters. Clicking the IME Pad button brings up a HandWriting window where HanGul or HanJa characters can be drawn with a mouse or drawing pad. The character is drawn on the left, then the computer brings up the most likely candidates on the right. Click on the correct character on the right. Note that you should use proper stroke direction and order to facilitate accurate automated recognition.

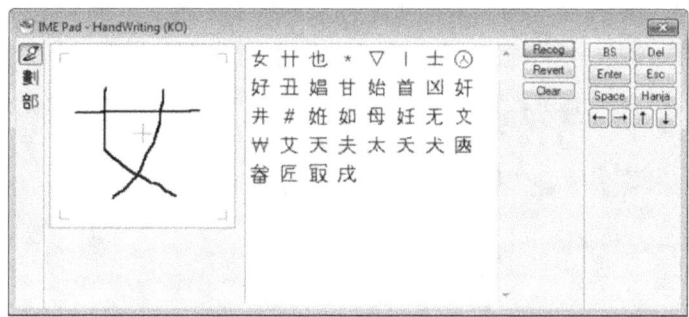

Korean on Mac OS X

Free Korean input methods can be enabled on OS X by following the instructions found at this web address:

http://support.apple.com/kb/PH4414

A language icon is placed in the upper right-hand corner of the desktop which can be used to access the following menu. The input language can be selected using this menu:

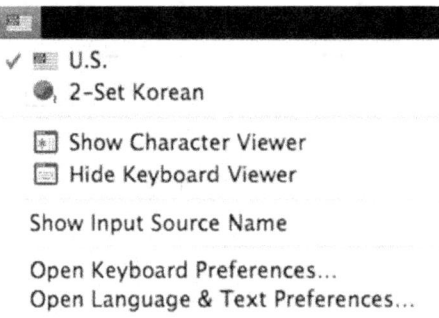

You can type Korean using a keyboard. If you don't have a Korean keyboard you can place stickers on the keys that show the Korean HanGul characters. You can also use the mouse and click an on-screen keyboard. Selecting the Korean language and "Show Keyboard Viewer" will display the following keyboard on the screen, shown with and without the shift key pressed below:

You can type a HanGul syllable and convert it into a HanJa character. Do this by first typing the HanGul syllable, pressing **option-return**, then selecting the desired HanJa character from the menu that appears:

Korean on the Internet

Regardless of what operating system you use, there are internet based methods to enter Korean characters into a computer. For example, you can use the following site to draw a HanJa character or type a HanGul syllable to find its definitions in Korean or learn the correct stroke order to draw the HanJa character.

http://hanja.naver.com

Translating HanJa and HanGul

Proficiency in HanGul is not required for researching Korean Genealogy, although it is very helpful. At a minimum, you should understand that Korean HanGul letters can be put together into syllables, and syllables/characters can be put together into words. If a word has HanJa roots, then each syllable could be represented in HanGul or HanJa. If the word does not have HanJa roots, then it can only be written in HanGul.

The first step in translating Korean genealogical records is translating the HanJa characters into HanGul syllables to determine the pronunciation. The next step is looking up the meanings of syllables and words (generally one, two, or three syllables per word). Even if you don't know where to break up words in a long string of HanJa that was written without spaces between words, you can get valuable insight into the overall meaning by looking up the meaning of each syllable.

The following websites are useful when converting between HanJa and HanGul.

http://hanja.naver.com/

http://hanjadic.bravender.us/

The following websites are useful when looking up the English meaning of HanGul words or HanJa syllables:

http://hanjadic.bravender.us/

http://translate.google.com/?langpair=zh%7Cen

Sometimes it can be useful to simply use a common search engine to find sample usages and translations of HanJa. This is particularly useful when a HanJa character, word, or phrase is found on Korean genealogy related sites. It is usually best to enter the HanJa into a Korean version of a search engine site to avoid being overwhelmed with Chinese rather than Korean results:

http://www.google.co.kr/

http://kr.yahoo.com/

http://www.naver.com/

2 - Names

Names

Korean names are usually three syllables that can be written in HanJa or HanGul characters.   The family name comes first and is normally one HanGul syllable or HanJa character.   The given name is listed last and is generally two HanGul syllables or HanJa characters.

There are rare exceptions to the most common pattern of three syllable names (one syllable family name with a two syllable given name). Some family names are two syllables, and some given names are just one syllable.   There is also a small but growing trend of pure Korean given names that don't have HanJa representations.

Children receive the family name of their father. When a woman gets married in Korea, she does not change her name. She keeps her family name, which is recorded in her husband's family registry. Her children are given her husband's family name.

Table 2.1 Examples of Korean Names

HanJa	HanGul	Pronunciation	Name
李明花	이명화	Lee MyungHwa	Family: Lee Given: MyeongHwa *Meaning: bright- flower*
朴琪顯	박기현	Pak GiHyeon	Family: Pak Given: GiHyeon *Meaning: jade-clear*
金하늘	김하늘	Kim HaNeol	Family: Kim Given: HaNeol *Meaning: heaven* *Note: The pure Korean given name "HaNeol" has no HanJa representation, so it is only written with HanGul Korean letters.*

Family Names

There are about 300 Korean family names. Many family names can be broken down into multiple clans (BoGuan). Normally the clans are not related, even if they have the same family name. Traditionally, people from the same clan cannot marry. Specifying clans is necessary when referring to family registries and genealogies, but generally clans aren't added to names for other purposes. The word "Shi" (씨, meaning Mr., Mrs., or family) is often placed as after the family name or full name.

The following table lists Korean family names. Note that there are many additional possible English spellings for the names. A good source of alternate popular English spellings of Korean family names is:

http://en.wiktionary.org/wiki/Appendix:Korean_surnames

Table 2.2 Korean Family Names (HanJa, HanGul, and English)

賈 가 Ga	簡 간 Gan	葛 갈 Gal	甘 감 Gam	剛 강 Gang	姜 강 Gang	康 강 Gang	疆 강 Gang	強 강 Gang	岡田 강전 GangJeon
綱切 강절 GangJeol	介 개 Gae	甄 견 Gyeon	堅 견 Gyeon	慶 경 Gyeong	景 경 Gyeong	京 경 Gyeong	桂 계 Gyae	高 고 Go	曲 곡 Gok
孔 공 Gong	公 공 Gong	郭 곽 Gwak	橋 교 Gyo	具 구 Gu	丘 구 Gu	邱 구 Gu	鞠 국 Guk	國 국 Guk	菊 국 Guk
君 군 Gun	弓 궁 Gung	鴌 궉 Gweok	權 권 Gweon	斤 근 Geun	琴 금 Geum	奇 기 Gi	箕 기 Gi	吉 길 Gil	金 김 Kim
羅 나 Na	欒 난 Nan	南 남 Nam	南宮 남궁 NamGung	浪 낭 Nang	乃 내 Nae	奈 내 Nae	盧 노 No	魯 노 No	盧 노 No
路 노 No	雷 뇌 Nwe	賴 뇌 Nwe	樓 누 Nu	段 단 Dan	單 단 Dan	端 단 Dan	譚 담 Dam	唐 당 Dang	大 대 Dae
都 도 Do	陶 도 Do	道 도 Do	獨孤 독고 DokGo	頓 돈 Don	敦 돈 Don	董 동 Dong	東方 동방 DongBang	杜 두 Du	頭 두 Du
羅 라 Ra	梁 량 Ryang	樑 량 Ryang	柳 류 Ryu	李 리 Lee	林 림 Rim	馬 마 Ma	麻 마 Ma	萬 만 Man	綱切 망절 MangJeol

55

梅 매 Mae	孟 맹 Maeng	明 명 Myeong	牟 모 Mo	毛 모 Mo	睦 목 Mok	苗 묘 Myo	墨 묵 Muk	文 문 Moon	門 문 Moon
米 미 Mi	閔 민 Min	朴 박 Pak	潘 반 Ban	班 반 Ban	方 방 Bang	房 방 Bang	邦 방 Bang	龐 방 Bang	裵 배 Bae
白 백 Baek	范 범 Beom	凡 범 Beom	卞 변 Byeon	邊 변 Byeon	卜 복 Bok	奉 봉 Bong	鳳 봉 Bong	夫 부 Bu	傅 부 Bu
丕 비 Pe	賓 빈 Pen	彬 빈 Pen	冰 빙 Peng	氷 빙 Peng	史 사 Sa	謝 사 Sa	舍 사 Sa	司空 사공 SaGong	森 삼 Sam
杉 삼 Sam	尚 상 Sang	徐 서 Seo	西 서 Seo	西門 서문 SeoMun	石 석 Seok	昔 석 Seok	宣 선 Seon	鮮于 선우 SeonU	高 설 Seol
薛 설 Seol	偰 설 Seol	葉 섭 Seop	成 성 Seong	星 성 Seong	蘇 소 So	邵 소 So	肖 소 So	召 소 So	素 소 So
逍 소 So	小峰 소봉 SoBong	孫 손 Son	宋 송 Song	松 송 Song	水 수 Su	洙 수 Su	筍 순 Sun	淳 순 Sun	舜 순 Sun
順 순 Sun	承 승 Seung	昇 승 Seung	施 시 Shi	柴 시 Shi	申 신 Shin	辛 신 Shin	愼 신 Shin	沈 심 Shim	辻 십 Ship

阿 아 A	安 안 An	艾 애 Ae	夜 야 Ya	梁 양 Yang	楊 양 Yang	樑 양 Yang	襄 양 Yang	魚 어 Eo	魚金 어금 EoGeum
嚴 엄 Eum	呂 여 Yeo	余 여 Yeo	汝 여 Yeo	延 연 Yeon	燕 연 Yeon	連 연 Yeon	廉 염 Yeom	葉 엽 Yeop	永 영 Yeong
榮 영 Yeong	影 영 Yeong	芮 예 Yae	吳 오 O	伍 오 O	玉 옥 Ok	溫 온 On	邕 옹 Ong	雍 옹 Ong	王 왕 Wang
姚 요 Yo	龍 용 Yong	禹 우 U	于 우 U	宇 우 U	雲 운 Un	芸 운 Un	元 원 Won	袁 원 Won	苑 원 Won
魏 위 We	韋 위 We	柳 유 Yu	劉 유 Yu	俞 유 Yu	庚 유 Yu	陸 육 Yuk	尹 윤 Yun	殷 은 Eun	恩 은 Eun
陰 음 Eum	李 이 Lee	異 이 Lee	伊 이 Lee	印 인 In	林 임 Im	任 임 Im	慈 자 Ja	張 장 Jang	蔣 장 Jang
章 장 Jang	莊 장 Jang	長谷 장곡 JangGok	邸 저 Jeo	全 전 Jeon	田 전 Jeon	錢 전 Jeon	占 점 Jeom	鄭 정 Jeong	丁 정 Jeong
程 정 Jeong	諸 제 Jae	齊 제 Jae	諸葛 제갈 JaeGal	趙 조 Jo	曹 조 Jo	鍾 종 Jong	宗 종 Jong	左 좌 Jwa	周 주 Ju

朱 주 Ju	俊 준 Jun	辻 즙 Jeup	曾 증 Jeung	增 증 Jeung	池 지 Ji	智 지 Ji	陳 진 Jin	秦 진 Jin	晉 진 Jin
眞 진 Jin	車 차 Cha	昌 창 Chang	倉 창 Chang	蔡 채 Chae	菜 채 Chae	采 채 Chae	千 천 Cheon	天 천 Cheon	楚 초 Cho
肖 초 Cho	初 초 Cho	崔 최 Choi	秋 추 Chu	鄒 추 Chu	椿 춘 Chun	卓 탁 Tak	彈 탁 Tak	太 태 Tae	判 판 Pan
彭 팽 Paeng	片 편 Pyeon	扁 편 Pyeon	平 평 Pyeong	包 포 Po	表 표 Pyo	馮 풍 Pung	皮 피 Pe	弼 필 Pel	河 하 Ha
夏 하 Ha	郝 학 Hak	韓 한 Han	漢 한 Han	咸 함 Ham	海 해 Hae	許 허 Heo	玄 현 Hyeon	邢 형 Heong	扈 호 Ho
胡 호 Ho	鎬 호 Ho	洪 홍 Hong	化 화 Hwa	桓 환 Hwan	黃 황 Hwang	皇甫 황보 HwangBo	侯 후 Hu	后 후 Hu	興 흥 Heung

Given Names

Given names are normally two HanJa characters. The HanJa versions of names aren't often used in daily life, but they are necessary for formal purposes, such as legal documents and genealogies.

Some given names are normally for boys while others are normally for girls, which is also a common practice with western given names. Unlike the western world, one syllable/character in the given name traditionally represents the family branch and generation. For example, the 37th generation of boys for a particular family branch (including cousins) may all start or end with the same syllable/HanJa character. Often the grandparents will select a HanJa character that will be used for the boys or girls born to their children. Not everyone follows this tradition and it wasn't always done for girls, but it is still widely practiced.

For names based on HanJa, each syllable has a meaning. The following table is based on a government issued listing of HanJa for use in given names (인명용 한자표). You can look up the meaning of each of the following HanJa by entering the HanJa or HanGul version into an online dictionary, such as http://hanjadic.bravender.us/. This powerful online dictionary translates any direction between English, Korean HanGul, and HanJa.

HanJa characters that share the same HanGul spelling have the same pronunciation. However, each HanJa character has a different meaning. http://hanja.naver.com/category/name is an excellent reference to learn more about the HanJa used in names. It includes the meaning, number of strokes in the HanJa character, and even the stroke order for drawing the HanJa character correctly. This will be particularly useful if you are drawing the character in Microsoft IME or another HanJa entry method on a computer.

If you know an ancestor's name in HanGul but do not know how to write their name in HanJa, the following list can help. It provides candidate HanJa versions of a syllable used in a given name. Each HanJa candidate has a different meaning. The HanJa version of the name is needed to find an ancestor's name in a Korean Family Registry genealogical record.

Table 2.3 HanJa Syllables Used in Korean Given Names

HanGul English	HanJa Used in Given Names
가 Ga	家 佳 街 可 歌 加 價 假 架 暇 嘉 嫁 稼 賈 駕 伽 迦 柯 呵 哥 枷 珂 痂 苛 袈 訶 跏 軻 茄 哿
각 Gak	各 角 脚 閣 却 覺 刻 珏 恪 殼 慤
간 Gan	干 間 看 刊 肝 幹 簡 姦 懇 艮 侃 杆 玕 竿 揀 諫 墾 栞 奸 柬 桿 澗 癇 磵 稈 艱
갈 Gal	渴 葛 曷 喝 曷 碣 竭 褐 蝎 鞨
감 Gam	甘 減 感 敢 監 鑑 鑒 勘 瞰 坎 嵌 憾 戡 柑 橄 疳 紺 邯 龕
갑 Gap	甲 鉀 匣 岬 胛 閘
강 Gang	江 降 講 强 康 剛 鋼 綱 杠 堈 岡 崗 姜 橿 疆 慷 罡 疅 糠 絳 羌 腔 肛 薑 襁 鱇 嫌
개 Gae	改 皆 個 箇 開 介 慨 槪 蓋 盖 价 凱 愷 漑 塏 愾 疥 芥 豈 鎧 玠
객 Gaek	客 喀

HanGul English	HanJa Used in Given Names
갱 Gaeng	更 坑 粳 羹
갹 Gyak	醵
거 Geo	去 巨 居 車 擧 距 拒 據 渠 遽 鉅 炬 倨 据 祛 踞 鋸
건 Geon	建 乾 件 健 巾 虔 楗 鍵 愆 腱 騫 蹇 漧
걸 Geol	傑 乞 杰 桀
검 Geom	儉 劍 劒 檢 瞼 鈐 黔
겁 Geop	劫 怯 迲
게 Gae	揭 偈 憩
격 Gyeok	格 擊 激 隔 檄 膈 覡
견 Gyeon	犬 見 堅 肩 絹 遣 牽 鵑 甄 繭 譴
결 Gyeol	訣 潔 缺 決 抉 結 潔
겸 Gyeom	慊 兼 鉗 箝 鎌 謙 嗛

HanGul English	HanJa Used in Given Names
경 Gyong	憬 灵 庚 烔 勍 瓊 梗 鯨 倞 慶 境 驚 痙 卿 耿 璥 更 徑 璟 坰 俓 儆 傾 竟 檠 競 冂 硬 囧 景 京 頸 絅 耕 敬 脛 憼 涇 莖 經 警 鶊 擎 勁 鏡 輕 逕 磬 頃 頸 暻 璄 京 橄 囧
계 Gyae	屆 系 悸 係 繼 溪 桂 計 鷄 季 誡 稽 啓 癸 榮 谿 界 械 烓 階 繫 戒 契 磎 堺
고 Go	顧 菰 故 皐 暠 藁 痼 姑 睾 沽 賈 枯 苽 固 鼓 稿 敲 古 孤 苦 考 尻 股 呱 高 錮 辜 杲 雇 拷 膏 庫 蠱 羔 袴 攷 皋
곡 Gok	谷 穀 哭 梏 曲 斛 鵠
곤 Gon	崑 坤 滾 昆 困 琨 錕 鯤 梱 棍 袞 衮
골 Gol	滑 骨 汩
공 Gong	空 拱 恐 鞏 珙 蚣 功 供 貢 孔 公 工 控 恭 攻 共

HanGul English	HanJa Used in Given Names
곶 Goj	串
과 Gwa	果 課 科 過 誇 寡 菓 鍋 顆 跨 戈 瓜
곽 Gwak	郭 廓 槨 藿
관 Gwan	官 觀 關 館 舘 管 貫 慣 冠 寬 款 琯 錧 灌 瓘 梡 串 棺 罐 菅
괄 Gwal	括 刮 恝 适
광 Gwang	光 廣 鑛 狂 侊 洸 珖 桄 匡 曠 眐 壙 筐 胱
괘 Gwae	掛 卦 罫
괴 Gwe	塊 愧 怪 壞 乖 傀 拐 槐 魁
굉 Gweng	宏 紘 肱 轟
교 Gyo	交 校 橋 敎 敎 郊 較 巧 矯 僑 喬 嬌 膠 咬 嶠 攪 狡 皎 絞 翹 蕎 蛟 轎 鮫 驕 餃 姣 佼

HanGul English	HanJa Used in Given Names
구 Gu	九 口 求 救 究 久 句 舊 具 俱 區 驅 苟 拘 狗 丘 懼 龜 構 球 坵 玖 矩 邱 銶 溝 購 鳩 軀 耈 枸 仇 勾 咎 嘔 垢 寇 嶇 廐 柩 歐 毆 毬 灸 瞿 絿 臼 舅 衢 謳 逑 鉤 駒 鷗 玽
국 Guk	國 国 菊 局 鞠 麴 鞫
군 Gun	君 郡 軍 群 窘 裙
굴 Gul	屈 窟 堀 掘
궁 Gung	弓 宮 窮 躬 穹 芎
권 Gweon	券 權 勸 卷 拳 圈 眷 倦 捲 淃
궐 Gweol	厥 闕 獗 蕨 蹶
궤 Gwae	軌 机 櫃 潰 詭 饋
귀 Gwe	貴 歸 鬼 龜 句 晷
규 Gyu	叫 規 糾 圭 奎 珪 揆 逵 窺 葵 槻 硅 竅 赳 閨 糺 邽 嫢
균 Gyun	均 菌 畇 鈞 勻 筠 龜

HanGul English	HanJa Used in Given Names
귤 Gyul	橘
극 Geuk	極 克 劇 剋 隙 戟 棘
근 Geun	近 勤 根 斤 僅 謹 漌 墐 槿 筋 瑾 女 菫 劤 懃 芹 堇 覲 饉
글 Geul	契
금 Geum	金 今 禁 錦 禽 琴 衾 襟 昑 妗 擒 檎 芩 衿
급 Geup	及 給 急 級 汲 伋 扱
긍 Geung	肯 亘 兢 矜
기 Gi	己 記 起 其 期 基 氣 技 幾 旣 紀 忌 旗 欺 奇 騎 寄 豈 棄 祈 企 畿 飢 器 機 淇 琪 璂 棋 祺 錤 騏 麒 玘 杞 埼 崎 琦 綺 錡 箕 岐 汽 沂 圻 耆 璣 磯 譏 冀 驥 嗜 曉 伎 夔 妓 朞 畸 碁 祁 祇 羈 穊 肌 饑 稘
긴 Gin	緊
길 Gil	吉 佶 桔 姞 拮

HanGul English	HanJa Used in Given Names
김 Kim	金
끽 Ggek	喫
나 Na	那 奈 奈 娜 挐 喇 懦 拿 儺 挐
낙 Nak	諾
난 Nan	暖 難 煖
날 Nal	捺 捏
남 Nam	南 男 楠 湳 枏
납 Nap	納 衲
낭 Nang	娘 囊
내 Nae	内 乃 奈 耐 柰
녀 Nyeo	女
년 Nyeon	年 秊 撚
념 Nyeom	念 恬 拈 捻
녕 Nyeong	寧 儜 獰

HanGul English	HanJa Used in Given Names
노 No	怒 奴 努 弩 瑙 駑
농 Nong	農 膿 濃
뇨 Nyo	尿 鬧 撓
눈 Nun	嫩
눌 Nul	訥
뇌 Noy	腦 惱
뉴 Nyu	紐 鈕 杻
능 Neung	能
니 Ne	泥 尼 柅 濔 膩
닉 Nek	匿 溺
다 Da	多 茶 爹
단 Dan	丹 但 單 短 端 旦 段 壇 檀 斷 團 緞 鍛 亶 象 湍 簞 蛋 袒 鄲 煓
달 Dal	達 撻 澾 獺 疸

HanGul English	HanJa Used in Given Names
담 Dam	談 淡 擔 譚 膽 澹 覃 啖 坍 憺 曇 湛 痰 聃 錟 蕁 潭 倓
답 Dap	答 畓 踏 沓 遝
당 Dang	堂 當 唐 糖 黨 塘 鐺 撞 幢 戇 棠 螳
대 Dae	大 代 待 對 帶 臺 貸 隊 垈 玳 袋 戴 擡 旲 坮 岱 黛
댁 Daek	宅
덕 Deok	德 悳
도 Do	刀 到 度 道 島 徒 圖 倒 都 桃 挑 跳 逃 渡 陶 途 稻 導 盜 塗 堵 棹 濤 熹 鍍 蹈 禱 屠 嶋 悼 掉 搗 櫂 淘 滔 睹 萄 覩 賭 韜
독 Dok	讀 獨 毒 督 篤 瀆 牘 犢 禿 纛
돈 Don	豚 敦 墩 惇 暾 燉 頓 旽 沌 焞
돌 Dol	突 乭

68

HanGul English	HanJa Used in Given Names
동 Dong	同 洞 童 冬 東 動 銅 凍 棟 董 潼 垌 瞳 蝀 仝 憧 疼 胴 桐 朣 曈 彤 烔
두 Du	斗 豆 頭 杜 枓 兜 痘 竇 荳 讀 逗 阧
둔 Dun	鈍 屯 遁 臀 芚 遯
득 Deuk	得
등 Deung	等 登 燈 騰 藤 膡 鄧 嶝 橙
라 Ra	羅 螺 喇 懶 癩 蘿 裸 邏 刺 覶 摞
락 Rak	落 樂 絡 珞 酪 烙 駱 洛
란 Ran	卵 亂 蘭 欄 瀾 丹 欒 鸞 爛
랄 Ral	剌 辣
람 Ram	覽 濫 嵐 擥 攬 欖 籃 纜 襤 藍
랍 Rap	拉 臘 蠟
랑 Rang	浪 郎 廊 琅 瑯 狼 螂 朗 烺

HanGul English	HanJa Used in Given Names
래 Rae	來 来 崍 萊 徠
랭 Raeng	冷
략 Ryak	略 掠
량 Ryang	良 兩 量 凉 梁 糧 諒 亮 倆 樑 涼 粮 梁 輛
려 Ryeo	旅 麗 慮 勵 呂 侶 閭 黎 儷 盧 戾 櫚 濾 礪 藜 驢 驪 蠣
력 Ryeok	力 歷 曆 瀝 礫 轢 靂
련 Ryeon	連 練 鍊 憐 聯 戀 蓮 煉 璉 攣 漣 輦 變
렬 Ryeol	列 烈 裂 劣 洌 冽
렴 Ryeom	廉 濂 斂 殮
렵 Ryeop	獵
령 Ryeong	令 領 嶺 零 靈 伶 玲 姈 聆 鈴 齡 怜 囹 岺 笭 羚 翎 聤 逞 泠 澪
례 Ryae	例 禮 隸 澧 醴

70

HanGul English	HanJa Used in Given Names
로 Ro	路 露 老 勞 爐 魯 盧 鷺 撈 擄 櫨 潞 濾 蘆 虜 輅 鹵 嚧
록 Rok	綠 祿 錄 鹿 彔 碌 菉 麓
론 Ron	論
롱 Rong	弄 瀧 瓏 籠 壟 朧 聾
뢰 Roy	雷 賴 瀨 儡 牢 磊 賂 賚
료 Ryo	料 了 僚 遼 寮 廖 燎 療 瞭 聊 蓼
룡 Ryong	龍 竜
루 Ru	屢 樓 累 淚 漏 壘 婁 瘻 縷 蔞 褸 鏤 陋
류 Ryu	柳 留 流 類 琉 劉 瑠 硫 瘤 旒 榴 溜 瀏 謬
륙 Ryuk	六 陸 戮
륜 Ryun	倫 輪 侖 崙 崘 綸 淪 錀
률 Ryul	律 栗 率 慄 嵂

HanGul English	HanJa Used in Given Names
릉 Ryung	隆
륵 Reuk	勒 肋
름 Reum	廩 凜
릉 Reung	陵 綾 菱 稜 凌 楞
리 Ri	里 理 利 梨 李 吏 離 裏 裡 履 俚 莉 离 璃 悧 俐 厘 唎 浬 犁 狸 痢 籬 罹 蠃 釐 鯉 浬
린 Rin	隣 潾 璘 麟 吝 燐 藺 躪 鱗 鄰
림 Rim	林 臨 琳 霖 淋 棽
립 Rep	立 笠 粒 砬
마 Ma	馬 麻 磨 瑪 摩 痲 碼 魔
막 Mak	莫 幕 漠 寞 膜 邈
만 Man	萬 晚 滿 慢 漫 万 曼 蔓 鏋 卍 娩 戀 彎 挽 灣 瞞 輓 饅 鰻 蠻
말 Mal	末 茉 耄 抹 沫 襪 靺

HanGul English	HanJa Used in Given Names
망 Mang	亡 忙 忘 望 茫 妄 罔 網 芒 莽 輞 邙
매 Mae	每 買 賣 妹 梅 埋 媒 寐 昧 枚 煤 罵 邁 魅 苺
맥 Maek	麥 脈 貊 陌 驀
맹 Maeng	孟 猛 盟 盲 萌 氓
몍 Myeok	冪 覓
면 Myeon	免 勉 面 眠 綿 冕 棉 沔 眄 緬 麵
멸 Myeol	滅 蔑
명 Myeong	名 命 明 鳴 銘 冥 溟 暝 椧 皿 瞑 茗 蓂 螟 酩 慏 洺 眀 鵬
몌 Myae	袂
모 Mo	母 毛 暮 某 謀 模 貌 募 慕 冒 侮 摸 牟 謨 姆 帽 摹 牡 瑁 眸 耗 芼 茅 矛
목 Mok	木 目 牧 睦 穆 鶩 沐

73

HanGul English	HanJa Used in Given Names
몰 Mol	沒 歾
몽 Mong	夢 蒙 朦
묘 Myo	卯 妙 苗 廟 墓 描 錨 畝 昴 杳 渺 猫 竗
무 Mu	戊 茂 武 務 無 无 舞 貿 霧 拇 珷 畝 撫 懋 巫 憮 楙 母 繆 蕪 誣 鵡
묵 Muk	墨 默
문 Mun	門 問 聞 文 汶 炆 紋 們 刎 吻 紊 蚊 雯
물 Mul	勿 物 沕
미 Mi	米 未 味 美 尾 迷 微 眉 渼 薇 彌 弥 媄 媚 嵋 楣 楣 湄 謎 靡 黴 躾 嫩 瀰
민 Min	民 敏 憫 玟 旻 旼 閔 珉 瑉 岷 忞 慜 憫 敃 愍 潤 暋 頤 泯 悶 緡 鈱 磻
밀 Mil	密 蜜 謐

74

HanGul English	HanJa Used in Given Names
박 Bak	泊 拍 迫 朴 博 薄 珀 撲 璞 鉑 舶 剝 樸 箔 粕 縛 膊 雹 駁
반 Ban	反 飯 半 般 盤 班 返 叛 伴 畔 頒 潘 磐 拌 搬 攀 斑 槃 泮 瘢 盼 磻 礬 絆 蟠 㔠
발 Bal	發 拔 髮 潑 鉢 渤 勃 撥 跋 醱 魃
방 Bang	方 房 防 放 訪 芳 傍 妨 倣 邦 坊 彷 昉 龐 榜 尨 幫 旁 枋 滂 磅 紡 肪 膀 舫 蒡 蚌 謗
배 Bae	拜 杯 盂 倍 培 配 排 輩 背 陪 裵 裴 湃 俳 徘 焙 胚 褙 賠 北
백 Baek	白 百 伯 佰 帛 魄 栢 柏
번 Beon	番 煩 繁 飜 翻 蕃 幡 樊 燔 磻 藩
벌 Beol	伐 罰 閥 筏
범 Beom	凡 犯 範 帆 机 氾 范 梵 泛 汎 釩
법 Beop	法 琺
벽 Byeok	壁 碧 璧 闢 僻 劈 擘 襞 癖 蘗 霹

75

HanGul English	HanJa Used in Given Names
변 Byeon	變 辯 辨 邊 卞 弁 便 采
별 Byeol	別 瞥 驚 鱉 徶 莂
병 Byong	丙 病 兵 竝 並 屛 抃 并 倂 瓶 軿 餠 炳 柄 昞 昺 秉 棅 餅 騈
보 Bo	保 步 報 普 補 譜 寶 宝 堡 甫 輔 菩 潽 洑 湺 珤 褓 俌
복 Bok	福 伏 服 復 腹 複 卜 覆 馥 鍑 僕 匐 宓 茯 蔔 轐 輻 鰒
본 Bon	本
볼 Bol	乶
봉 Bong	奉 逢 峯 峰 蜂 封 鳳 俸 捧 琒 烽 棒 蓬 鋒 熢 縫 漨
부 Bu	夫 扶 父 富 部 婦 否 浮 付 符 附 府 腐 負 副 簿 赴 賦 孚 芙 傅 溥 敷 復 不 俯 剖 咐 埠 孵 斧 缶 腑 腒 訃 荂 賻 趺 釜 阜 駙 鳧 膚 膞
북 Buk	北

HanGul English	HanJa Used in Given Names
분 Bun	分 紛 粉 奔 墳 憤 奮 汾 芬 盆 吩 噴 忿 扮 盼 焚 糞 賁 雰
블 Bul	不 佛 拂 彿 弗
붕 Bung	朋 崩 鵬 棚 硼 繃
비 Bi	比 非 悲 飛 鼻 備 批 卑 婢 碑 妃 肥 祕 秘 費 庇 枇 琵 扉 譬 丕 匕 匪 憊 斐 榧 毖 毗 緄 沸 泌 痺 砒 秕 粃 緋 翡 脾 臂 菲 蜚 裨 誹 鄙 棐
빈 Bin	貧 賓 頻 彬 斌 濱 嬪 儐 璸 玭 嚬 檳 殯 浜 瀕 牝 邠 繽 份 豳 霦 贇 鑌
빙 Bing	氷 聘 憑 騁
사 Sa	四 巳 士 仕 寺 史 使 舍 射 謝 師 死 私 絲 思 事 司 詞 蛇 捨 邪 賜 斜 詐 社 沙 似 查 寫 辭 斯 祀 泗 砂 糸 紗 娑 徙 奢 嗣 赦 乍 些 伺 俟 傞 唆 柶 梭 渣 瀉 獅 祠 肆 莎 蓑 裟 飼 駟 麝 篩

77

HanGul English	HanJa Used in Given Names
삭 Sak	削 朔 數 索
산 San	山 産 散 算 珊 傘 刪 汕 疝 蒜 霰 酸
살 Sal	殺 薩 乷 撒 煞
삼 Sam	三 參 蔘 杉 衫 滲 芟 森
삽 Sap	挿 澁 鈒 颯
상 Sang	上 尚 常 賞 商 相 霜 想 傷 喪 嘗 裳 詳 祥 象 像 床 牀 桑 狀 償 庠 湘 箱 翔 爽 塽 孀 峠 廂 橡 觴
새 Sae	塞 璽 賽
색 Saek	色 索 嗇 穡 塞
생 Saeng	生 牲 甥 省 笙
서 Seo	西 序 書 署 紋 叙 徐 庶 恕 暑 緒 誓 逝 抒 舒 瑞 棲 栖 曙 壻 婿 惰 諝 墅 嶼 捿 犀 筮 絮 胥 薯 鋤 黍 鼠 嶼 揟 恕

HanGul English	HanJa Used in Given Names
석 Seok	石 夕 昔 惜 席 析 釋 碩 奭 汐 淅 晳 祏 鉐 錫 潟 蓆 舃
선 Seon	先 仙 線 鮮 善 船 選 宣 旋 禪 扇 渲 瑄 愃 膳 墡 繕 琁 璿 璇 羨 嬋 銑 珗 嫙 傓 敾 煽 癬 腺 蘇 詵 跣 鐥 饍 蟬 洒
설 Seol	雪 説 設 舌 卨 薛 楔 屑 泄 洩 渫 褻 齧 䚄 契
섬 Seom	纖 暹 蟾 剡 殲 贍 閃 陝
섭 Seop	涉 攝 燮 葉
성 Seong	姓 性 成 城 誠 盛 省 聖 聲 星 晟 珹 娀 瑆 惺 醒 宬 猩 筬 腥 胜
세 Sae	世 洗 税 細 勢 歲 貰 笹 説 洒
소 So	小 少 所 消 素 笑 召 昭 蘇 騷 燒 訴 掃 疏 疎 蔬 沼 炤 紹 邵 韶 巢 遡 招 玿 嘯 塑 宵 搔 梳 溯 蕭 甦 瘙 篠 簫 逍 銷 蕭 愫 穌 卲
속 Sok	俗 速 續 束 粟 屬 涑 謖 贖

HanGul English	HanJa Used in Given Names
손 Son	孫 捐 遜 巽 蓀 飡
솔 Sol	率 帥
송 Song	松 送 頌 訟 誦 宋 淞 悚
쇄 Swae	刷 鎖 殺 灑 碎
쇠 Swe	衰 釗
수 Su	水 手 受 授 首 守 收 誰 須 雖 愁 樹 壽 數 修 脩 秀 囚 需 帥 殊 隨 輸 獸 睡 遂 垂 搜 洙 琇 銖 粹 穗 穗 繡 隋 髓 袖 嗽 嫂 岫 峀 戍 燧 漱 狩 璲 瘦 竪 綏 綬 羞 茱 蒐 瘶 藪 讐 邃 酬 銹 隧 鬚 潍
숙 Suk	叔 淑 宿 孰 熟 肅 塾 琡 璹 橚 夙 潚 莍
순 Sun	順 純 旬 殉 循 脣 瞬 巡 洵 珣 荀 筍 舜 淳 錞 諄 醇 焞 徇 恂 栒 楯 橓 蕈 蕣 詢 馴 盾
술 Sul	戌 述 術 鉥

HanGul English	HanJa Used in Given Names
승 Sung	崇 嵩 崧
슬 Seul	瑟 膝 瑟 蝨
습 Seup	習 拾 濕 襲 褶
승 Seung	乘 承 勝 昇 僧 丞 陞 繩 蠅 升 丞 塍
시 Shi	市 示 是 時 詩 施 試 始 矢 侍 視 柴 恃 匙 嘶 媤 尸 屎 屍 弑 柿 猜 翅 蒔 蓍 諡 豕 豺 偲 毸 諰 媞
식 Shik	食 式 植 識 息 飾 栻 埴 殖 湜 軾 寔 拭 熄 篒 蝕
신 Shin	身 申 神 臣 信 辛 新 伸 晨 愼 紳 莘 薪 迅 訊 侁 呻 娠 宸 燼 腎 藎 蜃 辰 璶
실 Shil	失 室 實 実 悉
심 Shim	心 甚 深 尋 審 沁 沈 瀋 芯 諶
십 Ship	十 什 拾
쌍 Ssang	雙

HanGul English	HanJa Used in Given Names
씨 Sshi	氏
아 A	兒 児 我 牙 芽 雅 亞 亜 餓 娥 峨 岈 衙 妸 俄 啞 莪 蛾 訝 鴉 鵝 阿 婀 娿 哦
악 Ak	惡 岳 樂 堊 嶽 幄 愕 握 渥 鄂 鍔 顎 鰐 齷
안 An	安 案 顔 眼 岸 雁 鴈 晏 按 鞍 鮟
알 Al	謁 斡 軋 閼
암 Am	暗 巖 岩 庵 菴 唵 癌 闇
압 Ap	壓 押 鴨 狎
앙 Ang	仰 央 殃 昂 鴦 怏 秧
애 Ae	愛 哀 涯 厓 崖 艾 埃 曖 碍 隘 靄
액 Aek	厄 額 液 扼 掖 縊 腋
앵 Aeng	鶯 櫻 罌 鸚
야 Ya	也 夜 野 耶 冶 倻 惹 揶 椰 爺 若 埜

HanGul English	HanJa Used in Given Names
약 Yak	弱 若 約 藥 躍 葯 蒻
양 Yang	羊 洋 養 揚 陽 讓 壤 樣 楊 襄 孃 漾 佯 恙 攘 敭 暘 瀁 煬 痒 瘍 禳 穰 釀 易
어 Eo	魚 漁 於 語 御 圉 瘀 禦 馭 齬 唹
억 Eok	億 憶 抑 檍 臆
언 Eon	言 焉 諺 彦 偃 堰 嫣
얼 Eol	孼 糱
엄 Eom	嚴 奄 俺 掩 儼 淹
업 Eop	業 嶪
엔 Aen	丹
여 Yeo	余 餘 如 汝 與 予 輿 歟 璵 礜 艅 茹 轝 妤 念
역 Yeok	亦 易 逆 譯 驛 役 疫 域 晹 繹

HanGul English	HanJa Used in Given Names
연 Yeon	然 煙 烟 研 延 燃 燕 沿 鉛 宴 軟 演 緣 衍 淵 淵 妍 娟 涓 沇 筵 王 奭 娫 嚥 堧 捐 挻 椽 涎 繎 鳶 硯 矊 醼 兗 兖 嬿 莚 瓀
열 Yeol	熱 悦 閱 説 咽
염 Yeom	炎 染 鹽 琰 艷 厭 焰 苒 閻 髥
엽 Yeop	葉 燁 曄 熀
영 Yeong	永 英 迎 榮 栄 泳 詠 營 影 映 漢 煐 瑛 暎 瑩 瀅 盈 鍈 嬰 楹 穎 瓔 咏 塋 嶸 潁 濚 瀛 霙 纓 嬴
예 Yae	藝 豫 譽 鋭 叡 睿 預 芮 乂 倪 刈 曳 汭 濊 猊 穢 薬 裔 詣 霓 堄 埶 榮 玭 嫕 蓺
오 O	五 吾 悟 午 誤 烏 汚 嗚 娛 傲 伍 吳 旿 珸 晤 奧 俉 塢 墺 寤 惡 懊 敖 熬 獒 筽 蜈 鰲 鼇 澳 梧 浯 燠
옥 Ok	玉 屋 獄 沃 鈺
온 On	溫 瑥 媼 穩 穩 瘟 縕 蘊 昷

HanGul English	HanJa Used in Given Names
올 Ol	兀
옹 Ong	翁 擁 雍 甕 瓮 甕 癰 邕 饔
와 Wa	瓦 臥 渦 窩 窪 蛙 蝸 訛
완 Wan	完 緩 玩 垸 浣 莞 琓 琬 婠 婉 宛 梡 椀 碗 翫 脘 腕 豌 阮 頑 妧 岏 鋺
왈 Wal	曰
왕 Wang	王 往 旺 汪 枉
왜 Wae	倭 娃 歪 矮
외 Oy	外 畏 嵬 巍 猥
요 Yo	要 腰 搖 遙 謠 夭 堯 饒 曜 耀 瑤 樂 姚 僥 凹 妖 嶢 拗 擾 橈 燿 窈 窯 繇 繞 蟯 邀
욕 Yok	欲 浴 慾 辱 縟 褥

85

HanGul English	HanJa Used in Given Names									
용 Yong	用	勇	容	庸	溶	鎔	瑢	榕	蓉	湧	涌
	埇	踊	鏞	茸	墉	甬	俑	傭	冗	憑	熔
	聳	俗	槦								
우 U	于	宇	右	牛	友	雨	憂	又	尤	遇	羽
	郵	愚	偶	優	佑	祐	禹	瑀	寓	堣	隅
	玗	釪	迂	旴	盂	禑	紆	芋	藕	虞	雩
	扜	圩	慪	燠							
욱 Uk	旭	昱	煜	郁	項	彧	勖	栯	稢	燠	
운 Un	云	雲	運	韻	沄	澐	耘	暈	会	暈	櫄
	殞	煩	芸	蕓	隕	篔					
을 Ul	蔚	鬱	乥								
웅 Ung	雄	熊									
원 Won	元	原	願	遠	園	怨	圓	員	源	援	院
	袁	垣	洹	沅	瑗	媛	嫄	愿	苑	轅	婉
	寃	湲	爰	猿	阮	鴛	褑	朊	杬	鋺	
월 Wol	月	越	鉞								

HanGul English	HanJa Used in Given Names
위 Wi	位 危 爲 偉 威 胃 謂 圍 衛 違 委 慰 偉 緯 尉 韋 瑋 暐 渭 魏 姜 葦 蔿 蝟 褘
유 Yu	由 油 酉 有 猶 唯 遊 柔 遺 幼 幽 惟 維 乳 儒 裕 誘 愈 悠 侑 洧 宥 庾 喩 兪 俞 楡 瑜 猷 濡 釉 愉 柚 攸 鈾 孺 揄 楢 游 癒 臾 萸 諛 諭 踰 鍮 蹂 逾 曘 婑 囿 牖 逌
육 Yuk	肉 育 堉 毓
윤 Yun	閏 潤 尹 允 玧 鈗 胤 阭 贇 贇 昀 筠 贇
율 Yul	聿 燏 汩
융 Yung	融 戎 瀜 絨
은 Eun	恩 銀 隱 垠 殷 誾 激 珢 慇 濦 听 蘟 檼 隢
을 Eul	乙 圪
음 Eum	音 吟 飮 陰 淫 蔭 愔

87

HanGul English	HanJa Used in Given Names
읍 Eup	邑 泣 揖
응 Eung	應 凝 膺 鷹
의 We	衣 依 義 議 矣 醫 意 宜 儀 疑 倚 誼 毅 擬 懿 椅 艤 薏 蟻
이 I	二 以 已 耳 而 異 移 夷 珥 伊 易 弛 怡 彛 彝 爾 頤 姨 痍 肄 苡 羡 貽 迤 飴 貳 嬰 柂
익 Ik	益 翼 翊 瀷 謚 翌 熤
인 In	人 引 仁 因 忍 認 寅 印 姻 咽 湮 絪 茵 蚓 靷 靭 刃 橉 茛 汭 牣
일 Il	一 日 逸 溢 鎰 馹 佾 佚 壹
임 Im	壬 任 賃 妊 姙 稔 恁 荏
입 Ip	入 廿
잉 Ing	剩 仍 孕 芿
자 Ja	子 字 自 者 姉 姊 慈 玆 紫 資 姿 恣 刺 仔 滋 磁 藉 瓷 咨 孜 炙 煮 疵 茨 蔗 諮 雌 秄

HanGul English	HanJa Used in Given Names
작 Jak	作 昨 酌 爵 灼 勺 雀 鵲 勺 嚼 斫 炸 綽 焉
잔 Jan	殘 屛 棧 潺 盞
잠 Jam	潛 潜 暫 箴 岑 簪 蠶
잡 Jap	雜
장 Jang	章 場 將 將 將 壯 壯 丈 張 帳 莊 庄 裝 奬 墙 牆 葬 粧 掌 藏 臟 障 腸 匠 杖 奘 漳 樟 璋 暲 薔 蔣 仗 檣 欌 漿 狀 獐 臧 贓 醬
재 Jae	才 材 財 在 栽 再 哉 災 裁 載 宰 梓 縡 齋 溨 滓 齎
쟁 Jaeng	爭 錚 箏 諍
저 Jeo	著 貯 低 底 抵 苧 邸 楮 沮 佇 儲 咀 姐 杵 樗 渚 狙 猪 疽 箸 紵 菹 諸 詛 躇 這 雎 齟
적 Jeok	的 赤 適 敵 滴 摘 寂 籍 賊 跡 積 績 迪 勣 吊 嫡 狄 炙 翟 荻 謫 迹 鏑 笛 蹟

HanGul English	HanJa Used in Given Names									
전 Jeon	田	全	典	前	展	戰	電	錢	傳	專	轉
	殿	佺	栓	詮	銓	琠	甸	塡	奠	荃	雋
	顚	佃	剪	塼	廛	悛	甎	澱	煎	畑	癲
	筌	箋	箭	篆	纏	輾	鈿	鐫	顴	餞	
절 Jeol	節	絶	切	折	竊	晢	截	浙	癤		
점 Jeom	店	占	點	点	漸	岾	粘	霑	鮎		
접 Jeop	接	蝶	摺								
정 Jeong	丁	頂	停	井	正	政	定	貞	精	情	静
	靜	淨	庭	亭	訂	廷	程	征	整	汀	玎
	町	呈	桯	珵	姃	偵	湞	幀	楨	禎	斑
	挺	綎	鼎	晶	聂	柾	鉦	淀	錠	鋌	鄭
	靖	靚	鋥	炡	釘	淳	婷	逛	爭	頁	旌
	檉	瀞	晴	碇	穽	艇	諄	酊	霆	埕	姸
	梃	胜									
제 Jae	弟	第	祭	帝	題	除	諸	製	提	堤	制
	際	齊	濟	濟	悌	梯	瑅	劑	啼	臍	薺
	蹄	醍	霽	媞							

HanGul English	HanJa Used in Given Names
조 Jo	兆 早 造 鳥 調 朝 助 弔 燥 操 照 條 潮 租 組 祖 彫 措 晁 窕 祚 趙 肇 詔 釣 曹 遭 眺 俎 凋 嘲 曺 棗 槽 漕 爪 璪 稠 粗 糟 繰 藻 蚤 躁 阻 雕 昭
족 Jok	足 族 簇 鏃
존 Jon	存 尊
졸 Jol	卒 拙 猝
종 Jong	宗 種 鐘 終 從 縱 悰 琮 淙 棕 倧 綜 璁 鍾 慫 腫 踵 踪 柊 樅
좌 Jwa	左 坐 佐 座 挫
죄 Jwe	罪
주 Ju	主 注 住 朱 宙 走 酒 晝 舟 周 株 州 洲 柱 奏 珠 鑄 胄 湊 炷 註 疇 週 遒 駐 姝 澍 姝 侏 做 呪 嗾 廚 籌 紂 紬 綢 蛛 誅 躊 輳 酎 燽 鉒 拄

91

HanGul English	HanJa Used in Given Names
죽 Juk	竹 粥
준 Jun	準 俊 遵 峻 浚 晙 埈 焌 竣 睃 駿 准 濬 雋 儁 埻 隼 寯 樽 蠢 逡 葰 儁
즐 Jul	茁
중 Jung	中 重 衆 仲
즉 Jeuk	卽 即
즐 Jeul	櫛
즙 Jeup	汁 楫 茸
증 Jeung	曾 增 證 憎 贈 症 蒸 烝 甑 拯 繒
지 Ji	只 支 枝 止 之 知 地 指 志 至 紙 持 池 誌 智 遲 旨 沚 址 祉 趾 祗 芝 摯 誌 脂 咫 枳 漬 肢 砥 芷 蜘 識 贄 洔 底 泜
직 Jik	直 職 織 稙 稷

92

HanGul English	HanJa Used in Given Names
진 Jin	辰 眞 真 進 盡 振 鎭 陣 陳 珍 震 晉 晋 瑨 王 晉 瑱 津 璡 秦 軫 塵 禛 診 縝 塡 賑 溱 抮 脣 嗔 搢 桭 榛 殄 疹 昣 瞋 縉 臻 蔯 袗 鉁 蓁 枃
질 Jil	質 秩 疾 姪 瓆 侄 叱 嫉 帙 桎 室 膣 蛭 跌 迭
집 Jip	集 執 什 潗 輯 楫 鏶 緝
징 Jing	徵 懲 澄
차 Cha	且 次 此 借 差 車 叉 瑳 侘 嗟 嵯 磋 箚 茶 蹉 遮 硨 韏 姹
착 Chak	着 錯 捉 搾 窄 鑿 齪
찬 Chan	贊 贄 讚 讃 撰 纂 粲 澯 燦 璨 瓚 纘 鑽 竄 篡 餐 饌 攢 巑 儹 儧
찰 Chal	察 札 刹 擦 紮
참 Cham	參 慘 塹 慚 僭 塹 懺 斬 站 讒 讖
창 Chang	昌 唱 窓 倉 創 蒼 暢 菖 昶 彰 敞 廠 倡 娼 漲 猖 愴 瘡 脹 艙 槍 滄

93

HanGul English	HanJa Used in Given Names
채 Chae	菜 採 彩 債 采 埰 寀 蔡 綵 寨 砦 釵 責 棌 婇 睬
책 Chaek	責 冊 策 栅
처 Chae	妻 處 凄 悽
척 Chaek	尺 斥 拓 戚 陟 坧 個 刺 剔 慽 擲 滌 瘠 脊 蹠 隻
천 Chaen	天 千 川 泉 淺 賤 踐 遷 薦 仟 阡 喘 擅 玔 穿 舛 釧 闡 韆 茜
철 Chael	鐵 哲 徹 喆 澈 轍 撤 綴 凸 輟 悊
첨 Chaem	尖 添 僉 瞻 沾 甛 簽 籤 詹 諂
첩 Chaep	妾 帖 捷 堞 牒 疊 睫 諜 貼 輒
청 Chaeng	青 靑 淸 清 晴 晴 請 請 廳 聽 菁 鯖
체 Chae	體 替 遞 滯 逮 締 諦 切 剃 涕 諟
초 Cho	初 草 艸 招 肖 超 抄 礎 秒 樵 焦 蕉 楚 剿 哨 憔 梢 椒 炒 硝 礁 稍 苕 貂 酢 醋 醮 岧

HanGul English	HanJa Used in Given Names
촉 Chok	促 燭 觸 囑 矗 蜀
촌 Chon	寸 村 忖 邨
총 Chong	銃 總 聰 聡 寵 叢 塚 恩 憁 摠 蔥
촬 Chwal	撮
최 Choy	最 催 崔
추 Chu	秋 追 推 抽 醜 楸 樞 鄒 錐 墜 椎 湫 皺 芻 萩 諏 趨 酋 鎚 雛 驅 鰍
축 Chuk	丑 祝 蓄 畜 築 逐 縮 軸 竺 筑 蹙 蹴
춘 Chun	春 椿 瑃 賰
출 Chul	出 朮 黜
충 Chung	充 忠 蟲 虫 衝 珫 沖 冲 衷
췌 Chwae	萃 悴 膵 贅
취 Chuy	取 吹 就 臭 醉 趣 翠 聚 嘴 娶 炊 脆 驟 鷲

HanGul English	HanJa Used in Given Names
측 Cheuk	側 測 仄 厠 惻
층 Cheung	層
치 Chi	治 致 齒 値 置 恥 熾 峙 雉 馳 侈 嗤 幟 梔 淄 痔 痴 癡 稺 緇 緻 蚩 輜 稚
칙 Chik	則 勅 飭
친 Chin	親
칠 Chil	七 漆 柒
침 Chim	針 侵 浸 寢 沈 枕 琛 砧 鍼 梣
칩 Chip	蟄
칭 Ching	稱 秤
쾌 Kwae	快 夬
타 Ta	他 打 妥 墮 咤 唾 惰 拖 朶 楕 舵 陀 馱 駝
탁 Tak	濁 托 濯 卓 度 倬 琸 晫 託 擢 鐸 拓 啄 坼 柝 琢

HanGul English	HanJa Used in Given Names
탄 Tan	炭 歎 彈 誕 吞 坦 灘 嘆 憚 綻
탈 Tal	脫 奪
탐 Tam	探 貪 耽 眈
탑 Tap	塔 榻
탕 Tang	湯 宕 帑 糖 蕩
태 Tae	太 泰 怠 殆 態 汰 兌 台 胎 邰 苔 苔 跆 颱 鈦
택 Taek	宅 澤 擇 垞
탱 Taeng	撑
터 Teo	攄
토 To	土 吐 討 兎
통 Tong	通 統 痛 桶 慟 洞 筒
퇴 Toy	退 堆 槌 腿 褪 頹
투 Tu	投 透 鬪 偸 套 妬

HanGul English	HanJa Used in Given Names
특 Teuk	特 慝
틈 Teum	闖
파 Pa	破 波 派 播 罷 頗 把 巴 芭 琶 坡 杷 婆 擺 爬 跛
판 Pan	判 板 販 版 阪 坂 辦 瓣 鈑
팔 Pal	八 叭 捌
패 Pae	貝 敗 霸 浿 佩 牌 唄 悖 沛 狽 稗
팽 Paeng	彭 澎 烹 膨
퍅 Pyak	愎
편 Pyeon	片 便 篇 編 遍 偏 扁 翩 鞭 騙
펀 Pyeon	貶
평 Pyeong	平 評 坪 枰 泙 萍
폐 Pyae	閉 肺 廢 弊 蔽 幣 陛 吠 嬖 斃

HanGul English	HanJa Used in Given Names
포 Po	布 抱 包 胞 飽 浦 捕 葡 褒 砲 鋪 佈 匍 匏 咆 哺 圃 怖 抛 暴 泡 疱 脯 苞 蒲 袍 逋 鮑
폭 Pok	暴 爆 幅 曝 瀑 輻
표 Pyo	表 票 標 漂 杓 豹 彪 驃 俵 剽 慓 瓢 颷 飄
픔 Pum	品 稟
풍 Pung	風 豐 豊 諷 馮 楓
피 Pi	皮 彼 疲 被 避 披 陂
필 Pil	必 匹 筆 畢 弼 泌 珌 苾 秘 鉍 佖 疋
핍 Pip	乏 逼
하 Ha	下 夏 賀 何 河 荷 廈 廈 昰 霞 瑕 蝦 遐 鰕 呀 碬 碬
학 Hak	學 学 鶴 慤 虐 謔 嗃
한 Han	閑 寒 恨 限 韓 漢 旱 汗 澣 瀚 翰 閒 悍 罕 澖

HanGul English	HanJa Used in Given Names
할 Hal	割 轄
함 Ham	咸 含 陷 函 涵 艦 喴 喊 檻 緘 街 鹹
합 Hap	合 哈 盒 蛤 閤 闔 陜
항 Hang	恒 巷 港 項 抗 航 亢 沆 姮 伉 嫦 杭 桁 缸 肛 行 降
해 Hae	害 海 海 亥 解 奚 該 偕 楷 諧 咳 垓 孩 懈 瀣 蟹 邂 駭 骸 哈
핵 Haek	核 劾
행 Haeng	行 幸 杏 倖 荇 涬
향 Hyang	向 香 鄉 響 享 珦 嚮 餉 饗 麘
허 Heo	虛 許 墟 噓
헌 Heon	軒 憲 獻 櫶
헐 Heol	歇
험 Heom	險 驗

HanGul English	HanJa Used in Given Names
혁 Hyeok	革 赫 爀 奕 侐 烼
현 Hyeon	現 賢 玄 絃 縣 懸 顯 見 峴 晛 炫 炫 玹 鉉 眩 眩 絢 呟 俔 睍 舷 衒 弦 儇 譞 儇
혈 Hyeol	血 穴 孑 頁
혐 Hyeom	嫌
협 Hyeop	協 脅 俠 挾 峽 浹 夾 狹 脇 莢 鋏 頰 冾
형 Hyeong	兄 刑 形 亨 螢 衡 型 邢 珩 泂 炯 瑩 瀅 馨 熒 滎 瀅 荊 逈 鎣
혜 Hyae	惠 恵 慧 兮 蕙 彗 譓 憓 暳 蹊 醯 鞋 譓 鏸
호 Ho	戶 乎 呼 好 虎 號 湖 互 胡 浩 毫 豪 護 晧 皓 澔 昊 淏 濠 灝 祜 琥 瑚 頀 扈 鎬 壕 壺 顥 濩 滸 岵 弧 狐 瓠 糊 縞 芦 葫 蒿 蝴 皜
혹 Hok	或 惑 酷

101

HanGul English	HanJa Used in Given Names
혼 Hon	婚 混 昏 魂 渾 琿
홀 Hol	忽 惚 笏
홍 Hong	紅 洪 弘 鴻 泓 烘 虹 鉷 哄 汞 訌
화 Hwa	火 化 花 貨 和 話 畵 畫 華 禾 禍 嬅 樺 譁 靴
확 Hwak	確 碻 穫 擴 廓 攫
환 Hwan	歡 患 丸 換 環 還 喚 奐 渙 煥 晥 幻 桓 鐶 驩 宦 紈 鰥
활 Hwal	活 闊 濶 滑 猾 豁
황 Hwang	黃 皇 況 荒 凰 堭 煌 晃 滉 榥 煌 璜 熀 幌 徨 恍 惶 愰 慌 湟 潢 晄 篁 簧 蝗 遑 隍
회 Hwe	回 會 悔 懷 廻 恢 晦 檜 澮 繪 絵 誨 匯 徊 淮 獪 膾 茴 蛔 賄 灰
획 Hwek	獲 劃
횡 Hweng	橫 鐄 宖

HanGul English	HanJa Used in Given Names
효 Hyo	孝 效 劾 曉 涍 爻 驍 斅 哮 嚆 梟 淆 肴 酵 晶 歆 寉
후 Hu	後 厚 侯 候 后 垕 逅 吼 嗅 帿 朽 煦 珝 喉
훈 Hun	訓 勳 勛 勲 焄 熏 薫 薰 壎 燻 塤 鑂 暈
흥 Hung	薨
홰 Hwae	毀 卉 喙
훤 Hwon	喧 暄 萱 煊
휘 Hwe	揮 輝 彙 徽 暉 煇 諱 麾
휴 Hyu	休 携 烋 畦 虧
휼 Hyul	恤 譎 鷸
흉 Hyung	凶 胸 兇 匈 洶
흑 Heuk	黑
흔 Heun	欣 炘 昕 痕 忻

103

HanGul English	HanJa Used in Given Names
흘 Heul	屹 吃 紇 訖
흠 Heum	欽 欠 歆
흡 Heup	吸 洽 恰 翕
흥 Heung	興
희 Heuy	希 喜 稀 戲 姬 晞 僖 熺 禧 檀 嬉 憙 熹 義 爔 曦 熙 俙 憘 犧 噫 熙 烯 嘻 熙
힐 Hil	詰

3 - Numbers and Dates

There are several modern and traditional ways to write numbers and dates in Korea. Each method is introduced here, including the traditional methods found in Korean genealogical records.

Pure Korean Numbers

Pure Korean numbers do not have HanJa representations. They are generally not used in genealogies.

Table 3.1 Pure Korean Numbers

HanGul	Pronunciation	Number
하나	HaNa	1
둘	Dul	2
셋	Saet	3
넷	Naet	4
다섯	DaSeot	5
여섯	YeoSeot	6
일곱	IlGop	7
여덟	YeoDeolp	8
아홉	AHop	9
열	Yeol	10
스물	SeuMul	20
서른	SeoReun	30
마흔	MaHeun	40
쉰	Swin	50
예순	YaeSun	60
일흔	IlHeun	70
여든	YeoDeun	80
아흔	AHeun	90

HanJa Numbers

HanJa numbers are used in genealogies to represent dates, page numbers, number of sons and daughters, and generations.

Table 3.2 HanJa Numbers

HanJa	HanGul	Pronunciation	Number
零 or ○	영 or 공	Yeong or Gong	0
一	일	Eel	1
二	이	Ee	2
三	삼	Sam	3
四	사	Sa	4
五	오	Oh	5
六	육	Yuk	6
七	칠	Chil	7
八	팔	Pal	8
九	구	Gu	9
十	십	Ship	10
百	백	Baek	100
千	천	Cheon	1,000
萬	만	Man	10,000

Here are some examples of how these HanJa characters can be used to represent numbers:

Table 3.3 Examples of HanJa Numbers

HanJa	Literal Translation	Number
十	10	10
十六	10 + 6	16
二十	2 10's	20
二十六	(2 10's) + 6	26
百	100	100
百二十六	100 + (2 10's) + 6	126
二百	2 100's	200
二百二十六	(2 100's) + (2 10's) + 6	226

Dates

In Korea dates are generally written in year-month-day order. This is true in both traditional and modern writings. Here are some important HanJa characters that are placed after HanJa numbers to specify the year, month, and day:

Table 3.4 HanJa Vocabulary for Dates

HanJa	HanGul	Pronunciation	Meaning
年	년	Nyeon	Year
月	월	Weol	Month *(Represented by the HanJa character for the moon)*
日	일	Eel	Day *(Represented by the HanJa character for the sun)*

The following is an example of a date written in HanJa characters, as you would typically find in genealogy records. Note however, that the example below is left-to-right (western or modern Korean style), but it would be formatted as top-to-bottom columns that are organized right-to-left across the page in a traditional genealogical record.

Table 3.5 Example HanJa Date

HanJa HanGul Literal Translation of HanJa Characters Meaning
一九八五 年 十一 月 二十四 日
1985 년 11 월 24 일
1985 year, 10 + 1 month, 2 10s + 4 day
1985th year, 11th month, 24th day

Lunar Calendar Years

Family genealogies often precede dates with the lunar calendar year. In some cases, only the lunar calendar year is given.

Lunar calendar (음력, EumNyeok) years are represented by two HanJa characters. The first HanJa character comes from a heavenly cycle of 10 characters. The second HanJa character comes from an earthly cycle of 12 characters. Together, these two characters form a 60-year cycle of lunar calendar years. Every sixty years the cycle repeats.

Within the heavenly cycle there are five elements and another cycle of opposites. The opposites Eum and Yang are represented in the Korean flag as the blue and red TaeGuk, meaning great extremes. The blue stands for Eum, which is negative, dark, and cold. The red stands for Yang, which is positive, bright, and hot. The philosophy behind this symbol is that the opposites are in balance and harmony. In the following table, Yang is represented as positive (+) and Eum is represented as negative (-).

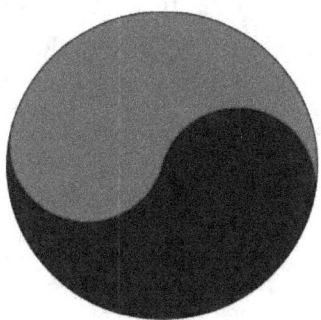

Table 3.6 Heavenly Cycle (1st HanJa Character in Lunar Year)

Heavenly Cycle	HanJa	HanGul	Pronunciation	Meaning
1	甲	갑	Gap	Wood (+)
2	乙	을	Eul	Wood (-)
3	丙	병	Byeong	Fire (+)
4	丁	정	Jeong	Fire (-)
5	戊	무	Mu	Earth (+)
6	己	기	Gi	Earth (-)
7	庚	경	Gyeong	Metal (+)
8	辛	신	Shin	Metal (-)
9	壬	임	Im	Water (+)
10	癸	계	Gyae	Water (-)

The Earthly cycle of 12 characters is similar to the Chinese zodiac. The zodiac uses 12 Chinese characters for animals that represent the 12-year cycle. The Chinese character representing these animals is shown in parentheses in the following Earthly Cycle table. Some traditions consider the characteristics of the zodiac animals for birth years when matchmaking in an attempt to create compatible matches for arranged marriages.

Table 3.7 Earthly Cycle (2ⁿᵈ HanJa Character in Lunar Year)

Earthly Cycle	HanJa	HanGul	Pronunciation	Chinese Zodiac
1	子	자	Ja	Rat (鼠)
2	丑	축	Chuk	Ox (牛)
3	寅	인	In	Tiger (虎)
4	卯	묘	Myo	Rabbit (兔)
5	辰	진	Jin	Dragon (龍)
6	巳	사	Sa	Snake (蛇)
7	午	오	Oh	Horse (馬)
8	未	미	Mi	Goat (羊)
9	申	신	Shin	Monkey (猴)
10	酉	유	Yu	Rooster (雞)
11	戌	수	Su	Dog (狗)
12	亥	해	Hae	Pig (豬)

The following table is very useful for translating years from Korean genealogy records. It shows sample years that are represented by each of the 60 combinations of heavenly and earthly cycles. To identify years earlier than shown in the following table, subtract multiples of 60 years. To go farther into the future than shown in the following table, add multiples of 60 years. Note that the first HanJa character cycles every 10 years (heavenly cycle) and the second cycles every 12 years (earthly cycle) to form every combination of the two preceding tables.

Note that the years listed in the following table are "approximate" due to the fact that a lunar year does not completely align with a western calendar solar year. Lunar years generally don't start or end on precisely the same day as solar years, although the majority of the days in a given lunar and solar year do overlap. Even today, many Koreans use traditional lunar calendars to celebrate Lunar New Year and lunar versions of birthdays.

Table 3.8 Lunar Calendar 60-Year Cycle

Lunar Year Cycle	Heavenly Cycle	Earthly Cycle	Lunar Year HanJa	Approximate Western Calendar Years (A.D.)
1	1	1	甲子	4, 64, 124, 184, 244, 304, 364, 424, 484, 544, 604, 664, 724, 784, 844, 904, 964, 1024, 1084, 1144, 1204, 1264, 1324, 1384, 1444, 1504, 1564, 1624, 1684, 1744, 1804, 1864, 1924, 1984
2	2	2	乙丑	5, 65, 125, 185, 245, 305, 365, 425, 485, 545, 605, 665, 725, 785, 845, 905, 965, 1025, 1085, 1145, 1205, 1265, 1325, 1385, 1445, 1505, 1565, 1625, 1685, 1745, 1805, 1865, 1925, 1985
3	3	3	丙寅	6, 66, 126, 186, 246, 306, 366, 426, 486, 546, 606, 666, 726, 786, 846, 906, 966, 1026, 1086, 1146, 1206, 1266, 1326, 1386, 1446, 1506, 1566, 1626, 1686, 1746, 1806, 1866, 1926, 1986
4	4	4	丁卯	7, 67, 127, 187, 247, 307, 367, 427, 487, 547, 607, 667, 727, 787, 847, 907, 967, 1027, 1087, 1147, 1207, 1267, 1327, 1387, 1447, 1507, 1567, 1627, 1687, 1747, 1807, 1867, 1927, 1987
5	5	5	戊辰	8, 68, 128, 188, 248, 308, 368, 428, 488, 548, 608, 668, 728, 788, 848, 908, 968, 1028, 1088, 1148, 1208, 1268, 1328, 1388, 1448, 1508, 1568, 1628, 1688, 1748, 1808, 1868, 1928, 1988
6	6	6	己巳	9, 69, 129, 189, 249, 309, 369, 429, 489, 549, 609, 669, 729, 789, 849, 909, 969, 1029, 1089, 1149, 1209, 1269, 1329, 1389, 1449, 1509, 1569, 1629, 1689, 1749, 1809, 1869, 1929, 1989
7	7	7	庚午	10, 70, 130, 190, 250, 310, 370, 430, 490, 550, 610, 670, 730, 790, 850, 910, 970, 1030, 1090, 1150, 1210, 1270, 1330, 1390, 1450, 1510, 1570, 1630, 1690, 1750, 1810, 1870, 1930, 1990
8	8	8	辛未	11, 71, 131, 191, 251, 311, 371, 431, 491, 551, 611, 671, 731, 791, 851, 911, 971, 1031, 1091, 1151, 1211, 1271, 1331, 1391, 1451, 1511, 1571, 1631, 1691, 1751, 1811, 1871, 1931, 1991

Lunar Year Cycle	Heavenly Cycle	Earthly Cycle	Lunar Year HanJa	Approximate Western Calendar Years (A.D.)
9	9	9	壬申	12, 72, 132, 192, 252, 312, 372, 432, 492, 552, 612, 672, 732, 792, 852, 912, 972, 1032, 1092, 1152, 1212, 1272, 1332, 1392, 1452, 1512, 1572, 1632, 1692, 1752, 1812, 1872, 1932, 1992
10	10	10	癸酉	13, 73, 133, 193, 253, 313, 373, 433, 493, 553, 613, 673, 733, 793, 853, 913, 973, 1033, 1093, 1153, 1213, 1273, 1333, 1393, 1453, 1513, 1573, 1633, 1693, 1753, 1813, 1873, 1933, 1993
11	1	11	甲戌	14, 74, 134, 194, 254, 314, 374, 434, 494, 554, 614, 674, 734, 794, 854, 914, 974, 1034, 1094, 1154, 1214, 1274, 1334, 1394, 1454, 1514, 1574, 1634, 1694, 1754, 1814, 1874, 1934, 1994
12	2	12	乙亥	15, 75, 135, 195, 255, 315, 375, 435, 495, 555, 615, 675, 735, 795, 855, 915, 975, 1035, 1095, 1155, 1215, 1275, 1335, 1395, 1455, 1515, 1575, 1635, 1695, 1755, 1815, 1875, 1935, 1995
13	3	1	丙子	16, 76, 136, 196, 256, 316, 376, 436, 496, 556, 616, 676, 736, 796, 856, 916, 976, 1036, 1096, 1156, 1216, 1276, 1336, 1396, 1456, 1516, 1576, 1636, 1696, 1756, 1816, 1876, 1936, 1996
14	4	2	丁丑	17, 77, 137, 197, 257, 317, 377, 437, 497, 557, 617, 677, 737, 797, 857, 917, 977, 1037, 1097, 1157, 1217, 1277, 1337, 1397, 1457, 1517, 1577, 1637, 1697, 1757, 1817, 1877, 1937, 1997
15	5	3	戊寅	18, 78, 138, 198, 258, 318, 378, 438, 498, 558, 618, 678, 738, 798, 858, 918, 978, 1038, 1098, 1158, 1218, 1278, 1338, 1398, 1458, 1518, 1578, 1638, 1698, 1758, 1818, 1878, 1938, 1998
16	6	4	己卯	19, 79, 139, 199, 259, 319, 379, 439, 499, 559, 619, 679, 739, 799, 859, 919, 979, 1039, 1099, 1159, 1219, 1279, 1339, 1399, 1459, 1519, 1579, 1639, 1699, 1759, 1819, 1879, 1939, 1999

Lunar Year Cycle	Heavenly Cycle	Earthly Cycle	Lunar Year HanJa	Approximate Western Calendar Years (A.D.)
17	7	5	庚辰	20, 80, 140, 200, 260, 320, 380, 440, 500, 560, 620, 680, 740, 800, 860, 920, 980, 1040, 1100, 1160, 1220, 1280, 1340, 1400, 1460, 1520, 1580, 1640, 1700, 1760, 1820, 1880, 1940, 2000
18	8	6	辛巳	21, 81, 141, 201, 261, 321, 381, 441, 501, 561, 621, 681, 741, 801, 861, 921, 981, 1041, 1101, 1161, 1221, 1281, 1341, 1401, 1461, 1521, 1581, 1641, 1701, 1761, 1821, 1881, 1941, 2001
19	9	7	壬午	22, 82, 142, 202, 262, 322, 382, 442, 502, 562, 622, 682, 742, 802, 862, 922, 982, 1042, 1102, 1162, 1222, 1282, 1342, 1402, 1462, 1522, 1582, 1642, 1702, 1762, 1822, 1882, 1942, 2002
20	10	8	癸未	23, 83, 143, 203, 263, 323, 383, 443, 503, 563, 623, 683, 743, 803, 863, 923, 983, 1043, 1103, 1163, 1223, 1283, 1343, 1403, 1463, 1523, 1583, 1643, 1703, 1763, 1823, 1883, 1943, 2003
21	1	9	甲申	24, 84, 144, 204, 264, 324, 384, 444, 504, 564, 624, 684, 744, 804, 864, 924, 984, 1044, 1104, 1164, 1224, 1284, 1344, 1404, 1464, 1524, 1584, 1644, 1704, 1764, 1824, 1884, 1944, 2004
22	2	10	乙酉	25, 85, 145, 205, 265, 325, 385, 445, 505, 565, 625, 685, 745, 805, 865, 925, 985, 1045, 1105, 1165, 1225, 1285, 1345, 1405, 1465, 1525, 1585, 1645, 1705, 1765, 1825, 1885, 1945, 2005
23	3	11	丙戌	26, 86, 146, 206, 266, 326, 386, 446, 506, 566, 626, 686, 746, 806, 866, 926, 986, 1046, 1106, 1166, 1226, 1286, 1346, 1406, 1466, 1526, 1586, 1646, 1706, 1766, 1826, 1886, 1946, 2006
24	4	12	丁亥	27, 87, 147, 207, 267, 327, 387, 447, 507, 567, 627, 687, 747, 807, 867, 927, 987, 1047, 1107, 1167, 1227, 1287, 1347, 1407, 1467, 1527, 1587, 1647, 1707, 1767, 1827, 1887, 1947, 2007

Lunar Year Cycle	Heavenly Cycle	Earthly Cycle	Lunar Year HanJa	Approximate Western Calendar Years (A.D.)
25	5	1	戊子	28, 88, 148, 208, 268, 328, 388, 448, 508, 568, 628, 688, 748, 808, 868, 928, 988, 1048, 1108, 1168, 1228, 1288, 1348, 1408, 1468, 1528, 1588, 1648, 1708, 1768, 1828, 1888, 1948, 2008
26	6	2	己丑	29, 89, 149, 209, 269, 329, 389, 449, 509, 569, 629, 689, 749, 809, 869, 929, 989, 1049, 1109, 1169, 1229, 1289, 1349, 1409, 1469, 1529, 1589, 1649, 1709, 1769, 1829, 1889, 1949, 2009
27	7	3	庚寅	30, 90, 150, 210, 270, 330, 390, 450, 510, 570, 630, 690, 750, 810, 870, 930, 990, 1050, 1110, 1170, 1230, 1290, 1350, 1410, 1470, 1530, 1590, 1650, 1710, 1770, 1830, 1890, 1950, 2010
28	8	4	辛卯	31, 91, 151, 211, 271, 331, 391, 451, 511, 571, 631, 691, 751, 811, 871, 931, 991, 1051, 1111, 1171, 1231, 1291, 1351, 1411, 1471, 1531, 1591, 1651, 1711, 1771, 1831, 1891, 1951, 2011
29	9	5	壬辰	32, 92, 152, 212, 272, 332, 392, 452, 512, 572, 632, 692, 752, 812, 872, 932, 992, 1052, 1112, 1172, 1232, 1292, 1352, 1412, 1472, 1532, 1592, 1652, 1712, 1772, 1832, 1892, 1952, 2012
30	10	6	癸巳	33, 93, 153, 213, 273, 333, 393, 453, 513, 573, 633, 693, 753, 813, 873, 933, 993, 1053, 1113, 1173, 1233, 1293, 1353, 1413, 1473, 1533, 1593, 1653, 1713, 1773, 1833, 1893, 1953, 2013
31	1	7	甲午	34, 94, 154, 214, 274, 334, 394, 454, 514, 574, 634, 694, 754, 814, 874, 934, 994, 1054, 1114, 1174, 1234, 1294, 1354, 1414, 1474, 1534, 1594, 1654, 1714, 1774, 1834, 1894, 1954, 2014
32	2	8	乙未	35, 95, 155, 215, 275, 335, 395, 455, 515, 575, 635, 695, 755, 815, 875, 935, 995, 1055, 1115, 1175, 1235, 1295, 1355, 1415, 1475, 1535, 1595, 1655, 1715, 1775, 1835, 1895, 1955, 2015

Lunar Year Cycle	Heavenly Cycle	Earthly Cycle	Lunar Year HanJa	Approximate Western Calendar Years (A.D.)
33	3	9	丙申	36, 96, 156, 216, 276, 336, 396, 456, 516, 576, 636, 696, 756, 816, 876, 936, 996, 1056, 1116, 1176, 1236, 1296, 1356, 1416, 1476, 1536, 1596, 1656, 1716, 1776, 1836, 1896, 1956, 2016
34	4	10	丁酉	37, 97, 157, 217, 277, 337, 397, 457, 517, 577, 637, 697, 757, 817, 877, 937, 997, 1057, 1117, 1177, 1237, 1297, 1357, 1417, 1477, 1537, 1597, 1657, 1717, 1777, 1837, 1897, 1957, 2017
35	5	11	戊戌	38, 98, 158, 218, 278, 338, 398, 458, 518, 578, 638, 698, 758, 818, 878, 938, 998, 1058, 1118, 1178, 1238, 1298, 1358, 1418, 1478, 1538, 1598, 1658, 1718, 1778, 1838, 1898, 1958, 2018
36	6	12	己亥	39, 99, 159, 219, 279, 339, 399, 459, 519, 579, 639, 699, 759, 819, 879, 939, 999, 1059, 1119, 1179, 1239, 1299, 1359, 1419, 1479, 1539, 1599, 1659, 1719, 1779, 1839, 1899, 1959, 2019
37	7	1	庚子	40, 100, 160, 220, 280, 340, 400, 460, 520, 580, 640, 700, 760, 820, 880, 940, 1000, 1060, 1120, 1180, 1240, 1300, 1360, 1420, 1480, 1540, 1600, 1660, 1720, 1780, 1840, 1900, 1960, 2020
38	8	2	辛丑	41, 101, 161, 221, 281, 341, 401, 461, 521, 581, 641, 701, 761, 821, 881, 941, 1001, 1061, 1121, 1181, 1241, 1301, 1361, 1421, 1481, 1541, 1601, 1661, 1721, 1781, 1841, 1901, 1961, 2021
39	9	3	壬寅	42, 102, 162, 222, 282, 342, 402, 462, 522, 582, 642, 702, 762, 822, 882, 942, 1002, 1062, 1122, 1182, 1242, 1302, 1362, 1422, 1482, 1542, 1602, 1662, 1722, 1782, 1842, 1902, 1962, 2022
40	10	4	癸卯	43, 103, 163, 223, 283, 343, 403, 463, 523, 583, 643, 703, 763, 823, 883, 943, 1003, 1063, 1123, 1183, 1243, 1303, 1363, 1423, 1483, 1543, 1603, 1663, 1723, 1783, 1843, 1903, 1963, 2023

Lunar Year Cycle	Heavenly Cycle	Earthly Cycle	Lunar Year HanJa	Approximate Western Calendar Years (A.D.)
41	1	5	甲辰	44, 104, 164, 224, 284, 344, 404, 464, 524, 584, 644, 704, 764, 824, 884, 944, 1004, 1064, 1124, 1184, 1244, 1304, 1364, 1424, 1484, 1544, 1604, 1664, 1724, 1784, 1844, 1904, 1964, 2024
42	2	6	乙巳	45, 105, 165, 225, 285, 345, 405, 465, 525, 585, 645, 705, 765, 825, 885, 945, 1005, 1065, 1125, 1185, 1245, 1305, 1365, 1425, 1485, 1545, 1605, 1665, 1725, 1785, 1845, 1905, 1965, 2025
43	3	7	丙午	46, 106, 166, 226, 286, 346, 406, 466, 526, 586, 646, 706, 766, 826, 886, 946, 1006, 1066, 1126, 1186, 1246, 1306, 1366, 1426, 1486, 1546, 1606, 1666, 1726, 1786, 1846, 1906, 1966, 2026
44	4	8	丁未	47, 107, 167, 227, 287, 347, 407, 467, 527, 587, 647, 707, 767, 827, 887, 947, 1007, 1067, 1127, 1187, 1247, 1307, 1367, 1427, 1487, 1547, 1607, 1667, 1727, 1787, 1847, 1907, 1967, 2027
45	5	9	戊申	48, 108, 168, 228, 288, 348, 408, 468, 528, 588, 648, 708, 768, 828, 888, 948, 1008, 1068, 1128, 1188, 1248, 1308, 1368, 1428, 1488, 1548, 1608, 1668, 1728, 1788, 1848, 1908, 1968, 2028
46	6	10	己酉	49, 109, 169, 229, 289, 349, 409, 469, 529, 589, 649, 709, 769, 829, 889, 949, 1009, 1069, 1129, 1189, 1249, 1309, 1369, 1429, 1489, 1549, 1609, 1669, 1729, 1789, 1849, 1909, 1969, 2029
47	7	11	庚戌	50, 110, 170, 230, 290, 350, 410, 470, 530, 590, 650, 710, 770, 830, 890, 950, 1010, 1070, 1130, 1190, 1250, 1310, 1370, 1430, 1490, 1550, 1610, 1670, 1730, 1790, 1850, 1910, 1970, 2030
48	8	12	辛亥	51, 111, 171, 231, 291, 351, 411, 471, 531, 591, 651, 711, 771, 831, 891, 951, 1011, 1071, 1131, 1191, 1251, 1311, 1371, 1431, 1491, 1551, 1611, 1671, 1731, 1791, 1851, 1911, 1971, 2031

Lunar Year Cycle	Heavenly Cycle	Earthly Cycle	Lunar Year HanJa	Approximate Western Calendar Years (A.D.)
49	9	1	壬子	52, 112, 172, 232, 292, 352, 412, 472, 532, 592, 652, 712, 772, 832, 892, 952, 1012, 1072, 1132, 1192, 1252, 1312, 1372, 1432, 1492, 1552, 1612, 1672, 1732, 1792, 1852, 1912, 1972, 2032
50	10	2	癸丑	53, 113, 173, 233, 293, 353, 413, 473, 533, 593, 653, 713, 773, 833, 893, 953, 1013, 1073, 1133, 1193, 1253, 1313, 1373, 1433, 1493, 1553, 1613, 1673, 1733, 1793, 1853, 1913, 1973, 2033
51	1	3	甲寅	54, 114, 174, 234, 294, 354, 414, 474, 534, 594, 654, 714, 774, 834, 894, 954, 1014, 1074, 1134, 1194, 1254, 1314, 1374, 1434, 1494, 1554, 1614, 1674, 1734, 1794, 1854, 1914, 1974, 2034
52	2	4	乙卯	55, 115, 175, 235, 295, 355, 415, 475, 535, 595, 655, 715, 775, 835, 895, 955, 1015, 1075, 1135, 1195, 1255, 1315, 1375, 1435, 1495, 1555, 1615, 1675, 1735, 1795, 1855, 1915, 1975, 2035
53	3	5	丙辰	56, 116, 176, 236, 296, 356, 416, 476, 536, 596, 656, 716, 776, 836, 896, 956, 1016, 1076, 1136, 1196, 1256, 1316, 1376, 1436, 1496, 1556, 1616, 1676, 1736, 1796, 1856, 1916, 1976, 2036
54	4	6	丁巳	57, 117, 177, 237, 297, 357, 417, 477, 537, 597, 657, 717, 777, 837, 897, 957, 1017, 1077, 1137, 1197, 1257, 1317, 1377, 1437, 1497, 1557, 1617, 1677, 1737, 1797, 1857, 1917, 1977, 2037
55	5	7	戊午	58, 118, 178, 238, 298, 358, 418, 478, 538, 598, 658, 718, 778, 838, 898, 958, 1018, 1078, 1138, 1198, 1258, 1318, 1378, 1438, 1498, 1558, 1618, 1678, 1738, 1798, 1858, 1918, 1978, 2038
56	6	8	己未	59, 119, 179, 239, 299, 359, 419, 479, 539, 599, 659, 719, 779, 839, 899, 959, 1019, 1079, 1139, 1199, 1259, 1319, 1379, 1439, 1499, 1559, 1619, 1679, 1739, 1799, 1859, 1919, 1979, 2039

Lunar Year Cycle	Heavenly Cycle	Earthly Cycle	Lunar Year HanJa	Approximate Western Calendar Years (A.D.)
57	7	9	庚申	60, 120, 180, 240, 300, 360, 420, 480, 540, 600, 660, 720, 780, 840, 900, 960, 1020, 1080, 1140, 1200, 1260, 1320, 1380, 1440, 1500, 1560, 1620, 1680, 1740, 1800, 1860, 1920, 1980, 2040
58	8	10	辛酉	61, 121, 181, 241, 301, 361, 421, 481, 541, 601, 661, 721, 781, 841, 901, 961, 1021, 1081, 1141, 1201, 1261, 1321, 1381, 1441, 1501, 1561, 1621, 1681, 1741, 1801, 1861, 1921, 1981, 2041
59	9	11	壬戌	62, 122, 182, 242, 302, 362, 422, 482, 542, 602, 662, 722, 782, 842, 902, 962, 1022, 1082, 1142, 1202, 1262, 1322, 1382, 1442, 1502, 1562, 1622, 1682, 1742, 1802, 1862, 1922, 1982, 2042
60	10	12	癸亥	63, 123, 183, 243, 303, 363, 423, 483, 543, 603, 663, 723, 783, 843, 903, 963, 1023, 1083, 1143, 1203, 1263, 1323, 1383, 1443, 1503, 1563, 1623, 1683, 1743, 1803, 1863, 1923, 1983, 2043

4 - History

Genealogical research is greatly enriched by the study of history. Coupling knowledge of when a Korean ancestor lived with a study of Korean history yields a dramatic increase in an understanding, appreciation, and attachment. Furthermore, the dates contained in older records often cannot be deciphered without a basic knowledge of Korean history. This is particularly true when dates are recorded based on the years of a monarch's reign. Therefore, this chapter introduces a basic Korean history timeline with particular emphasis on the years that monarchs reigned in the Wang and Yi dynasties.

Founding Legends

There are several theories about the origin of the Korean people. A root grammar that differs from surrounding nations makes the quest to discover the oldest Korean roots quite interesting. Theories cover a wide range of possibilities, including Mongolian roots, ties to ancient Norway, and even a lost tribe of Israel mixed with ancient Asian cultures. Traditional legends of Korea's founding also add to the variety.

One of the earliest surviving records of a Korean founding legend is found in a 13th century A.D. record called SamGukYuSa (三國遺事, 삼국유사). The god HwanIn (桓因, 환인) had a son named HwanUng (桓雄, 환웅). HwanUng became the Heavenly King and founded God City (신시, ShinShi) located at White-Head Mountain (白頭山, 백두산, BaekDuSan), which is in modern day North Korea on the northern border by China. A heavenly lake fills a volcanic crater at the top of BaekDuSan. HwanUng granted the wish of a bear and transformed her into a woman named UngNyeo (熊女, 웅녀), meaning "bear woman." UngNyeo prayed for a child beneath the Godly Birch Tree (神檀樹, 신단수). The Heavenly King took her as his wife, and she had a son named DanGun WangGeom (檀君王儉, 단군왕검). DanGun founded the walled city of ASaDal (阿斯達, 아사달), the predecessor of the modern-day North Korean capital city PyungYang. This was the legendary start of the earliest Korean kingdom called Ancient JoSeon or GoJoSeon. GoJoSeon was believed to have been established by DanGun in 2333 B.C., which is why the early DanGi (檀紀, 단기) calendar starts with that year.

Early Kingdoms

Korea was made up of smaller kingdoms before becoming one unified empire. GoGuRyeo, a northern kingdom, had many wars with China and ultimately was weakened and conquered. That led to a period when Korea was divided into three kingdoms: GaYa, SilLa, and BaekJae. SilLa, in the south east, was a strong sea power that defeated Japanese pirates. GaYa was between SilLa and BaekJae. GaYa was rich in iron, which helped it develop the tools necessary to thrive in agriculture. GaYa was taken over by SilLa in 562 A. D. SilLa drove the Chinese kingdoms out of Korea in 676.

GoRyeo

The GoRyeo Empire unified all of Korea. GoRyeo is the source of the modern day word "Korea." GoRyeo was founded in 918 A.D. Buddhism was the primary religion during this period, which resulted in the publication of the Tripitaka Koreana Buddhist scriptures that were carved into 81,258 wooden blocks. A printing press with movable-metal type was also developed during this time period. GoRyeo leadership established a clear Korean identity that continues even today.

The GoRyeo Empire was ruled by the Wang (王, 왕) Dynasty. The Wang Dynasty monarchs are listed in the following table. The rulers were given temple or posthumous names after their deaths, which are usually the names used when referencing years. Emperor names ending in "Jo" (祖, 조) began eras, while those ending in "Jong" (宗, 종) followed them. "Wang" (王, 왕) is also the Korean word for "king."

Table 4.1 GoRyeo Monarchs' Ruling Years

Ruling Years (Years in A.D.)	Living Names and Titles HanJa (HanGul, Romanized)	Posthumous Temple or Era Names HanJa (HanGul, Romanized)
918–943	王建 (왕건, WangGeon) 若天 (약천, YakCheon)	太祖 (태조, TaeJo)
943–945	王武 (왕무, WangMu) 承乾 (승건, SeungGeon)	惠宗 (혜종, HyaeJong)
945–949	王堯 (왕요, WangYo) 천의 (천의, CheonUi)	定宗 (정종, JeongJong)
949–975	王昭 (왕소, WangSo) 日華 (일화, IlHwa)	光宗 (광종, GwangJong) 光德 (광덕, GwangDeok) 峻豊 (준풍, JunPung)

Ruling Years (Years in A.D.)	Living Names and Titles HanJa (HanGul, Romanized)	Posthumous Temple or Era Names HanJa (HanGul, Romanized)
975–981	王伷 (왕유, WangYu) 長民 (장민, JangMin)	景宗 (경종, GyeongJong)
981–997	王治 (왕치, WangChi) 溫古 (온고, OnGo)	成宗 (성종, SeongJong)
997–1009	王誦 (왕송, WangSong) 孝伸 (효신, HyoShin)	穆宗 (목종, MokJong)
1009–1031	王詢 (왕순, WangSun) 安世 (안세, AnSae)	顯宗 (현종, YeonJong)
1031–1034	王欽 (왕흠, WangHeum) 元良 (원량, WonRyang)	德宗 (덕종, DeokJong)
1034–1046	王亨 (왕형, WangHyeong) 申照 (신조, ShinJo)	靖宗 (정종, JeongJong)
1046–1083	王徽 (왕휘, WangHwi) 燭幽 (촉유, ChokYu)	文宗 (문종, MunJong)
1083	王勳 (왕훈, WangHun) 義恭 (의공, UiGong)	順宗 (순종, SunJong)
1083–1094	王運 (왕운, WangUn) 繼天 (계천, GyaeCheon)	宣宗 (선종, SeonJong)
1094–1095	王昱 (왕우, WangUk)	獻宗 (헌종, HeonJong)
1095–1105	王熙 (왕희, WangHui) 天常 (천상, CheonSang)	肅宗 (숙종, SukJong)
1105–1122	王俁 (왕우, WangU) 世民 (세민, SaeMin)	睿宗 (예종, YaeJong)
1122–1146	王楷 (왕해, WangHae) 仁表 (인표, InPyo)	仁宗 (인종, InJong)

Ruling Years (Years in A.D.)	Living Names and Titles HanJa (HanGul, Romanized)	Posthumous Temple or Era Names HanJa (HanGul, Romanized)
1146–1170	王晛 (왕현, WangHyeon) 日升 (일승, IlSeung)	毅宗 (의종, UiJong)
1170–1197	王晧 (왕호, WangHo) 之旦 (지단, JiDan)	明宗 (명종, MyeongJong)
1197–1204	王晫 (왕탁, WangTak) 至華 (지화, JiHwa)	神宗 (신종, ShinJong)
1204–1211	王韺 (왕영, WangYeong) 不陂 (불피, BulPi)	熙宗 (희종, HuiJong)
1211–1213	王晶 (왕오, WangO) 王璹 (왕숙, WangSuk) 王貞 (왕정, WangJeong) 大華 (대화, DaeHwa)	康宗 (강종, GangJong)
1213–1259	王㬚 (왕철, WangCheol) 天祐 (천우, CheonU)	高宗 (고종, GoJong)
1259–1274	王倎 (왕식, WangShik) 日新 (일신, IlShin)	元宗 (원종, WonJong)
1274–1308	王椹 (왕거, WangGeo)	忠烈王 (충렬왕, ChungRyeolWang)
1308–1313	王璋 (왕장, WangJang) 仲昻 (중앙, JungAng)	忠宣王 (충선왕, ChungSeonWang)
1313–1330 1332–1339	王燾 (왕만, WangMan) (의효, EuiHyo)	忠肅王 (충숙왕, ChungSukWang)
1330–1332 1339–1344	王禎 (왕정, WangJeong) 普塔失里 (보탑실리, BoTapShilLi)	忠惠王 (충혜왕, ChungHyaeWang)

Ruling Years (Years in A.D.)	Living Names and Titles HanJa (HanGul, Romanized)	Posthumous Temple or Era Names HanJa (HanGul, Romanized)
1344–1348	王昕 (왕흔, WangHeun) 八思麻朶兒只 (팔사마타아지, PalSaMaTaAJi)	忠穆王 (충목왕, ChungMokWang)
1348–1351	王蚳 (왕저, WangJeo) 迷思監朶兒只 (미사감타아지, MiSaGamTaAJi)	忠靖王 (충정왕, ChungJeongWang)
1351–1374	王祺 (왕전, WangJeon) 伯顏帖木兒 (바얀테무르, BaYanTaeMuReu) (이재, IJae) (익당, IkDang)	恭愍王 (공민왕, GongMinWang)
1374–1388	王禑 (왕우, WangU)	禑王 (우왕, UWang)
1388–1389	王昌 (왕창, WangChang)	昌王 (창왕, ChangWang)
1389–1392	王瑤 (왕요, WangYo)	恭讓王 (공양왕, GongYangWang)

JoSeon

The JoSeon Empire was ruled by the Yi (李, 이) Dynasty beginning in 1392. JoSeon is also frequently spelled "Chosun" or "Choson." TaeJo was powerful in the previous GoRyeo Empire and lead a coup that began the Yi Dynasty and the JoSeon Empire. The JoSeon Empire had a strong government and class system. The culture focused on morality with a Confucius influence. The modern-day Korean focus on scholarship, standardized tests, and the honoring of teachers has many of its roots in this period. One of the most honored rulers of this period is the fourth ruler -- The Great King SaeJong. King SaeJong is known for adopting the Korean HanGul alphabet. The scientific and phonetic HanGul alphabet is still credited for Korea's record-setting literacy rate.

Table 4.2 JoSeon Monarchs' Ruling Years

Ruling Years (Years in A.D.)	Personal Names and Titles HanJa (HanGul, Romanized)	Temple/Era Names HanJa (HanGul, Romanized)
1392–1398	李成桂 (이성계, ISeongGyae) 李旦 (이단, IDan)	太祖 (태조, TaeJo) 天授 (천수, CheonSu)
1398–1400	李芳果 (이방과, IBangGwa)	定宗 (정종, JeongJong)
1400–1418	李芳遠 (이방원, IBangWon)	太宗 (태종, TaeJong)
1418–1450	李祹 (이도, IDo)	世宗 (세종, SaeJong)
1450–1452	李珦 (이향, IHyang)	文宗 (문종, MunJong)
1452–1455	李弘暐 (이홍위, IHongWui)	端宗 (단종, DanJong)
1455–1468	李瑈 (이유, IYu)	世祖 (세조, SaeJo)
1468–1469	李晄 (이광, IGwang)	睿宗 (예종, YaeJong)
1469–1494	李娎 (이혈, IHyeol)	成宗 (성종, SeongJong)
1494–1506	李隆 (이융, IYung)	燕山君 (연산군, YeonSanGun)
1506–1544	李懌 (이역, IYeok)	中宗 (중종, JungJong)
1544–1545	李峼 (이호, IHo)	仁宗 (인종, InJong)
1545–1567	李峘 (이환, IHwan)	明宗 (명종, MyeongJong)
1567–1608	李蚣 (이연, IYeon)	宣祖 (선조, SeonJo)
1608–1623	李琿 (이혼, IHon)	光海君 (광해군, GwangHaeGun)
1623–1649	李倧 (이종, IJong)	仁祖 (인조, InJo)

Ruling Years (Years in A.D.)	Personal Names and Titles HanJa (HanGul, Romanized)	Temple/Era Names HanJa (HanGul, Romanized)
1649–1659	李淏 (이 호, IHo)	孝宗 (효종, HyoJong)
1659–1674	李棩 (이 연, IYeon)	顯宗 (현종, HyeonJong)
1674–1720	李焞 (이 순, ISun)	肅宗 (숙종, SukJong)
1720–1724	李昀 (이 윤, IYun)	景宗 (경종, GyeongJong)
1724–1776	李昑 (이 금, IGeum)	英祖 (영조, YeongJo)
1776–1800	李祘 (이 산, ISan)	正祖 (정조, JeongJo)
1800–1834	李玜 (이 공, IGong)	純祖 (순조, SunJo)
1834–1849	李奐 (이 환, IHwan)	憲宗 (헌종, HeonJong)
1849–1863	李昪 (이 변, IByeon)	哲宗 (철종, CheolJong)
1863–1907	李命福 (이 명 복, IMyeongBok)	高宗 (고종, GoJong)
1907–1910	李坧 (이 척, ICheok)	純宗 (순종, SunJong)

GoRyeo was renamed the Korean Empire in 1897. Korea was modernizing heavily during this time. Russian influence grew until the Korean Empire was defeated by Japan in 1905.

Japanese Occupation

The Japanese annexed Korea in 1905 and conquered Korea in 1916. The annexation was generally considered illegal by the Korean people. The treaty was not signed with the emperor's seal. The annexation treaty was internationally determined to be false in 1965.

The occupation was brutal. The Korean culture was declared illegal. Koreans were required to adopt Japanese names. Korean history was banned from being taught in schools. Some areas reported people being publicly executed for speaking Korean. Natural resources and in some cases even people were sent to Japan. The mountains, once full of trees, were bald. Today you see many mountains covered with trees in straight lines because of modern re-planting efforts to recover.

The Korean people refused to let their language and culture die. They formed strong liberation movements. The March First Movement was the most famous event in the liberation struggle, which took place in 1919 A. D. Thousands were killed in demonstrations. This movement was inspired by a speech by President Woodrow Wilson on the right of self-determination, which began Korea's close ties to the U.S. The Provisional Government of Korea was set up in China and formally petitioned the U.S. government for help. Many of those involved were Presbyterians who later helped establish the South Korean government. The influence of Presbyterians and Christianity are still strong in South Korean culture.

The end of World War II and the surrender of Japan finally enabled Korean liberation. Due to political struggles between the U.S. and the Soviet Union, Korea was temporarily divided at the 38th parallel. The U.S. and Soviet Union could not agree on how to set up a unified Korean government, so the issue was taken to the United Nations (U.N.). Although the U.N. recognized the Republic of Korea (ROK) as the government for all of Korea, Cold War tensions prevented Korea from regaining its unified independence.

Korean War

North Korea attacked the south in 1950, which started the Korean War. They drove the U.S. and South Korean forces to the southeast corner in PuSan. General MacArthur, who is still a revered figure in South Korea, led an amphibious attack that trapped the attackers and then drove north. China joined the north, which quickly destabilized the situation. The fighting stopped in 1953 with the signing of an armistice agreement. The agreement did not officially declare the war over, however.

North and South Korea

The Soviet Union set up a communist dictatorship in the north called the Democratic People's Republic of Korea (DPRK). The Republic of Korea (ROK) was established in the south. South Korea modeled its constitution and government after the U.S. This division remains to the present day without formally closing the Korean War.

Hopes for Reunification

Many Korean songs and proverbs reflect the long struggles of the Korean people to maintain their culture, language, and independence. One saying reflects the Korean honor particularly well: a mighty tree can break and fall when hit by the wind of a terrible storm, but the humble rice bows its head and rises again when the storm passes. One can almost feel the pain and wisdom of a peaceful-loving people struggling to maintain their culture and identity as neighboring empires invade and interrupt their peace. If there is one thing Korean history has taught, it is that the Korean people will bond together and survive despite outside attempts to conquer and divide them. One can feel the suspense as the world watches to see if the Korean people will ultimately overcome the tensions set up during the Cold War to once again unite as an independent nation.

It is the author's hope and prayer that the path for a peaceful reunification will one day be realized. The world watched miraculous events in Europe reunite a divided Germany; perhaps a similar miracle is waiting to unite the humble and deserving people of Korea. The figurative rice field may have been beaten down by the storm of the Cold War, but surely each stalk of rice will eventually stand again when the storm passes.

5 - Family Registries

Family Records

Many Korean clans pass down genealogies and family histories that are kept by the eldest sons. These family registries are called JokBo (族譜, 족보). Many families have a formal family run organization that collects and publishes genealogy updates to the family. These organizations identify and take care of family historical sites, including grave sites and ancestral homes. Some families are starting to publish this information on the internet. Donating records to public online archives to preserve Korean history is also a wonderful growing trend. There have never been so many resources available to genealogists, and the future is even brighter.

There is also a new movement to preserve and publicly publish family histories as national treasures. For example, the Inje University Genealogy Library collects and publishes Korean genealogical records at http://genealogy.inje.ac.kr. The software used to view these records requires a Korean version of Microsoft Windows (not just an English version of Windows with Korean fonts installed), however, which can be a barrier for researchers outside of Korea.

Family Search also makes genealogical records available at http://familysearch.org. Fortunately, these records are viewable by almost any computer with a web browser. At the time this book was written, Korean records can be located on Family Search by navigating to "Records", "Browse by Location," "Asia and Middle East", "Korea, Collection of Genealogies, 1500-2009," "Browse through 171,982 images." The number of published records is continually growing. No doubt, this will eventually include indexing, which enables text-based searches, rather than just images. Although searchable indexed records would be very helpful, the currently available images of genealogical records are all that is needed to find ancestors using the methods presented in this book. From there you can navigate to specific clan records by selecting the family name, country, province, and city/county, and town that identify the clan. You will often find many volumes of records for clans in the collection.

Family genealogies often start with family histories. Some records contain the valiant acts of the ancestors. Some also contain maps and pictures of family graves and historical sites, photos or paintings of prominent ancestors, and photos and information about family historical treasures.

Page Structure

When viewing pages of a family registry, imagine the pages as being cut out from one giant scroll. The following diagrams represent a simplified version of that visualization. First, imagine a giant scroll with information about family members recorded on it. The scroll has horizontal rows that each represent a generation. In this simplified example there are only 4 generations, but in a real Korean genealogical record there could be over 30 generations recorded. Note that each entry shows a married couple or an individual child. Also note that the record starts in the upper right and is read top-to-bottom, right-to-left, in traditional style.

Diagram 5.1 Visualization of a Genealogy Scroll:

Generation 1							Great Grandparents			
Generation 2			Grandparents B					Grandparents A		
Generation 3		Parents B-2		Parents B-1			Parents A-2		Parents A-1	
Generation 4	Child B-2-2	Child B-2-1	Child B-1-2	Child B-1-1	Child A-2-4	Child A-2-3	Child A-2-2	Child A-2-1	Child A-1-2	Child A-1-1

Next, imagine that there are lines showing parent-child relationships. The actual records do not include these lines, but this visualization clarifies how to identify parent-child relationships. Children are generally located just below their parents in the records. They don't always line up exactly, but there will be enough clues in the text to identify where one couple's children end and the next begin. For example, each parent record lists the number of sons and daughters, which will helps identify where that family's record ends in the next row of children.

Diagram 5.2 Visualization of Lineage on a Genealogy Scroll:

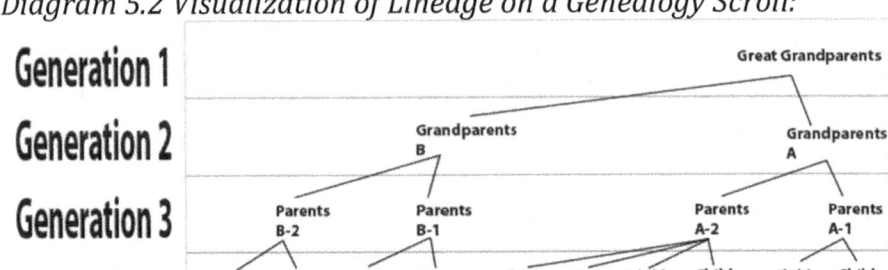

Next, imagine cutting the scroll into pages. In this simplified example there are two generations per page. In actual records you typically find about 6 generations per page. Also, the pages could be organized into multiple volumes of books.

Diagram 5.3 Visualization of a Genealogy Scroll Cut into Pages:

Generation 1	Page 6	Page 5	Page 4	Page 3	Page 2	Page 1
Generation 2						
Generation 3	Page 12	Page 11	Page 10	Page 9	Page 8	Page 7
Generation 4						

Note that not every page has every generation row populated. In the simplified example above, Page 3 and 6 have no records, and therefore may be excluded from the actual record. Page 9 only has records on the row for the 4th generation and is blank for the 3rd generation; in that case you would need to turn to page 8 and move up a row to locate the children's parents. Also, it is not uncommon to see the text of the bottom generation overflow across the bottom row's boundaries somewhat; some dates and text might overflow a bit into the row below in an effort to fit all of the children on same page as their parents. Sometimes that still doesn't get the whole family on one page, so you may have to turn to the next page to see the rest of a parent's children. Remember that pages are numbered from back-to-front in eastern style, unlike western books that number pages front-to-back.

Facing pages are generally organized as follows. The facing pages can be considered to be one page read from right-to-left across the binding and top-to-bottom thru the generations listed on the right page (elements D-I on the following diagram). All of the structural elements labeled below are normally written in HanJa from top-to-bottom.

Locating individuals in a 12-page record would be easy, but it would be considerably more difficult when the record count grows to tens of thousands of individuals in the clan. A method of linking pages across generations helps simplify navigation. The following example describes links up and down generations that span multiple pages for Diagram 5.3. The names of Parents A-1 and Parents A-2 from pages 7 and 8 would also be listed at the bottom of Page 1 under Grandparents A in an appreviated record showing just the gender, name, and often even the volume and page number where their full record can be found (page 1, in this case). The opposite direction is also linked. The name of the grandfather from Grandparents A on page 1 would be listed above Parents A1 and Parents A2 on pages 7 and 8. Similar links would be included between page 4, 12, and 10 to link the children of Grandparents B to the page with their father.

Generation numbers are shown in locations D thru I in the following diagram. The earliest founder of the clan is generation 1. Generations are generally formatted as HanJa numbers followed by the HanJa character 世, meaning generation:

HanJa	HanGul	Pronunciation	Meaning
世	세	Sae	Generation

Diagram 5.4 Structure of Facing Pages of a Family Registry:

A – Book Title and Volume (read top-to-bottom)
B – Page #
C – Page # (one page greater than B; book pages arranged right-to-left)
D, E, F, G, H, I – Generation # (increasing down the page)

When the book is bound, the book is read in the opposite direction as western or even modern Korean books. Genealogical records follow the traditional method of the "back" cover being the "front." Pages are numbered back-to-front. Facing pages are numbered from the right page to the left page, but they function as one large page.

Linking Individual Records

Records of individuals follow some common patterns. They start by indicating if the individual is a son (子, 자, Ja) or a daughter (女, 녀, Nyeo). The family name is not specified in individual records of children born into the clan, but the family name is specified in the title of the registry book. It is assumed that all sons and daughters of the clan in the entire family registry share the family name. Note that married women do not change their family name when they are married, unlike in western cultures. Accordingly, women who are married into the family have their family names and sometimes even their father's names specified in the record.

When a son marries, his children are listed in his father's family registry. This makes it possible to find a full paternal line in one family registry by following a linked chain of fathers.

Following maternal links to a mother's parents requires jumping to another family's registry book. When a daughter marries, she is given to her husband's family. Her children will be listed under her in her husband's family registry. She will usually still be listed in her father's registry as his daughter, and normally her husband's name will be listed, too. This provides genealogists with a precious link between the two clans. The daughter and even her husband may be in both families' registries, but her children are only listed in her husband's family registry. These maternal links bind together the family registries of all the clans in Korea into one people with a common history.

Linking Individuals Across Pages and Volumes

The top and bottom generation rows of each page serve as a link to the same individual on another page of the family registry, except in cases where the start or end of a family line has been reached. The top parent generation on a page is represented by generation row D in the previous diagram, and the bottom generation row of children on a page is represented by generation row I. Listing an individual twice (as the parent on one page and the child on another) links pages of a registry together when moving up or down to generations that can't all fit on one page.

In some newer publications, individual records on the top and bottom generation rows include volume and page numbers to aide in locating the linked page for that individual. The volume number is often prefixed with the HanJa character 正 and followed by the volume number and page number, all typically written in HanJa. If volume and page number links are not included, you can still find the linked page by searching all pages of the family registry for the linked record of that individual. It helps to narrow down the search by only searching pages with the correct generation number. If you are linking down a generation, the name of a child on the bottom generation row of one page is included in the top parent row of another page; both of those linked records represent the same individual and will have the same generation number. If you are linking up a generation, a parent name on the top generation row of a page is also listed as a child on the bottom row of another page; that page continues the line up to earlier generations.

In these cases where a person is listed twice (the top parent generation of one page and the bottom child generation of another page), their full record is shown in the parent version of the record (top generation row of a page) and an abbreviated record is shown in the child version of the record (bottom generation row of a page). The full record includes information like the date of birth, spouse, number of children, or grave site. The abbreviated child version of such a record may only show the gender and name and is included just as a link to the full record on the other page. Note that the two pages that are linked together could be in different volumes/books of the same family registry.

Records of Married Sons

The following table is a typical individual record formatted traditionally as you would find in a family registry. The text is mostly HanJa and is read top-to-bottom, then right-to-left. It is followed by another table that breaks down and interprets each element of the individual record.

Table 5.1 Sample Married Son

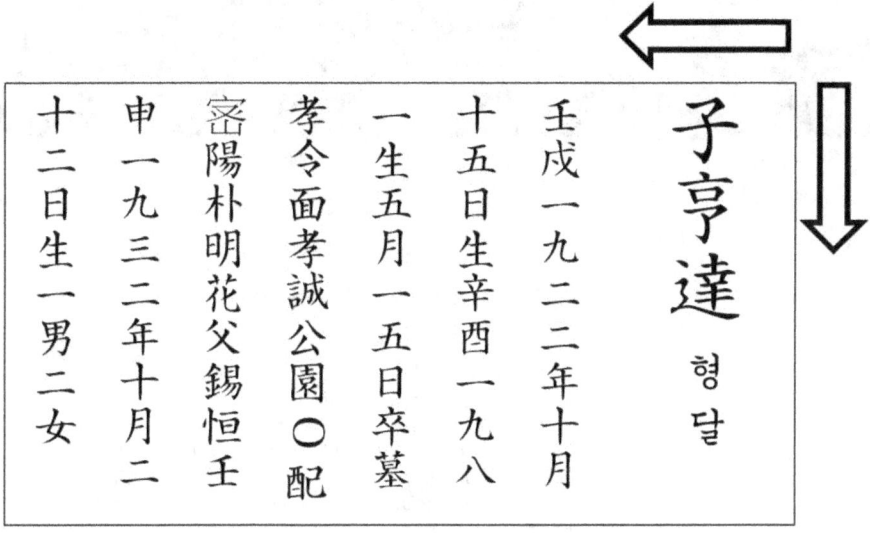

The following divides the sample record into lettered sections. Key common HanJa characters that can help you identify sections are circled. The sections are interpreted in table 5.2.

Table 5.2 Interpretation of a Sample Married Son

Section	HanJa (from the table above) HanGul ---------------- Interpretation Notes

Section A: Gender and Given Name	子亨達 형달
	
	자 형 달 형 달
	
	--- 	
	
	• A son (子, 자, Ja) with the given name of HyeungDal (亨達, 형달).
	
	   - *Note that the given name is listed in HanJa then repeated in HanGul, which is becoming common in some modern editions of family registries. The HanGul version is much easier to read when uncommon HanJa characters are used, and the HanGul version shows the pronunciation. The HanJa version of the name specifies the precise meaning.*
	   - *Note that the last name was not specified. It is assumed that this son has the same family name as every child born into this family. The family name is in the title of the family registry itself and is not repeated for each individual.*
	   - *Note that you can find both of the HanJa characters in the given name in the "HanJa Syllables Used in Korean Given Names" table in chapter 2. You can look them each up in an online Korean-English HanJa dictionary to find the meanings. http://hanjadic.bravender.us defines the syllables of HyeongDal's given name as follows: Hyeong (亨, 형) means smoothly progressing, or no trouble. Dal (達, 달) means arrive at, reach, or intelligent. HyeongDal could be translated as "reaching tranquility."*

Section	HanJa (from the table above) HanGul -------------- Interpretation Notes
Section B: Birth Date	壬戌一九二二年十月十五日生 임수 1 9 2 2 년 10 월 10 5 일생 -- • Born October 15, 1922 • ImSu (壬戌, 임수) is the 59th year of the lunar year cycle: 1922 A.D. • 1922 (一九二二) year (年, 년, Nyeon) • 10th (十) month (月, 월, Weol) • 15th (十五) day (日, 일, Eel) • Birth (生, 생, Saeng) - *Note that you can look up the HanJa numbers, vocabulary for dates, and lunar years in chapter 3.* - *ImSu (壬戌, 임수) could represent the years 1802, 1862, 1922, 1982 and others (see the table of lunar calendar years in chapter 3). In this case, it clearly represents 1922 A.D. because "1922" follows it in HanJa (一九二二). It is common to see both lunar and solar years listed, like the record above, for modern records. Older records may only contain the lunar year, which requires looking for other clues in the text to narrow down the exact year. If you know the year a child was born, for example, the parent's birth and death years would have to fall before and after the child's brith; that clue would help narrow down which of the possible solar years to select for the lunar year specified.*

Section	HanJa (from the table above) HanGul --------------- Interpretation Notes
Section C: Death Date	辛酉一九八一生五月一五日卒 신유 1 9 8 1 년 5 월 1 5 일졸 -- • Passed away May 15, 1981 • ShinYu (辛酉, 신유) is the 58th year of the lunar year cycle: 1981 A.D. • 1981 (一九八一) year (年, 년, Nyeon) • 5th (五) month (月, 월, Weol) • 15th (十五) day (日, 일, Eel) • Death (卒, 졸, Jol) - *Note that you can look up the HanJa numbers, vocabulary for dates, and lunar years in chapter 3.* - *ShinYu (辛酉, 신유) could represent the years 1801, 1861, 1921, 1981 and others (see the table of lunar calendar years in chapter 3). In this case, it clearly represents 1981 A.D. because "1981" follows it in HanJa (一九八一). It is common to see both lunar and solar years listed, like the record above, for modern records. Older records may only contain the lunar year, which requires looking for other clues in the text to narrow down the exact year. If you know the year a child was born, for example, the parent's birth and death years would have to fall before and after the child's brith; that clue would help narrow down which of the possible solar years to select for the lunar year specified.*
Section D: Grave Location	墓孝令面 孝誠公園 묘 효령면 효성공원 -- • Grave (墓, 묘, Myo) located at the town HyoRyeongMyeon (孝令面, 효령면) at HyoSeong Park (孝誠公園, 효성공원)

Section	HanJa (from the table above) HanGul -------------- Interpretation Notes
Section E: Section Divider	**O** -- • This circle symbol separates sections of the record. In this case it is the end of the husband's information and the start of the wife's information. - *Note that if there was more than one wife, each wife has their own section and each section is separated by this symbol.*
Section F: Wife and Father in Law Names	**配密陽朴明花父錫恒** 배밀양박명화부석항 -- • Wife (配, 배, Bae) from the MilYang Pak clan (密陽朴, 밀양박) with the family name Pak (朴, 박) and the Given name MyeongHwa (明花, 명화) who is the daughter of Pak SeokHang (錫恒, 석항). - *Note that in this case the given name of the wife is listed. If only her family name was listed, she would be referred to as Mrs. Pak (朴氏, 박씨, Pak Sshi). Even without the wife's given name, her family name and clan with the given name of her father is enough to trace the maternal family link thru her father's family registry.* - *Note that the father's given name, SeokHang, is listed but his family name is not. You can assume that he has the same family name (and clan) as his daughter, in this case Pak.* - *The family name (in this case Pak, 朴, 박) can be located in the "Korean Family Names" table in chapter 2.* - *The HanJa for the given names of the wife and the father can be located in the "HanJa Syllables Used in Korean Given Names" table in chapter 2.*

Section	HanJa (from the table above) HanGul --------------- Interpretation Notes
Section G: Wife Birth Date	壬申一九三二年十月二十二日生 임신 1 9 3 2 년 10 월 2 10 2 일생 --- • Born October 22, 1932: • ImShin (壬申, 임신) is the 9th year of the lunar year cycle: in this case 1932 A.D. • 1932 (一九三二) year (年, 년, Nyeon) • 10th (十) month (月, 월, Weol) • 22nd (二十二) day (日, 일, Eel) • Birth (生, 생, Saeng) - *In this sample the wife's death date is not listed. That may be because she was still living at the time the record was printed. If she had passed away, her death date and grave location would be recorded in a style similar to the husband's record in sections C and D.*
Section H: Number of Sons and Daughters	一男 二女 1 남 2 녀 --- • This couple had 1 (一) son (男, 남, Nam) and 2 (二) daughters (女, 녀, Nyeo).

Records of Married Daughters

Daughters are usually recorded in a family record. Usually their given names are listed, but sometimes only their husband's names are listed. Their records are not as detailed because their full information is recorded as part of their husband's record in his family's registry, similar to the wife in the previous example of a married son. A daughter's record should contain enough information to locate her husband's record in his family registry. Sometimes her birth date and some other information is also included. In the following example a daughter's given name, birth date, and husband's name and clan are listed.

Table 5.3 Sample Married Daughter

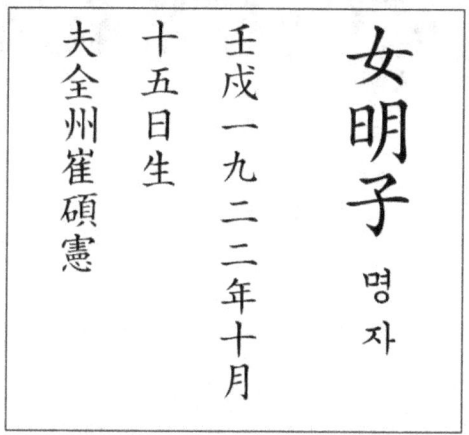

The following divides the sample record into lettered sections. Key HanJa characters that can help you identify sections are circled. The sections are interpreted in table 5.4.

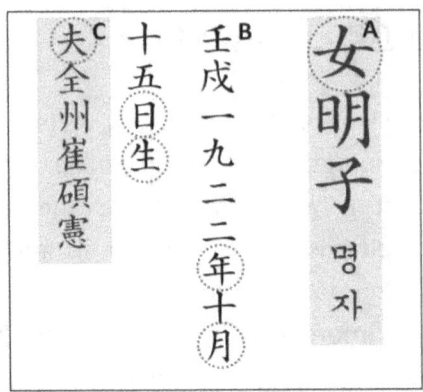

Table 5.4 Interpretation of a Sample Married Daughter

Section	HanJa (from the table above) HanGul -------------- Interpretation Notes
Section A: **Gender and** **Given Name**	**女明子 명자** 여 명 자 명 자 --- • A daughter (女, 여, Yeo) with the given name of MyeongJa (明子, 명 자) - *Note that the given name was repeated in HanGul, which is becoming common in some modern editions of family registries.* - *Note that the last name was not specified. It is assumed that this daughter has the same name as every child born into this family. The family name is in the title of the family registry itself and is not repeated for each individual. A woman does not change her family name when she is married.* - *Note that you can find the both of the HanJa characters in the given name in the "HanJa Syllables Used in Korean Given Names" table in chapter 2. You can look them each up in an online Korean-English HanJa dictionary to find the meanings.* *http://hanjadic.bravender.us defines the syllables of MyeongJa's given name as follows: Myeong (明, 명) means bright, light, brilliant, or clear. Ja (子, 자) means offspring, child, fruit, or seed of. MyeongJa could be translated as "bright child."*

Section	HanJa (from the table above) HanGul -------------- Interpretation Notes

Section B:
Birth Date
	壬戌一九二二年十月十五日生
	임수 1 9 2 2 년 10 월 10 5 일생
	--- 	
	
	• Born October 15, 1922
	• ImSu (壬戌, 임수) is the 59th year of the lunar year cycle: 1922 A.D.
	• 1922 (一九二二) year (年, 년, Nyeon)
	• 10th (十) month (月, 월, Weol)
	• 15th (十五) day (日, 일, Eel)
	• Birth (生, 생, Saeng)
	
	   - *Note that you can look up the HanJa numbers, vocabulary for dates, and lunar years in chapter 3.*
	   - *ImSu (壬戌, 임수) could represent the years 1802, 1862, 1922, 1982 and others (see the table of lunar calendar years in chapter 3). In this case, it clearly represents 1922 A.D. because "1922" follows it in HanJa (一九二二). It is common to see both lunar and solar years listed, like the record above, for modern records. Older records may only contain the lunar year, which requires looking for other clues in the text to narrow down the exact year. If you know the year a child was born, for example, the parent's birth and death years would have to fall before and after the child's brith; that clue would help narrow down which of the possible solar years to select for the lunar year specified.*

Section	HanJa (from the table above) HanGul --------------- Interpretation Notes
Section C: **Husband** **Name and** **Clan**	夫全州崔碩憲 부전주최석헌 --- • Husband Choi SeokHeon from the JeonJu clan of the Choi family. • Husband (夫, 부, Bu) • JeonJu clan (전주, JeonJu) of the Choi family name (崔, 최, Choi) • Given name SeokHeon (碩憲, 석헌, SeokHeon) - Note that JeonJu (全州, 전주) is the name of the city where the JeonJu Choi clan originated. - The clan name can be used to identify the correct family registry for the JeonJu clan of the Choi family. This daughter's full record, including her children, can be found under her husband's record in the JeonJu Choi family registry -- they are generally not recorded in the daughter's father's family registry because she moves to her husband's registry. Her abbreviated information in this sample record is listed in her parent's registry with the name of her husband as a link to her record in her husband's registry where her full record with her children can be found. - Note that you can find the Choi (崔, 최) family name in the "Korean Family Names" table in chapter 2. - Note that you can find the both of the HanJa characters in the given name in the "HanJa Syllables Used in Korean Given Names" table in chapter 2. You can look them each up in an online Korean-English HanJa dictionary to find the meanings. http://hanjadic.bravender.us defines the syllables of SeokHeon's given name as follows: Seok (碩, 석) means great, eminent, large, or big. Heon (憲, 헌) means constitution, statute, or law. His name could be interpreted "the great law."

Records of Single Children

Records of unmarried sons and daughters resemble the previous two sections without the information about spouses or children. Just like the previous two examples, a son's record will start with 子 (자, Ja) and a daughter's record will start with 女 (여, Yeo). It will then have the HanJa version of their given names. Usually at least a birth date follows the given name, but sometimes only the gender and given name are provided.

Blood-Line Adoptions

Traditionally, it is very important to have a son in Korea. A son carries on the family line in the family registry. Family registries are paternal – building maternal lines requires multiple registries from each family in the line. It is particularly important for the eldest son to have a son, as he will inherit leadership of the extended family. However, there are cases where the eldest son does not have a son of his own. A common remedy for this problem is a "blood-line adoption" where one of the eldest son's siblings gives him their second son. When this takes place, the son of a sibling becomes the son and inheritor of the eldest son.

Family registries record blood-line adoptions. The adopted son is placed under the eldest son, to designate his new adopted father, but the fact that it is a blood-line adoption is clearly indicated. The real father is also recorded.

An adopted son's record has some additional elements that aren't found in the previous examples. The son-less father records the adoption of his sibling's son under his line. However, instead of the adopted son's record starting with the HanJa for son 子 (자, Ja), as seen in previous examples, it starts with 子系 (자계, JaGyae), literally meaning "child line" or "child connection." Next, the adopted child's given name is recorded.

151

Following the given name, you will find the HanJa version of the word 生父 (생부, SaengBu), meaning "birth father" or real father, and the birth father's given name. Since the real father is a sibling of the adopted father (generally the eldest son), you already know the family name of the real father. They are all from the same family and share the family name that is in the title of the family registry for the clan. The rest of the adopted son's record follows the same patterns as previous examples.

The son-less father who adopts the son of his sibling also has a difference in his record. At the end of the adopting father's record, instead of recording 一男 (1 남, 1 Nam) to indicate one son, the record says 系男 (계남, GyaeNam), literally meaning "line son" and indicating a blood-line adoption that continues the family line.

Starting Point

There are two important pieces of information that will get you started on your search for Korean ancestors. The first is the name of a Korean ancestor written in HanJa characters. The second is the name of the clan associated with that ancestor's family name. These two pieces of information are needed to find an individual in family genealogical records available online. If that information is not available for the clan, then turn to government records related to family registries, clan websites, or even request to obtain access to the records from the family directly.

If an ancestor's name in English or HanGul is known but the HanJa version is unknown or if the clan is unknown, then the search will be more challenging, but it is not impossible. Use the table of family names from chapter 2 to find the all of the possible HanJa versions of the family name. Note that there are a variety of English spellings for each HanGul version of a family name, but it is generally not difficult to find the right HanGul version of a Korean family name from the English version. Next, take each possible HanJa version of the name and find all of the online records associated with each of those as a good starting place. For some HanGul family names with many HanJa versions this may result in several volumes to start with, but at least it is a good starting point.

The following example is from the YeoSan clan of the Song family. This older edition of the Song records is divided into two books. Of course, newer editions could include information about living people that could cause privacy concerns – a genealogist should always respect the privacy and wishes of individuals when researching. Clan records broken into more than two books will often number the volumes. In this case there are only two books, so they are identified as the "above" (上, 상, Sang) and "below" (下, 하, Ha) books (卷, 권, Gweon). In the following picture from the Family Search website, you see the title of the two family registry volumes (in HanGul and HanJa) followed by the volume identifier. The table after the picture breaks down the title of the family registry.

Picture 5.1 Locating a Family Registry Online

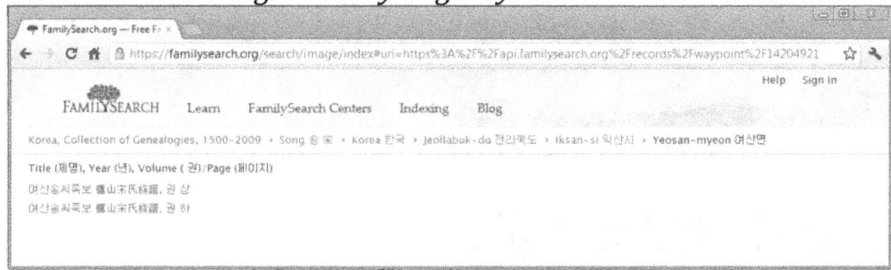

Table 5.5 Family Registry Title Translation

HanJa	HanGul	Pronunciation	Meaning
礪山	여산	YeoSan	Yeo Mountain (the location where the YeoSan Song family clan originated)
宋氏	송씨	Song SShi	Song Family
族譜	족보	JokBo	Family Registry
卷上	권상	Gweon Sang	Scroll/Book Above/Before *(First Volume)*
卷下	권하	Gweon Ha	Scroll/Book Below/After *(Second Volume)*

Family registries follow the traditional book orientation by starting from the back and working forward as you read the book. The front cover is where western books would have placed the back cover, and the book is read in the opposite direction of western books. Accordingly, in the YeoSan Song family registry below, you'll notice that the cover page has the binding on the right. Family Search correctly designates this as page or image 1.

Picture 5.2 Viewing a Family Registry Online

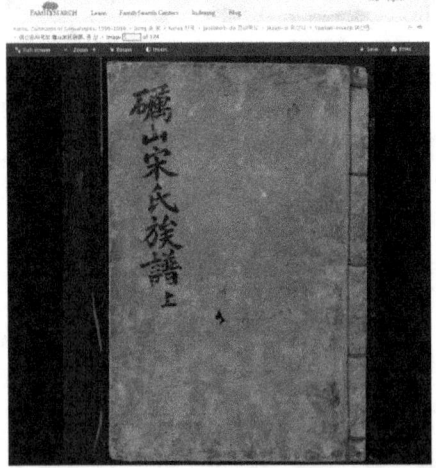

The genealogical record is primarily written in HanJa characters. Some modern records also translate portions of the record into HanGul, but the bulk of the records are still in HanJa. Pages of traditional records are read back-to-front, top-to-bottom, right-to-left. In the example above, "礪山宋氏族譜上" (YeoSan Song Family Registry, First Volume) is written top-to-bottom on the cover page, in traditional style.

Discovery Approach

Start with identifying the page structure of the records. Identify how many generations are represented by each book in the volume by looking at the generation numbers on the right sides of pages. After becoming familiar with the page structure, search each page for an individual's gender and name. Try using row generation numbers to narrow down which pages to search. Find some sample birth dates for generation numbers to get a feel for which generations may contain the individual being searched for. Birth dates can be quickly identified by looking for the 生 (생, Saeng) character after dates. See the previous examples for date formats.

When the record of an individual is found, identify the record structure. Find the common vocabulary covered in this book to identify sections, birth and death dates, etc. Look for HanJa representing lunar years and vocabulary representing births, deaths, marriages, or children. Determine if the individual was married and how many children they had. Look up one generation row to identify their parents. Look next to them on the same row to identify siblings after identifying how many children the parents had. Determine if there were blood-line adoptions. Look down one generation row to identify children.

Generally, in recent generations the year is specified in HanJa as well as in lunar years. As you move up to older generations only the lunar years are listed. Use the known solar years for lower generations to narrow down which solar years are represented by lunar years in earlier generations. For example, if the solar birth year of a child is known, select solar years for the parents' birth and death years that make sense and bound their children's birth years. Go up one generation at a time to accurately select the correct solar years for given lunar years using this method.

When faced with unknown HanJa, search the tables of this book or draw the HanJa at http://hanja.naver.com following the stroke order and direction taught in chapter 1. Find and copy the HanJa character, then paste it into http://hanjadic.bravender.us to discover the English meaning of the character. Search for groups of characters on http://hanjadic.bravender.us or http://www.google.co.kr to discover the meaning of words made up of multiple syllables.

Look for grave site locations to identify where the individuals lived. Use online searches to learn more about those regions. Fortunately, most Korean city names haven't changed thru history, so it is normally easy to find information about where they lived. Also look up the information about the city or town where the clan began. Generally this city is in the clan title, which is also the title of the family registry.

Finally, learn about the history that took place during the time that the individuals lived. This enriches understanding of their lives and intensifies the lessons of Korean history.

Discovering Korean ancestors is a challenging and rewarding endeavor. The fundamentals introduced by this book provide a good foundation. Learn, collaborate, and share as you discover Korean ancestors and history. May your journey of discovery richly bless you as you discover the rich history of Korea.

BIBLIOGRAPHY

2000 South Korean Census. (2000). South Korea: Korean National Statistical Office.

Korea, Collection of Genealogies, 1500-2009. Family Search.
https://familysearch.org/search/collection/show#uri=http://familysearch.org/searchapi/search/collection/1398522

List of Monarchs of Korea; Korean Mythology; Dangun; Korean History. http://en.wikipedia.org

Hanja Dictionary. http://hanjadic.bravender.us

네이버 한자사전. http://hanja.naver.com

인명용 한자표. (2011). South Korea.

ABOUT THE AUTHOR

Jason Howard grew up in South Korea, where he developed a deep love for the Korean people, culture, and language. He soon returned to serve as a missionary for two years. He received a B.S. in Computer Science from Illinois Institute of Technology, and then returned again to Korea. He married his sweetheart, a native Korean. Together they are raising four wonderful daughters. The author served as a Marine, worked in the defense industry, and received an MBA from the University of Dallas.

Jason began studying the genealogy of his family. This endeavor was motivated by love for his children. He desired to pass on to them a precious connection to their ancestors. Genealogical research enables them to appreciate and honor those who came before them and intensifies the meaning and lessons of history. This ancestral connection is truly rewarding.

Locating records of his wife's Korean ancestors was exciting, and interpreting them was fascinating. The author recognized that his children and their children would need a guide to help them continue to treasure and research the family genealogical records. He dedicated himself to this task.

The author realized that this guide could also benefit others with similar goals, so he published it. He hopes to help fill the void of resources to help English speakers discover Korean ancestors, enable the use of family registries for educational research into Korean history and culture, and honor the heritage of Korea.

The author administers a website dedicated to helping people succeed in Korean genealogical research. Visit http://KoreanGenealogy.org or other online communities dedicated to genealogy to receive help or serve those who need help with Korean genealogical research.